FINDING MONEY

FINDING MONEY

THE SMALL BUSINESS GUIDE TO FINANCING

KATE LISTER

TOM HARNISH

JOHN WILEY & SONS, INC.

New York • Chichester • Brisbane • Toronto • Singapore

aap - 9040

For our inspiration

Ethel and Charlie, Jane and Tom

Library of Congress Cataloging-in-Publication Data:

Lister, Kate, 1959
    Finding money : the small business guide to financing / Kate
Lister, Tom Harnish.
       p.   cm. — (Wiley small business editions)
    Includes bibliographical references and index.
    ISBN 0-471-10983-5 (cloth: alkaline paper) —
    ISBN 0-471-10984-3 (paperback: alkaline paper)
    1. Small business—United States—Finance. 2. Business
enterprises—United States—Finance.   I. Harnish, Tom, 1945-
II. Title. III. Series.
HG4027.7.L58   1995
658.15'92—dc20   95-878

Printed in the United States of America

10 9 8 7 6 5 4 3 2 1

PREFACE

This book was written to help you cope with the unique financing problems of a new or growing small business. While the federal government says "Financing is amply available" for small business, their definition of a *small business* includes some with as many as 500 employees. In fact, over 98 percent of the nation's small businesses employ less than 100 people, and almost 90 percent employ less than 20.[1] Finding money can be difficult for these smaller small businesses, and especially difficult for new businesses, service businesses, retailers, high-technology firms, and fast-growing companies.

The good news is that lenders *do* want to lend, and investors *do* want to invest; that's their business, after all. The bad news is that most business owners don't know how to ask for money. We've met literally dozens of business owners who've had loans declined and investments rejected that would otherwise have met with a much happier fate if they'd simply done two things right: found the right lender or investor, and then approached that source of funds in the right way.

So that's what we wrote about in this book—insights and insider secrets about the lenders and investors who have money, how they operate, and how you can convince them to lend to or invest in your business.

In Section One—Who Has Money?—we offer a smorgasbord of financing sources that are available to you including private investors and venture capital funds, banks and finance companies, leasing companies, the U.S. Small Business Administration and government lenders, and others.

In Section Two—Finding Money from Lenders—we reveal how banks and other lenders evaluate your loan request, how loans are commonly structured, how to choose a lender, what to include in a loan proposal, what goes on behind closed doors when lenders consider your loan request, and what to do if you're declined or if your company runs into trouble after you've received a loan.

In Section Three—Finding Money from Investors—we focus on who invest, how they evaluate your plans, what kind of investments are possible and what different approaches will cost you, how to navigate through the legal requirements of equity financing, and how to choose an investor that's right for your business.

In Section Four—How Much Money Do You Need?—we help you avoid cash drains on a new company or spot cash leaks within an existing operation. Either problem will divert the only thing that can keep you alive—precious cash flow. Then, with all the holes plugged, we show you how to figure the amount of money you really need to establish or grow your business. You don't want to go through the whole process and not ask for enough!

We've been helping business owners (including ourselves) find financing for over a decade. During that time, we've played the role of banker, venture capitalist, private investor, and financial advisor. So we have experience finding money, but we also have experience using it. As entrepreneurs, we've started and run a range of enterprises from a decidedly low-tech barnstorming business flying vintage airplanes to a high-tech CD-ROM publishing company.

What we've learned from helping dozens of companies find millions of dollars is that finding money is an art. That's right, it's an *art* not a *science*. True, there's a fair level of number-crunching involved in loan and investment decisions, but success in finding money requires a major dose of finesse too.

So if you're looking for money to start a new business or to expand an existing one, you've come to the right place. There are lots of ways to find money, you just need to know how to find it, you need to know how to ask for it, and you need to have the stamina to go the distance.

> *Far better it is to dare mighty things,*
> *to win glorious triumphs even though checkered by failure,*
> *than to rank with those poor spirits who neither enjoy nor suffer much*
> *because they live in the gray twilight that knows neither victory nor defeat.*

Theodore Roosevelt

ACKNOWLEDGMENTS

Throughout this book, wherever necessary, we've tried to round out our experience with contributions from industry's leaders. Special thanks go to the following individuals and organizations for their valuable contributions.

Kristine Anderson, Vice President, Union Bank
Latimer Asch, The Fair Isaac Company, Inc.
Dave Bartram, Executive Vice President, Bank of Commerce
Fred Beste, Managing Partner, NEPA Venture Fund
Diana Bukaty, Manager, *Inc.* magazine
Dave Clark, Owner, Riviera Finance
Pete Collins, Director of Entrepreneurial Services, Coopers & Lybrand LLP
H. Michael Cushinsky, President, American Credit Indemnity
Tom DeFilipps, Esq., Partner, Wilson, Sonsini, Goodrich & Rosati
Mace Edwards, President, The Edwards Research Group
David Gerhardt, Executive Director, The Capital Network
David Gleba, President, Venture One
Rosemarie Greco, President and CEO, CoreStates Bank
Cindy Harper, GE Capital
Mark Hill, President, Baker Hill Financial
Susan Kelsay, Editor, Annual Statement Studies, Robert Morris Associates
Dan Morefield, Senior Vice President, First Interstate Bank of California
Greg Myers, Public Relations Manager, CFI ProServices, Inc.
Matt Quilter, Esq., Partner, Heller, Ehrman, White & McAuliffe
Don Schmoll, Acting Branch Manager, Export-Import Bank of the United States

Hans Schroeder, President, Business Equity Appraisal Reports
Rolf S. Selvig, Jr., Marketing Director, Venture One
Donald Sontag, Partner, Sontag & Associates
William E. Wetzel, Director Emeritus, Center for Venture Research
Mark Zmiewski, Information Products Manager, Robert Morris Associates

Addresses and telephone numbers for these individuals and organizations are provided in the Appendix.

KATE LISTER
TOM HARNISH

CONTENTS

SECTION ONE

WHO HAS MONEY?

Starting or growing a business, and you need money to turn your dreams into reality? You have several options:

- You can borrow the money you need and incur a debt, which you'll have to repay.
- You can sell part of your company to investors and exchange equity for the money you need.
- You can do both.

How much debt you can take on and how much equity you should sell are tough decisions, because the right mix varies from industry to industry and from business to business. In any case, the decision is often made for you based on what a given source will qualify you for, rather than what you might want. So what kind of financing *do* you qualify for, and where can you find it?

1 LESSONS FROM SUCCESS

As a starting point, it's worth taking a look at where successful companies found the money they needed. Coopers & Lybrand, one of the nation's largest accounting firms, recently conducted a study of 328 fast-growing manufacturing and service companies. Interestingly, they found that most of them started *without* the help of outside capital. These highly successful companies, it turns out, were usually started with the founder's own money and with help from family and friends:

Start-Up Funding Sources	
Owner, friends, family	71%
Investors	13%
Bank loans	8%
Supplier/customer alliances	8%

Source: Trendsetter Barometer, Coopers & Lybrand, Philadelphia, PA, 1994. Used with permission.

Inc.'s most recent annual survey (top of p. 3) of the 500 fastest growing U.S. companies (of any kind) shows the same general breakdown.

The *Inc.* survey also provides a breakdown (bottom of p. 3) of how much money was available to start. Over a quarter of the *Inc.* 500 companies started with $5,000 or less, and more than half started with less than $50,000.

Inc. 500
Sources of Seed Capital

Source	%
Personal savings	78.5
Bank loans	14.3
Family	12.9
Employees/partners	12.4
Friends	9.0
Venture capital	6.3
Mortgaged property	4.0
Govt. guaranteed loans	0.1
Other	3.4

* The percentages don't add up to 100%, because most companies start with money from several sources.

Source: Martha E. Mangelsdorf, ``Behind the Scenes," *Inc.,* October 1992, pp. 72–80. Reprinted with permission, *Inc.* Magazine, (October 1992). Copyright 1992 by Goldhirsh Group, Inc., 38 Commercial Wharf, Boston, MA 02110.

Inc. 500
Start-Up Funding

Amount	%
$1000 or less	13.0
$1000–$5000	12.6
$5000–$10,000	8.3
$10,000–$25,000	13.3
$25,000–$50,000	12.0
$50,000–$100,000	15.6
$100,000–$500,000	17.8
$500,000–$1,000,000	2.8
$1,000,000–$2,000,000	1.3
$2,000,000–$5,000,000	1.3
$5,000,000 and more	1.1

Source: Martha E. Mangelsdorf, "Behind the Scenes," *Inc.,* October 1992, pp. 72–80. Reprinted with permission, *Inc.* magazine, (October 1992). Copyright 1992 by Goldhirsh Group, Inc., 38 Commercial Wharf, Boston, MA 02110.

❑ Secret

> You really don't need megabucks to start even a fast-growing business. The Coopers & Lybrand study also observed, however, that growth companies that did receive money from outside investors typically started with three times more money and went on to produce 30 percent more revenue. Even more interesting was their finding that those companies that started with bank loans raised only slightly more capital than the norm to start out, but went on to produce 76 percent more revenue than the average growth company surveyed.

Now, does that mean that if you want to make more money you should go after a bank loan to start? Not really. These figures are probably more a reflection of cause than effect: Better grounded firms are more likely to qualify for a bank loan at start-up, and thus are likely to make more money in the long run. Either way, it's clear that outside funding—if you can obtain it—will help you grow faster.

Even though, as we've seen, most company founders used their own money for start-up, they probably would have preferred to use someone else's. The problem is most start-ups are simply unable to attract lenders or investors. But, as companies grow and prove their ability to generate cash flow and operate successfully, their financing needs and options begin to change—typically within two to three years of start-up.

The Coopers & Lybrand study showed that, on average, by their 28th month in business, two out of three surveyed companies were funded primarily by outside sources such as banks, venture capital, and alliances. Significantly, those companies that received funding from investors two to three years after start-up raised nearly five times more money than those receiving bank financing, and today they're producing, on average, 30 percent higher revenues than their surveyed peers.

DEBT OR EQUITY?   2

What kind of money is right for *your* business? Debt capital is generally cheaper than equity capital in the long run, and it's typically quicker and easier to find. Plus the real advantage to debt financing is that it doesn't dilute your ownership. The bad news about debt capital is that lenders require regular monthly payments of principal and interest regardless of your profitability. When you're just cranking up, or if things aren't going well later, don't expect a lender to cut you some slack.

Investors on the other hand are, almost by definition, willing to gamble on your success. Early in the life of your company investors usually don't expect a return on their money, because they're really hoping for a huge success in three to seven years. Of course, as owners, investors also share in the risk of failure. They may not require monthly payments, but you can be sure they'll be checking on your performance to make sure the company is doing what you promised it would.

Incidentally, while the concept of financing your business purely on other people's money (OPM) has been widely touted by a number of self-appointed gurus, it rarely works that way in the real world. First, the Coopers & Lybrand study found that only about 13 percent of companies found someone to invest money in their start-up. And remember, those statistics were based on fast-growing manufacturing and service companies. The chance of a slow-growth retail or distribution company being financed by an investor is much lower. Which leaves lenders—and lenders shy away from what they call an "undercapitalized" company (one where the owners have too little of their own money at risk). Your investment in your company is a lender's best guarantee of your commitment through thick and thin.

Here are some questions to consider when deciding between debt and equity financing (we'll help you with the answers as we continue):

Debt

- Will my company qualify for debt financing?
- What terms and conditions will be placed on the debt?
- Am I willing to personally guarantee the debt?
- Am I willing to pledge company and personal assets as collateral?
- Will we have the cash flow to support new debt?
- Will we be able to afford the new debt if interest rates rise or business slows?
- What's my after-tax cost of borrowing money?
- Can we produce the necessary reports to comply with loan terms?
- Can we accurately predict our future cash flow?
- Can we comply with all covenants and conditions?
- Can we obtain enough debt financing to achieve our growth plans?
- Will new debt increase our leverage so much that it will hurt our credit rating with vendors and others?

Equity

- Can we attract investors?
- Will we be happy with the terms and conditions that investors are likely to place on us?
- Am I willing to share control with others?
- Am I willing to risk losing control of my company?
- Are we willing to share confidential information with potential investors?
- Do our financial statements and internal records accurately reflect our operation?
- Can we keep up with the ongoing demand for information from investors?
- Am I willing to share future profits with investors?

To summarize, then, if you finance your company with debt and you're successful, everything you make is yours after you pay off the debt. On the other hand, with equity capital you may grow larger or more quickly, but you'll have to share the wealth and some control with investors. If the thought of sharing ownership and control bothers you, but your company really needs the money, you have to ask yourself: "Would I rather own 1 percent of General Motors, or 100 percent of

I-Wanna-Be-General-Motors?" It's an individual decision that has to be weighed against the possibilities and potential tradeoffs.

❑ **Secret**

> This is one you probably don't want to hear, but the fact is you're probably better off to struggle through start-up on your own nickel, perhaps with some money from a bank if you can qualify. If you can put a couple of years of success under your belt before you approach investors, you'll be able to attract more money, at a lower cost, than you would have at start-up.

In the end, the best approach will be one that fits you and your company's needs, wants, personality, and financial realities. And if you haven't already gathered, by financial realities, we mean the Golden Rule of Finance applies: *Those who have the gold rule.*

The rest of this section is devoted to giving you an insider's look at a variety of sources of debt and equity. Read about each one in light of your own particular cash flow needs. Then, once you've targeted your search, later sections will help you hone your approach and, ultimately, find the money you need.

<table>
<tr><td>**3**</td><td># WHO ARE THE LENDERS AND INVESTORS?</td></tr>
</table>

Believe it or not, there actually are *lots* of lenders and investors out there, and they really do want to lend to, or invest in, your business. That's how they make money, after all. But they each have their own unique way of packaging their product—money.

Some sources are cheap, and some are expensive. Some sources will be slow to deliver the money you need, and some work quickly. Some will try to avoid all risk, and some are adrenaline junkies looking to achieve a new nervous high by investing in risky propositions. And while some sources are far more accessible than others, it's best to consider all the alternatives. Just keep in mind that finding the *ideal* source may take some time and will require that you do your homework. In the end, though, the paperwork you prepare will literally be worth its weight in gold.

OVERVIEW

Where *do* you find money? Most companies find at least some of the money they need from company founders and investors. Beyond that, banks supply the bulk of the capital to small businesses. Finance companies run a distant third. It might surprise you to know that, in spite of their visibility, less than 1 percent of small businesses get money from the U.S. Small Business Administration (SBA), other government programs, venture capitalists, mortgage bankers, insurance companies, public markets, or grants. While all that may sound discouraging, remember that 1 percent of U.S. businesses is still roughly 200,000 companies. Your chance of finding money through one of those sources is far better than theirs after reading this book.

Let's take a closer look, then, at all the investors and lenders who can provide the money you need.

INDIVIDUAL INVESTORS

Individual investors include two types of people: those who know you, like you, or love you enough to provide money with few or no strings attached, or successful folks who invest in businesses, because they believe it will beat the return they could see from more traditional investments. Often referred to as *angels*, these investors are a huge source of informal venture capital.

Angel investments appear to be the largest source of risk capital in the small business economy, but the extent isn't well known because transactions tend to be kept private. Some estimates put the annual volume of private investor deals in the $30 to $50 billion range. The size of this capital pool dwarfs that of the formal venture capital community, which invests between $3 and $5 billion annually.

William Wetzel, Director of the Center for Venture Research at the University of New Hampshire is well known for his research on private investors. Information compiled from several of his studies shows that the "average" private investor is 47 years old, has an annual income of $90,000, a net worth of $750,000, is college educated, has been self-employed, and invests $37,000 per venture.

Most angels invest close to home, and rarely put in more than a few hundred thousand dollars. Exhibit 3.1 offers some additional information about the nature of informal capital.

Only one problem. Angels don't wear signs proclaiming that they're investors! But angels can be found among your family, friends, acquaintances, professionals, customers, suppliers, and even competitors. Some invest in groups with other angels (whom, by the way, they'll usually bring to the party).

In some parts of the country, *angel networks* have formed to improve their access to deals, which of course means that the networks also can help you find money. Angel networks, like angels, tend to keep a low profile, but here's a list of some of the better known angel networks to help you start tracking down this elusive bunch.

The Capital Network
8920 Business Park Drive,
Suite 160
Austin TX 78759
512-794-9398

Technology Capital Network at M.I.T.
201 Vassas Street
Cambridge MA 02139
617-253-7163

Pennsylvania Private Investors
  Network
Technology Council of Greater
  Philadelphia
435 Devon Park Drive
Wayne PA 19087-1945
215-975-9430

Northwest Capital Network
P.O. Box 6650
Portland OR 97228
503-282-6273

The Enterprise Corporation of
  Pittsburgh
4516 Henry Street, Suite 201
Pittsburgh PA 15213
412-578-3481

Capital Resource Network
11140 Lackman Road
Lenexa KS 66219
913-888-6807

Kentucky Investment Capital
  Network
2326 Capital Plaza Tower
Frankfort KY 40601
502-564-7140

The Investors' Circle
31W007 North Avenue,
Suite 101
W. Chicago IL 60185
708-876-1101
(members invest only in socially
  responsible business
  opportunities)

The Capital Circle
31W007 North Avenue,
Suite 101
W. Chicago IL 60185
708-876-1101
(members invest only in women-
  led business opportunities)

Most angel networks are nonprofit organizations that charge between $50 and $1,500 to circulate your business plan to their investors.
The average fee charged by the most successful of these networks is
around $450 per year. Investors pay similar fees to belong to these net-
works giving them access to business opportunities like yours. Some
networks offer monthly forums where, once your deal's been screened,
it can be pitched to a roomful of potential angels. Others, like the Capital Network, based in Austin, Texas, offer computerized matchmaking.
Due to securities laws, most angel networks stop short at the introduction stage. If an investor, or group of them, is interested in your deal, the
follow-up and negotiations will be up to you and the investor(s). Section
Three offers secrets and advice on how to approach and structure deals
with private investors or angels.

But first, a word from the lawyers: Equity transactions must comply
with all federal and state securities laws. The Securities Act of 1933 offers a number of exemptions that allow for relatively uncomplicated private placements when the deal and investors meet certain criteria. More
about those later; for now, recognize that even a seemingly harmless ad

EXHIBIT 3.1   Findings of Various Studies of Informal Capital

- Informal investment appears to be the largest source of external equity capital for small businesses. Nine out of ten investments are devoted to small, mostly start-up firms with fewer than twenty employees.

- Nine out of ten investors provide personal loans or loan guarantees to the firms they invest in. On average, this increases the available capital by 57%.

- Informal investors are older, have higher incomes, and are better educated than the average citizen, yet they are not often millionaires. They are a diverse group, displaying a wide range of personal characteristics and investment behavior.

- Seven out of ten investments are made within fifty miles of the investor's home or office.

- Investors expect an average 26% annual return at the time they invest, and they believe that about one-third of their investments are likely to result in a substantial capital loss.

- Investors accept an average of three deals for every ten considered. The most common reasons given for rejecting a deal are insufficient growth potential, overpriced equity, lack of sufficient talent of the management, or lack of information about the entrepreneur or key personnel.

- There appears to be no shortage of informal capital funds. Investors included in this study would have invested almost 35% more than they did if acceptable opportunities had been available.

Source: Information in this exhibit is taken from *The State of Small Business: A Report of the President,* transmitted to Congress 1993, GPO ISSN 0735-1437, Table A-5, p. 156.

in a newspaper promoting your need for an investor or partner can get you into big trouble with the securities sheriff. Naïveté in such matters could cost you your company and worse!

BANKS

When asked by a newspaper reporter why he robbed banks, infamous bank robber Willie Sutton is alleged to have replied, "Because that's where the money is." As you continue reading, you'll find that Willie was only partially right. Nevertheless, banks do supply the bulk of the money for small businesses. A significant portion of this book, therefore, focuses on bank financing. And most of what you'll read about how bankers think, for the most part, applies to other types of lenders as well.

In effect, bankers are financial intermediaries. They're a little like Robin Hood except that banks take from the cash-rich and give, er . . . lend, to the cash-poor. They borrow from individuals, companies, and institutions that deposit money in their bank. In exchange, banks pay them interest for the use of their money. The bank then turns around and rents the money to you in the form of a loan at an interest rate that's high enough to cover the interest they pay on the money they borrow from depositors, plus the bank's fixed expenses, and some level of profit.

Banking Environment

Today, it's more important than ever to know the rules and realities of the banking environment. Major changes occurred in the U.S. banking system in the 1980s and 1990s. Probably the most significant change came as a result of the savings and loan crisis. Federal regulators, embarrassed by their handling of that debacle, were determined not to let the banking system follow suit. They instituted a variety of new rules, regulations, and performance standards on banks that, of course, also affected borrowers. The result of these changes is that bankers are more cautious than ever about lending to companies that lack a demonstrated cash flow. Loan prices, bank service fees, collateral requirements, collateral scrutiny, and emphasis on cash flow analysis have all been escalated as a result of the S&L crisis. Cash flow, credit quality, and caution are the watchwords in banking today.

Another factor that's helped to shape the current banking scene dates back to the late 1970s when commercial banks found themselves in big trouble as a result of rapidly rising interest rates. They had, in effect, borrowed short term (in the form of checking and savings accounts) at variable rates of interest, and they loaned long term (for mortgages and other loans) at fixed rates of interest. As a result, they saw the rates they had to pay on short-term money go way up, while the rate they received on long-term money stayed about the same. So their net interest income, a bank's primary source of income, declined dramatically. These days, banks are reluctant to fix an interest rate for more than three to five years, and for the same reason they prefer shorter terms over longer ones.

Section Two offers details on how to deal with banks and other lenders, including how to select a bank, how loan officers will evaluate your loan request, how to develop your loan request package, and how to negotiate your deal. For now, here's a summary of their lending activities.

Commercial Loans

The types of service that a particular bank offers is influenced by commercial banking regulations designed to protect the deposits (maybe *your* deposits) that the bank is lending. The bank's size, its own asset/liability mix, and their management preferences all influence what the bank will do. As a result, banks vary widely in their product offerings and risk appetite, and it's not at all unusual for the same loan request to be approved at one bank and declined at several others.

Business loans from banks range from a minimum of a few thousand dollars to a maximum based on the size of the bank and their risk appetite. Smaller banks are therefore more limited than larger ones in the amount they can lend an individual borrower. But smaller banks solve this problem by sharing larger loans with other banks, through what are called *participations*.

While some unsecured commercial loans are extended by banks, most small-business loans are secured with liens on company and personal assets. Lenders will often require personal guarantees (joint with spouses) and personal collateral from anyone who owns more than 20 percent of the company—especially if they feel that the business doesn't have a strong credit history, reliable cash flow, or offer enough collateral. This is typically the case with young businesses, service businesses, retailers, and fast-growing businesses. The owner's home is often taken as additional collateral on such loans, so don't feel as if you're being singled out should they want you to pledge everything you own including your firstborn. Just about every business owner goes through the same thing at some point. Think of it from the bank's perspective: If you don't think it's worth the risk, why should they?

Expect the loan approval process to take several weeks at a minimum. For loans over $100,000, a four- to eight-week approval process is not unusual. Once the loan is approved, it may take several days or even weeks to actually receive the funds, so don't spend it before you have it. Complex loans that require nonstandard loan documents will take longer.

During the 1980s, many S&Ls expanded their consumer lending activities to include business loans. While recent problems in the industry have dampened the commercial lending activities of many, some S&Ls still offer small business loans. Their fees, approval process, and rates are similar to banks, though some are more willing to provide longer terms and better rates for real-estate loans.

Consumer Loans

Many business start-ups are funded by people who found the money they needed through home equity loans, second mortgages, first mortgage refinancings, and personal loans from banks. These differ from commercial or business loans in that they are often handled by the consumer lending side of the bank rather than the commercial lenders. For applicants with good credit and a strong income history (that will continue in the future), consumer loans are easier to obtain than commercial loans, they're governed by consumer protection regulations, and they have fewer strings attached.

Many lenders don't care if you use a consumer loan for business purposes, but others will send you to straight to their commercial loan division if you indicate the money is for a business. So shop around before you try the old "I just want the money for a vacation and to fix up some stuff around the house" trick—it's fraud, although that doesn't seem to stop a lot of people.

Consumer lenders don't require that you submit a business plan, company financial information, or most of the other documentation that business lenders require. Typically consumer loan applications are less than four pages including a personal financial statement. Approval within days and even hours of application is often possible. And thanks to consumer protection laws, as long as you continue to make your payments, even if your business falls on tough times, you probably won't run the risk of having the bank require that you immediately pay off the loan—something *that can and does happen* with business loans. In addition, consumer lenders may or may not require collateral depending on your credit and income history. Consumer loans come in a variety of shapes and sizes including:

Uncollateralized Personal Loan

If your credit history and income are strong, you may qualify for an uncollateralized personal loan or line of credit. These are often called signature loans, because they are granted primarily on the strength of your word that you'll pay them back. You can apply for these loans over the telephone, at your local bank branch, or through the mail. Such loans are usually granted for amounts of less than $10,000 and a maximum term of five years. Interest rates are similar to those for credit cards. Approvals are often granted in a matter of days or even hours.

First Mortgage Refinance (with cash out)

Some lenders will refinance your first mortgage for an amount greater than its remaining balance, thus providing you with some walkaway funds. You may need to snoop around to find such lenders, but this is often a good way to find money. Lenders limit the cash you can take out to some dollar amount or to a percentage of the mortgage value.

The primary advantage to these loans is that they provide maximum cash flow by allowing you to spread your payments over a 15-, 25-, or 30-year term. On the other hand, this may not feel like much of an advantage 10 years from now when you're still paying interest on the money you spent long ago. You can solve this problem by shopping for a loan with no prepayment penalty. Then, if you want to, you can pay the business portion of the loan off as your cash flow allows.

First mortgage rates are often several percentage points cheaper than second mortgages and home equity loans, but closing costs of up to 3 percent may apply. First mortgage refinances may take longer than other consumer loans, because they require an appraisal. In times of low interest rates having your property appraised can delay the process by several weeks, or even months, because everyone else is trying to refinance too. First mortgage refinancing makes sense when current mortgage rates are at least 2 percent lower than the rate on your existing mortgage debt.

Second Mortgages and Home Equity Loans

These loans leave your first mortgage in place by taking a second- and sometimes even a third-mortgage position. They're generally higher priced than first mortgages and are offered with 15- to

25-year repayment terms. Such loans often require less time to close than first mortgages.

Home Equity Lines of Credit

Some home equity lenders offer lines of credit. Such loans allow you to borrow when you need extra cash, and pay the money back when you can. Monthly payments are based on a 36- to 60-month repayment schedule. You may need to shop around for such loans, but their flexibility makes them handy for the small business owner.

No-Income-Verification Loans

No-doc (no documentation) or low-doc loans were extremely popular prior to the shake-up of the savings and loan industry. Such loans don't require borrowers to provide tax returns as verification of income. You simply fill out an application stating your current income, and the lender bases a decision on the information submitted.

No-doc loans are intended to expedite loan approvals for people who have good credit but whose tax returns do not reflect their current earnings. Submitting incorrect information on loan applications *is* fraudulent, and lenders are more careful than ever about extending these loans. Most, but not all, carry higher rates and fees than conventional loans. And due to the changes in the S&L industry and financial markets, you'll need to shop hard to find them. But, at least as of this writing, they do still exist. Try the mortgage lenders section of your local newspaper, or call a few mortgage lenders and ask if they know anyone who is doing them.

Personal Loan Qualifications　Determining what size personal or home loan you'll qualify for is simple. First, your monthly rent or mortgage payments, homeowner's insurance, and real estate taxes should total no more that 28 to 30 percent of your monthly gross income.

Housing Cost Test

Projected rent or mortgage	$1,000
Insurance	25
Real estate taxes	100
Total housing expense	$1,125

Second, your housing costs plus all other lease, credit card, and loan payments (including the one you're applying for) should total no more than 38% of your monthly income.

Consumer Debt Test

Consumer loans	$ 50
Credit card payments	$ 50
Total housing and debt service	$1,225

Depending on the nature of the loan and the strength of the borrower, some lenders will stretch to even 55 percent of monthly income on the consumer debt test.

❑ Secret

Most lenders focus more on the second cash flow test rather than the first so if you pass the latter, but not the former, they'll often do the deal anyway.

For real estate secured loans, once you've passed the preceding consumer debt tests, you'll also have to pass a collateral test that will be based on the value of your home and any existing mortgages. For home equity loans and mortgages, you can determine the amount you'll qualify for by taking 75 to 85 percent of your house's value less your existing mortgage. If that total exceeds the amount that you qualify for from the consumer debt test, you'll be entitled to borrow only up to the lesser amount. Conversely, if the amount determined in this test is less than what you'd qualify for on the consumer debt test, then the collateral test will establish your limit.

Collateral Value Test for Home Equity Loans			
House value	$200,000	$200,000	$200,000
Lender's maximum loan to value	75%	80%	85%
House collateral value	$150,000	$160,000	$170,000
Less existing mortgage(s)	($50,000)	($50,000)	($50,000)
Maximum loan amount	$100,000	$110,000	$120,000

Credit guidelines, consumer debt test standards, and loan-to-value criteria vary from one lender to the next. Some lenders will stretch on the collateral test, others will stretch on the cash flow test especially if you have good credit, lots of equity, a small mortgage balance, strong personal cash balances, or a high score on the consumer debt test.

Determining which lenders will stretch the most will require some sleuthing.

❑ Secret

In general, the lenders who write your loan and then immediately sell it to a servicing organization are the least flexible. This is because the companies that buy mortgages in what's called the secondary mortgage market have established a set of standards for the loans that they buy. If your loan doesn't meet those standards, your lender is stuck with it. Some of the more flexible lenders are known as portfolio lenders, because they hold (or portfolio) their loans rather than selling them in the secondary market. As a result, these lenders can, to some extent, set their own lending guidelines, but they often (though not always) charge premium rates and fees.

A word of caution in selecting a mortgage lender. If it sounds too good to be true, it probably is. Not all lenders are as reputable as you might think. Be cautious about deals that require higher than average up-front, nonrefundable application fees, or those where the terms seem unrealistically attractive. Some low-life lenders have been known to change terms and conditions at the last minute—after you've already invested a month or more of your time and who knows how much money in their loan approval process. If you have any doubts, call other lenders in your area and the Better Business Bureau to see if they can tell you anything about the lender you're considering.

FINANCE COMPANIES

Commercial finance companies often take on higher risk commercial loans than banks. Besides the more visible auto loan side of their business, commercial finance companies can sometimes handle the tougher commercial loans. Companies in high-growth situations, where traditional lenders are unwilling to continually increase their loans; companies whose ability to cover loan payments can't be demonstrated in historical financial statements; companies with erratic financial performance; or companies with high debt-to-worth ratios but strong cash flow may be able to find money through commercial finance companies.

Most finance companies prefer larger deals (in excess of $500,000), but some have divisions that will handle smaller transactions too. Because their cost of funds and risk of default are higher than a bank's, finance companies tend to charge rates and fees 2 to 10 percent higher. Collateral and lending preferences vary, but finance companies will usually consider loans secured by accounts receivables, inventory, equipment, or real-estate. Finance companies may be willing to place liens on just the assets being financed rather than on all company and personal assets.

Finance companies will take about the same time to process your loan request as banks, and they may require greater detail about your cash flow and collateral. Extremely detailed field audits of collateral (for which you'll pay thousands of dollars) are not unusual. Weekly and even daily cash flow projections are required in some situations.

LEASING

Almost any fixed asset can be leased, right down to the silverware in a restaurant. Leasing often provides an advantage over the purchase of an asset because it requires a lower initial cash outlay, because it can result in off-balance-sheet financing, and because it mitigates the risk of equipment obsolescence.

The concept of leasing is simple—someone else buys an asset on your behalf and essentially rents it to you for some period of time. The lease versus buy decision, on the other hand, is anything but simple. It's virtually impossible to make an unequivocal statement about how and when leasing could be more attractive than buying because tax, accounting, legal, cash flow, and credit factors vary from time to time and from business to business. But let's take a look at what's possible.

Leasing Basics

There are two types of leases for financial accounting purposes, operating leases and capital leases. Operating leases allow the lessee (you) to treat the lease payment as an expense for financial reporting purposes. As a result, your financial statements will show neither the leased asset nor the lease liability on your balance sheet. So your ability to borrow money in the future is preserved, because the transaction will

not increase your debt-to-equity ratio (you'll read more about the importance of this ratio in Section Two).

Capital leases, on the other hand, treat the leased asset as though
you bought it and financed it with a loan. The asset is depreciated, and
the loan appears on your balance sheet as a liability. On the income
statement, the interest portion of the loan and the amortization of the
lease are shown as an expense (similar to depreciation). If a lease meets
any one of the following criteria, it will be considered a capital lease for
the purpose of financial statement presentation:

- The lease transfers ownership of the property to the lessee by the
  end of the lease term.
- The lease contains an option to purchase the leased property at a bargain price.
- The lease term is greater than or equal to 75 percent of the estimated
  economic life of the leased property (this criterion does not apply if
  the lease term falls within the last 25% of the total estimated economic life of the leased property).
- The present value of rental or other minimum lease payments equals
  or exceeds 90 percent of the fair value of the leased property less any
  investment tax credit retained by the lessor (this criterion does not
  apply if the lease term falls within the last 25% of the total estimated
  economic life of the leased property).

Exhibit 3.2 compares the treatment of an operating lease and a capital lease on a financial statement.

With a Capital Lease, your Balance Sheet will look weaker than it
would with an Operating Lease, since the item treated as an asset will
decline in value quicker than the same item treated as a liability. In addition, your Income Statement will show a deduction for depreciation of
the asset and the interest portion of the lease payment under a Capital
Lease. Therefore, early in the lease, your Income Statement will look
weaker with a Capital Lease than it would with an Operating Lease. In
fact, both your Income Statement and the Balance Sheet will look just
like they would if you'd purchased the asset outright and financed it
with a commercial loan.

Now that you have an idea of the difference between an Operating
Lease and a Capital Lease for financial statement purposes, we have to
confuse the situation a little. You see, the IRS uses different rules than
those used by the people who prepare financial statements in confor-
mance with generally accepted accounting principles (GAAP). Conse-
quently, the same lease can be treated one way on your financial
statements and another way on your tax returns.

EXHIBIT 3.2 Operating Lease versus Capital Lease (Example Based on Leasing $1 Million Asset)

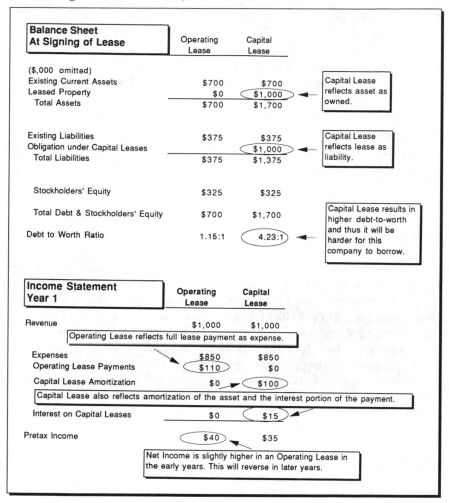

Both the lessor and the lessee have to agree on the treatment of the leased asset for tax-reporting purposes so that only one party takes the related tax deductions. If your lease meets all the following guidelines, the lessor, not your company, will usually treat the lease as though it were owned (and thus show it as an asset on their Balance Sheet and deduct depreciation on their Income Statement). Your company can then show the lease payment as an expense on your income statement for federal tax purposes if:

- The lease term does not exceed 80% of the estimated useful life of the asset.
- The leased asset's estimated residual value, at the expiration of the lease term, must be projected to equal at least 20 percent of its original value.
- Neither the lessee nor any related party can have a right to purchase the property from the lessor at a price *less* than its fair market value at the time of the purchase.
- The lessee or any related party may not pay or guarantee payment of any part of the original purchase price of the leased asset.
- The leased equipment must not be so specialized that no one other than the lessee could use it in a commercially feasible manner at the end of the lease.

Leasing Companies

Leasing companies come in a variety of shapes and sizes. Many are subsidiaries of banks, some are owned by large corporations (like General Electric), some are related to equipment vendors, some specialize in certain types of equipment (like trucks, cars, computer equipment, aircraft, telecommunications, furniture, etc.). Others focus on a variety of equipment, but specialize in certain size transactions.

In general, leasing companies can be more creative, move quicker, and be more aggressive than commercial banks. Therefore, it really pays to shop for the best lease. And while lessors talk in terms of lease payments rather than interest rates, be sure you compare the full cost of the lease before you make a decision.

Lease/Buy Comparison   While every lease versus buy decision will differ, Exhibit 3.3, prepared by GE Capital, the largest equipment lessor in the world, demonstrate a typical lease versus buy decision for a $30,000 truck.

So what can you conclude about leasing? Whether leasing is right for you will depend on your particular financial situation, and the specific terms of your purchase or lease; but, in general, leasing is a good idea when:

- You're short on cash and the lease allows a lower down payment or lower monthly payments than lenders would require on a commercial loan. You can usually enter a lease for one or two payments up front. If you borrow the money, you'll have to come up with 10 to 30 percent of the whole amount as a down payment.

EXHIBIT 3.3   Lease versus Buy Decision: $30,000 Truck

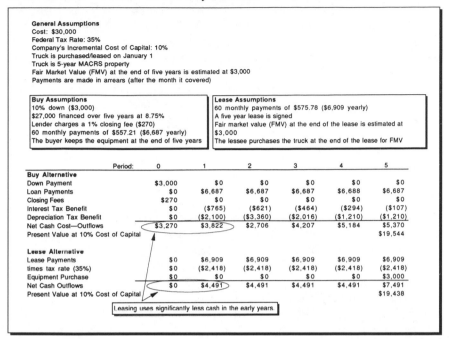

General Assumptions
Cost: $30,000
Federal Tax Rate: 35%
Company's Incremental Cost of Capital: 10%
Truck is purchased/leased on January 1
Truck is 5-year MACRS property
Fair Market Value (FMV) at the end of five years is estimated at $3,000
Payments are made in arrears (after the month it covered)

Buy Assumptions	Lease Assumptions
10% down ($3,000)	60 monthly payments of $575.78 ($6,909 yearly)
$27,000 financed over five years at 8.75%	A five year lease is signed
Lender charges a 1% closing fee ($270)	Fair market value (FMV) at the end of the lease is estimated at
60 monthly payments of $557.21 ($6,687 yearly)	$3,000
The buyer keeps the equipment at the end of five years	The lessee purchases the truck at the end of the lease for FMV

Period:	0	1	2	3	4	5
Buy Alternative						
Down Payment	$3,000	$0	$0	$0	$0	$0
Loan Payments	$0	$6,687	$6,687	$6,687	$6,688	$6,687
Closing Fees	$270	$0	$0	$0	$0	$0
Interest Tax Benefit	$0	($765)	($621)	($464)	($294)	($107)
Depreciation Tax Benefit	$0	($2,100)	($3,360)	($2,016)	($1,210)	($1,210)
Net Cash Cost—Outflows	$3,270	$3,822	$2,706	$4,207	$5,184	$5,370
Present Value at 10% Cost of Capital						$19,544
Lease Alternative						
Lease Payments	$0	$6,909	$6,909	$6,909	$6,909	$6,909
times tax rate (35%)	$0	($2,418)	($2,418)	($2,418)	($2,418)	($2,418)
Equipment Purchase	$0	$0	$0	$0	$0	$3,000
Net Cash Outflows	$0	$4,491	$4,491	$4,491	$4,491	$7,491
Present Value at 10% Cost of Capital						$19,438

Leasing uses significantly less cash in the early years.

- You're short on borrowing capacity or want to preserve your balance sheet for future financing needs. Only an operating lease fits this criterion.

- Time is of the essence and the lessor can move quicker than a commercial lender.

- The risk of equipment obsolescence is high. In a lease transaction, the lessor usually bears the brunt of this risk.

- The lessor is willing to offer a flexible payment schedule that matches your cash flow needs.

- The lessor has a vested interest in wanting you to use its equipment and has a secondary market for it at the end of the lease. An equipment vendor is often much more eager and capable of putting together an attractive deal than a disinterested third party, in part because that vendor knows, understands, and appreciates the value of the equipment. Therefore, you won't have to spend hours trying to convince a vendor that the equipment is worth the amount you suggest, as you may with a banker.

- You're not sure you can really use the equipment. Better to risk a little money in a lease than a lot of money in a purchase. Just be sure that you can back out of the lease that you sign, perhaps with an upgrade in equipment.
- Your lessor's package offers other benefits such as maintenance, repair, replacement, or backup services.

In addition to conventional leases, a couple of unique lease financing alternatives are available including sale-leasebacks and venture leasing.

Sale-Leaseback Financing

Sale-leasebacks, as the name implies, involve selling your assets to a third party and then leasing them back. If your business is cash-poor but asset-rich, this form of financing will allow you to unlock the value of your buildings and equipment. In addition, a sale-leaseback can improve your financial statement ratios, preserve your credit lines and borrowing capacity, and result in a variety of tax benefits.

Let's say you own a building that has very little debt, but due to historical losses, you're not in a position to take advantage of the tax benefits of owning the building. You don't want to sell it outright because you don't want to move. Instead, you sell it to a third party such as an individual, another company, or a leasing company, and lease it back over some period. Now you have the cash from the sale of the building to fund your business, and you continue to use the building just as you did before the transaction.

Venture Leasing

Recently, a new form of leasing has emerged, called venture leasing. This nontraditional form of leasing allows venture-capital-backed companies to qualify for leases that would otherwise be impossible. Venture leasing companies work closely with a venture financing firm to structure a lease that works for both the lessor and the lessee. Typically, the lessor eases its standard underwriting criteria in exchange for an equity position or rights to a future equity position in the lessee's company. Such transactions are only available to fast-growing companies with a strong potential for future success.

As we've said, leasing is a complex and dynamic topic. Be sure to consult your tax, legal, and/or accounting advisors for advice about your specific situation and the lease that you're considering.

U.S. SMALL BUSINESS ADMINISTRATION (SBA)

Most small businesses are eligible for SBA assistance. The bulk of SBA lending is accomplished through authorized bank and nonbank lenders with the SBA guaranteeing a portion of the deal. In addition, some loans are available directly from the SBA in situations where no other financing is available. A list of SBA-authorized bank and nonbank lenders is available from your local SBA office or by calling their Small Business Answer Desk at 1-800-827-5722.

SBA Loans Profile[1]

88% between $100,000 and $750,000.

56% went to retail and service businesses.

83% went to existing companies.

35% went to companies less than eight years old.

To qualify for an SBA loan, a business must meet the criteria in Exhibit 3.4.

In general, SBA funds may be used for the purchase of equipment, supplies, inventory, and commercial/industrial real estate; or for working capital, leasehold improvements, business start-ups, buy-outs, construction and under certain programs, some forms of debt repayment. SBA funds may not be used to pay unsecured creditors, for speculative endeavors, to cash out owners or investors, for gambling operations, for lending and investment, or for investment real estate.

SBA loans are basically intended for businesses that do not qualify for "reasonable" financing from other sources. Borrowers are encouraged to apply through authorized bank and non-bank lenders, but as a last resort and in some special circumstances, the SBA may consider a direct loan. Business owners that have significant cash resources (unless earmarked for retirement or family education) will not qualify for SBA financing. Likewise, companies with "excessive" cash balances or assets that could be converted to cash will not qualify for SBA loans.

The SBA frequently introduces new programs, places greater emphasis on certain existing programs or types of businesses, and restructures program terms, conditions and guidelines. Be sure to keep in touch with your local SBA office for up-to-date information.

A breakdown of the number and dollar value of loans granted under each program, along with details about the kinds of businesses receiving SBA loans is summarized in Exhibit 3.5.

EXHIBIT 3.4 SBA Loan Qualification Requirements

- Business must be organized as a for-profit entity.
- Business can't be dominant in its field.
- Business must be independently owned and operated.
- Business must meet size limits set by SBA:*
    —Manufacturers cannot have more than 500–1500 employees.
    —Retailers must have sales of less than $5–$17 million.
    —Service businesses must have sales of less than $2.5–$14.5 million.
    —Agricultural businesses must have sales of less than $500,000–$7 million.
    —Wholesalers must have less than 100 employees.
    —Special trade construction firms' average annual receipts may not exceed $7 million.
    —Construction firms' average annual receipts may not exceed $13.5–$17 million.

* The size limits vary depending on the nature of the business, change from time to time, and differ from state to state.

7(a) Loan Guarantee Program

The 7(a) Loan Guarantee Program is the SBA's most active program. In 1992, this program guaranteed $6.1 billion in loans that went to about 25,000 recipients. The average 7(a) loan was just over $240,000.

You apply for a 7(a) loan at a bank or other designated SBA lender rather than through the SBA. In the past, you had to be formally declined for a loan before you could apply for 7(a) assistance. Now the SBA lending officers will determine for themselves that you don't qualify for conventional financing concurrent with their consideration of your application.

Banks and others participate in the SBA Guaranteed Loan Program because it allows them to make loans to businesses that wouldn't otherwise qualify. Loans made through the 7(a) programs are guaranteed by the SBA for up to 90 percent of the loan amount (or 85% for loans under $155,000). This means that if the borrower fails to pay the loan, the lender can recover the majority of its principal from the SBA.

EXHIBIT 3.5   SBA Loan Demographics

SBA Loans By Program	1992 $ Millions	1992 #	1993 $ Millions	1993 #
7(a) Loan Guarantee Program	$5,100.0	22,753	$6,100.0	25,011
504 CDC Program	$843.0	2,503	$806.9	2,501
Handicapped Loan Program	$11.6	119	$7.0	123
Guaranty Export Revolving Line	$25.0	81	$17.2	57
Guaranty Seasonal Line	$56.6	228	$61.0	227
Surety Bond Program (Bid Bonds)			$5,000.0	23,996
Small Business Investment Corps	$544.3	1,999	$806.3	1,992
Contract Loan Program	$78.5	521	$60.7	380
Small Loans Program	$124.0	3,288	$106.3	3,316
Vietnam and Disabled Vet Program	$16.0	196	$15.8	209
International Trade Loans	$33.6	58	$30.2	48
8a Loans	$4.7	28	$4.7	29

1994 Data Based on 1992 Loans

Type of organization

Corporation:	67%
Individuals	25%
Partnerships	9%

By Minority Group

Asian	8%
Hispanic	3%
Black	2%
Puerto Rican	1%

By Special Category

Veterans	14%
Vietnam Veterans	9%
Franchise	6%

Percentage of Total $ of Loans

Up to $50,000	2%
$50-$75,000	3%
$75-$100,000	4%
$100-250,000	27%
$250-$500,000	31%
$500-$750,000	30%
Over $750,000	2%

Percentage of Total # of Loans

Up to $50,000	15%
$50-$75,000	10%
$75-$100,000	10%
$100-250,000	35%
$250-$500,000	19%
$500-$750,000	9%
Over $750,000	less than 1%

By Type of Industry

Service	32%
Retail	24%
Manufacturing	20%
Wholesale	12%
Construction	5%
Transportation	3%
Agriculture	3%
Finance, Insurance, Real Estate	1%
Mining	less than 1%

By SBA Region

San Francisco	23%
Atlanta	13%
Chicago	12%
Dallas	12%
Boston	7%
New York	7%
Kansas City	7%
Denver	7%
Seattle	6%
Philadelphia	5%

By Original Loan Term

4-5 Years	6%
6-7 Years	5%
8-10 Years	16%
11-15 Years	15%
16-20 Years	24%
21-25 Years	21%
Over 25 Years	1%

New vs. Existing Businesses

New Businesses	17%
Existing Businesses	83%

Loans By # Employee

1-3 Employees	17%
4-7 Employees	18%
8-19 Employees	28%
20-49 Employees	24%
50-99 Employees	9%
100-249 Employees	3%
Over 250 Employees	less than 1%

SBA Loans by Year

	$ Million	#
1960	$167.6	3,659
1970	$527.1	8,695
1980	$3,611.3	28,192
1990	$3,545.7	15,698
1991	$3,858.1	16,442
1992	$5,599.7	22,459

Source: Information in this exhibit is taken from *Loan Profiles Fiscal Year 1992,* SBA Office of Financial Assistance, Washington, DC, 1993.

You might think that the SBA's guarantee would provide a larger incentive than it does to lenders. In reality, no lender wants a loan to go bad. In spite of the guarantee, the lender still has to chase down the defaulted borrower and try to recover the loan. All of that is very hard work, time consuming, expensive, and takes a lender away from the more productive business of booking good loans. In addition, even if they collect on the guarantee, they're still out the unguaranteed portion of the loan, the lost interest, and their collection expenses. All of which is to say that while the SBA guarantee program does allow lenders to stretch a little further, it isn't a miracle cure.

Many banks and other financing organizations provide 7(a) loans through special SBA loan divisions. Each lender establishes its own internal approval criteria, minimum loan amounts, and collateral preferences, so it's not at all unusual to be approved by one SBA lender and declined by another.

SBA lenders are given certain distinctions based on the volume of loans they process and their history with the SBA. Your local SBA office can provide you with a list of the most active lenders under the following programs:

- *Preferred SBA Lenders.* These lenders don't have to go to the SBA for approval prior to granting a loan. They actually make loan decisions on the SBA's behalf; and, therefore, the process generally doesn't take any longer than conventional bank loans. Loans handled through the Preferred Lender process carry a maximum SBA guarantee of 70 percent, although Preferred Lenders can follow standard processing rules for deals requiring a larger guarantee.

- *Certified SBA Lenders.* These lenders process your loan request, but the SBA does the approval. Guarantees for loans handled in this way can be for up to 85 percent of the loan amount for loans over $155,000 (with loan terms of 10 years or less), up to 75 percent for loans over $155,000 (with loan terms of 10 years or more), or 90 percent for loans up to $155,000 (regardless of their term). According to the SBA, loan requests submitted for approval through the Certified Lender process are promised three-day turnaround versus three-week turnaround for lenders who are neither Preferred nor Certified. In reality, the process can take much longer.

7(a) Loan Guarantee Terms and Conditions   The guaranteed portion of an SBA 7(a) loan can't exceed $750,000. Minimum loan sizes vary from lender to lender, but since it takes just as much time to do a small loan as it does a large one, most prefer loans greater than $50,000.

Loan terms are set to match the life of the asset being financed and the ability of the borrower to repay the loan. Generally, loan maturities will be between five and ten years for working capital loans, up to 10 years for machinery and equipment loans, and up to 25 years for real estate or new construction loans. SBA loans are fully amortizing, meaning there are no balloon payments. And there are no prepayment penalties on SBA loans.

Interest rates on SBA loans can be fixed or variable. Rates on loans with terms greater than seven years cannot exceed 2.75 percent over the prime rate of interest, or 2.25 percent over prime if the loan term is less than seven years. The SBA charges lenders a fee of 2 percent of the guaranteed portion of the loan for long-term loans over $50,000, 1 percent of the guaranteed portion of the loan for long-term loans under $50,000, and .25 percent of the guaranteed portion of the loan for short-term loans (with maturities of less than 12 months). These fees are passed on to the borrower. Lenders often collect additional packaging fees of $750 to $1,500 (which must be disclosed to the SBA and must pass the SBA's test of "reasonableness"), plus actual costs for title searches, appraisals, recording fees, and other out-of-pocket expenses. Such fees can usually be paid out of loan proceeds.

While the SBA does not require a minimum equity contribution from the business owner, most lenders who participate in the SBA loan program like to see new businesses contribute at least 20 to 30 percent of the project cost in cash. Existing businesses will sometimes qualify for 100 percent financing if their ratio of total debt to total equity does not exceed four to one.

SBA loans are generally secured by collateral equal to the loan amount. Some lenders will allow less than 100 percent collateralization, but this is rare. Loans are generally secured by all business assets and often personal assets including the owner's home. Certain lenders strongly prefer real estate collateral while others are much more creative in what they'll accept. Some will even accept paintings, classic cars, jewelry, antiques, and so forth.

The SBA requires personal and spousal guarantees from anyone with over 20 percent ownership. In addition, guarantees from nonowners may strengthen a marginal request. SBA lenders will usually want to be named as beneficiary on the life insurance policy of all significant owners.

Borrowers will be required to prove that the company has sufficient cash flow to support the loan payments. If the company's historical cash flow does not demonstrate the ability to support the new debt, a secondary source of repayment, such as a spouse's income, might add additional comfort for the lender.

Recent changes in SBA rules allow their 7(a) loan funds to be used to pay off existing debt in some circumstances such as loans with an upcoming balloon payment or loans made on unfavorable terms (high rate of interest or short loan term). The 7(a) loans may also be used in conjunction with other federal loan programs such as the 504 Certified Development Corporation Loan Program.

Processing the SBA 7(a) Loan   When processed by Preferred Lenders, the whole loan approval process and related paperwork is only slightly more involved than a bank loan request. Funding is typically available four to six weeks after the lender receives all required information.

Dave Bartram, Executive Vice President of the Bank of Commerce, the largest bank SBA lender in the western United States, suggests including the following information in your loan request:

- 7(a) loan application.
- Personal financial statements for all significant owners.
- Current business financial statements.
- Business tax returns (3 years, signed) for existing businesses.
- Personal tax returns (3 years, signed) for all significant owners.
- Accounts receivable and accounts payable agings.
- Schedule of existing term debt.
- Projected financial balance sheet, income statement, cash flow (one year with assumptions).
- Business plan.

A Preferred Lender for over seven years and an SBA lender since 1976, the Bank of Commerce is delighted by its participation in the program. "It really helps us stretch our conventional lending limits," according to Mr. Bartram. "Several years ago, we helped a company that makes glass-mirrored signs buy their first building so they could move the business out of the owner's garage. Since that time, we've done several other SBA loans for the company to help them expand. Today, they are producing over $20 million in revenue, and they employ over 200 people. We couldn't have helped them without the SBA program."

Low Doc 7(a) Guarantee Loan

These special 7(a) loans offer a low documentation approach for loans of less than $100,000. From the SBA's point of view, the only information they require is a one-page application, personal financial statements from all guarantors, and a business tax return. Lenders may need more information, but the program still offers quicker, simpler approvals. Qualifying businesses must have average annual sales of less than $5 million and less than 100 employees.

Small Loan Program

To encourage lenders to make smaller loans, the SBA created the Small Loan Program, which allows lenders to charge higher rates and fees than are allowed under the 7(a) loan program. For loans between $25,000 and $50,000, lenders may charge up to prime plus 3.25 percent when the loan term is less than seven years, and up to prime plus 3.75 percent when the loan term is more than seven years. On loans of less than $25,000, lenders may charge an additional 1 percent. As an incentive to do these smaller loans, the lender is also allowed to keep up to 1 percent of the 2 percent fee that's normally charged on the guaranteed portion of the loan.

Qualifying criteria, collateral, eligibility requirements, and other terms are similar to those of 7(a) loans. Your local SBA office can provide you with a list of organizations that offer these small loans.

Microloan Program

Recognizing the need for very small loans, the SBA also recently created the Microloan Program. Under this program, loans that range from $100 to $25,000 are offered through responsible private, nonprofit groups. The Microloan Program provides short-term loans of up to $25,000 (with a maximum maturity of six years) for the purchase of machinery, equipment, furniture, fixtures, inventory, supplies, and working capital. These funds are not available for debt replacement. Interest rates on these loans are set at a maximum of prime plus 4.25 percent. Fees up to 2 percent of the guaranteed portion of the loan may be charged.

During 1993, a total of 3,316 microloans were granted. Your local SBA office can provide you with a list of organizations that administer microloans.

Women's Prequalification Pilot Loan Program

At the time of this writing, the SBA was piloting a program to assist businesses that are at least 51 percent owned, operated, and managed by women, by streamlining the loan application process. Through this program, businesses are prequalified by the SBA before they approach an SBA lender.

Loans of up to $250,000 are eligible; the SBA will guarantee up to 85 percent for loans between $155,000 and $250,000, or up to 90 percent of smaller loans. Rates are similar to those of 7(a) loans, although loans of less than $50,000 may be subject to slightly higher rates. Normally business assets will be pledged as collateral, personal guarantees will be required of all significant owners, and personal collateral may be required as well. Loans will not be declined if inadequate collateral is the only unfavorable factor.

Applications for this program are coordinated by designated technical assistance organizations who help prepare business plans and complete the prequalification forms. These organizations submit the required information to the SBA for preapproval. Once approved, they can help applicants locate an appropriate lender.

For loans of less than $100,000, the SBA will rely on the applicant's personal and business credit history as the principal indication of ability and willingness to repay. For loans between $100,000 and $250,000, required documents include resumes of the principals, personal financial statements, and business financial statements or tax returns. Lenders may require additional information.

Like other SBA programs, the SBA may be willing to guarantee your loan, but you'll still have to find a lender to actually do the deal. The guarantee will provide them some comfort, but it won't replace their own credit underwriting standards. Lenders will require additional information and may or may not be willing to write the loan regardless of the prequalified guarantee.

As a pilot program, the Women's Prequalification Program is being tested statewide in Colorado, Maine, Montana, New Mexico, and Utah and locally in San Francisco, California; Chicago, Illinois; New Orleans, Louisiana; Buffalo, New York; Columbus, Ohio; Louisville, Kentucky; and Charlotte, North Carolina. Assuming a successful test, the program will likely be introduced in other communities in the mid-1990s.

504 Certified Development Company Program (CDCs)

The SBA's Development Company Program is administered through private Certified Development Companies (CDCs). The program is designed to assist small businesses in financing projects that involve the purchase, construction, or improvement of land, buildings, equipment, and other long-term fixed assets (called 504 projects). Some construction "soft costs" such as surveying, engineering, and professional fees may qualify for funding as well, but working capital loans are not available through this program. CDCs can finance up to 40 percent of the project cost. Up to 50 percent of the balance of the project cost may be financed by another, nonfederal lender, and at least 10 percent must be contributed by the applicant. The CDC acts as an agent for the loan, and will package and submit the loan request to the SBA.

Just over 2,500 CDC loans were extended in 1993 at an average of approximately $322,000 each (which, remember, represents only 40% of the total project cost). A list of CDCs in your area is available from your local SBA office.

As with many government programs, the primary goal is to create or retain jobs. Therefore the project financed must demonstrate a positive impact on the economy. Normally, the project must create or retain one job for every $35,000 of the government's share of the loan. Thus, a $300,000 project, with $120,000 of government money (the 40% CDC portion) should create at least four new jobs ($120,000/$35,000) within two years following the project completion.

This fixed rate, long-term lending program, is an excellent choice for financing real estate or equipment. Loan terms of 10 and 20 years are available. Typically, a 504 project includes two separate loans, one for the bank portion of the loan and one for the CDC portion. The CDC rates are set at the time of funding, and are based on the market rate for U.S. Treasury bonds (which, if you can believe it, is established the third Wednesday following the second Sunday of the month). This usually results in a rate that's lower than conventional fixed rate financing. In the fall of 1994, the CDC rate for 20-year loans was 8.49 percent. Twenty-year, fixed-rate loans are practically nonexistent from conventional lenders, but if they were, they'd carry a rate of at least prime plus 1 to 3 percent (8.75% to 10.75%). The bank's rate, for their portion of the loan, is set at their own discretion. Prime plus 1.5 percent to prime plus 2.5 percent is typical for the bank portion.

Loan fees on 504 projects include the following: 2.8 percent of the 40 percent CDC portion of the loan, plus $800, plus 1 to 2 percent of the 50 percent bank portion of the loan. Legal fees related to loan closing (which, as with all loans, will be charged to you) may not exceed $2,500.

CDC loans require collateralization by the project being financed, personal guarantees of all significant owners, and cash flow coverage of the new debt. On rare occasions, liens will also be placed on other business and personal assets. A qualifying business's net worth cannot exceed $6 million and average net profit after taxes cannot exceed $2 million. Loan minimums are officially $50,000 for the CDC portion of the loan ($25,000 in some special cases), but more often range from $200,000 to $600,000. Projects of any size may qualify for funding, but the CDC's portion can't exceed $750,000 ($1,000,000 in certain circumstances) for their 40 percent of the project.

This type of loan is appropriate for expanding businesses with proven cash flow and good credit, versus start-up or turnaround businesses. Banks are inclined to participate in such loans because they have first rights to collateral in the event of default. Since their portion of the loan is only 50 percent, collateral coverage is quite strong.

As an example of a CDC loan, consider a successful five-year-old printing company that needed to acquire a $300,000 piece of equipment that would create four new jobs. The company's bank was unwilling to loan it money for more than five years, but a shorter period would have created a cash flow pinch due to the larger payments required. Instead, the company went to a CDC lender for 40 percent of the loan. The company contributed $30,000 (10%) to the project and the bank funded the $150,000 balance. The useful life of the asset was determined to be 10 years so the loan was set for that term. The bank was happy because it had a $150,000 loan secured by a $300,000 asset. The company was happy because it had a 10-year term loan at a blended rate between the bank's own rate and the CDC rate, which helped the company's cash flow.

CDC lending has an undeserved bad reputation for being complicated. But, according to Kristine Anderson, Vice President for Union Bank in San Diego (an active 504 lender) the process shouldn't take much longer than any other loan.

❑ Secret

Lenders are often inclined to suggest financing your real estate or equipment under the 7(a) program rather than the CDC program, because they make more money on the former. Lenders can make as much as 10 points or 10 percent of the loan amount selling loans to another lender who's deposit-rich but loan-poor. CDC loans, on the other hand, are almost never sold, which may explain why some lenders prefer 7(a) loans.

If you think your loan will qualify for CDC financing, contact CDC lenders in your area and see what they have to say. The SBA can provide you with a list of these lenders. Try to choose the lender who has the most experience with the program in order to avoid unnecessary processing delays.

Surety Bond Guarantee Program

Approximately $5 billion went to 23,996 recipients in 1993 for an average of $208,368 per Surety Bond Guarantee Program loan. This program can provide guarantees for bid bonds, performance bonds, and payment bonds for small and emerging contractors who cannot obtain surety bonds through regular commercial channels. Construction and service businesses with less than $3.5 million in revenue are eligible for this program. Application for guarantees under this program can be submitted by commercial sureties only after the applicant has been declined for conventional bonding. The recipient pays a fee to the SBA of $6 per $1,000 of bonding plus the surety's bonding fee. The bonding company also pays a guarantee fee to the SBA that generally is passed on to the recipient.

Small Business Investment Companies (SBICs)

About $806.3 million went to 1,992 recipients in 1993 for an average of $404,769 per SBIC loan. This program provides a form of venture capital for later stage companies. A detailed description of the SBIC program is included in Section Three.

Contract Loan Program

In 1993, $60.7 million went to 380 recipients for an average of $159,737 per Contract Loan Program loan. This program provides guarantees on short-term lines of credit that can be used to cover the estimated cost of labor and materials needed to perform a specific contract. Financing is provided on a contract-by-contract basis rather than through a revolving line of credit. Businesses may have more than one Contract Loan outstanding so long as the SBA's exposure does not exceed $750,000. Guarantees of 85 to 90 percent are typically available for a maximum term of twelve months (18 months in some circumstances). The maximum rate for these loans is prime plus 2.25 percent. Fees are usually capped at 2 percent of the guaranteed portion of the loan or 0.25 percent if the loan is for a period of less than 12 months. Loans requiring extraordinary servicing may be charged additional fees of up to 2 percent. Qualifying businesses must be at least one year old. These loans require business and sometimes personal collateral in addition to the assignment of the financed contract. As with other SBA programs, personal guarantees are required.

Guaranty Seasonal Line of Credit

About $61 million went to 227 recipients in 1993 for an average of $268,722 per Guaranty Seasonal Line of Credit loan. This program helps highly seasonal businesses finance their receivables and inventory. Applicants must demonstrate a minimum one-year history of seasonal activity. Guarantees of up to 85 percent are available for up to $750,000, and up to 90 percent on loans under $155,000. The maximum term for these loans is 12 months with rates capped at prime plus 2.25 percent and maximum fees of 0.25 percent of the guaranteed portion of the loan. Loans requiring extraordinary servicing may be charged additional fees of up to 2 percent. Business collateral, often personal collateral, and personal guarantees are required.

Vietnam and Disabled Veterans Program

In 1993, $15.8 million went to 209 recipients for an average of $75,598 per Vietnam and Disabled Veterans Program loan. Applicants must prove that they do not qualify for conventional financing before they can apply directly to the SBA for a loan under this program. Qualifying businesses must be at least 51 percent owned and operated by Vietnam-era veterans or at least 30 percent owned and operated by disabled veterans of any era. Loans range from $1,000 to $150,000 and may be used for construction, expansion, leasehold improvements, equipment, inventory, or working capital. Loan rates are set at the federal government's cost of money plus 1 percent. No fees are charged on these loans. Collateral requirements, loan maturities, and other conditions are similar to those of 7(a) loans.

Handicapped Loan Program (HAL-1 and HAL-2)

About $7 million went to 123 recipients in 1993 for an average of $56,910 per Handicapped Loan Program loan. Guarantees and direct loans from this program are available to establish, acquire, and operate a small business owned and managed by or for the benefit of disabled persons.

HAL-1 funds are available to state and federally chartered organizations that operate in the interest of disabled persons. Eligibility rules specify that the applying organization's net income cannot benefit any stockholder or other individual, and that 75 percent of the direct work involved must be done by handicapped persons.

HAL-2 loans are available to businesses that are 100 percent owned by handicapped individuals. Absentee-owned businesses do not qualify.

Under the Handicapped Loan Programs, the Administration can guarantee loans of up to $750,000 made by SBA lenders. If the applicant cannot qualify for other financing, the SBA will consider a direct loan of up to $150,000. Direct loans from the SBA bear an interest rate of 3 percent per year. Guarantee loan rates are set by the lending institution. Funds may be used for the purchase of equipment, inventory, or working capital.

Guaranty Export Revolving Line of Credit

In 1993, $17.2 million went to 57 recipients for an average of $301,754 per Guaranty Export Revolving Line of Credit loan. These loan guarantees provide short-term financing for exporting companies that wish to develop or penetrate foreign markets or that need to finance their exported product. Funds from this program may be used to finance labor, inventory, foreign accounts receivable, or foreign market development. Companies should be established for at least one year. Guarantees of up to 85 percent are available for lines of credit of up to $750,000, and guarantees of up to 90 percent are available on loans of less than $155,000. Loans are established for a maximum of 36 months with options to renew.

Due to the increased role of international trade in the economy, changes in this program are being considered at the time of this writing. Contact your local SBA office for updated information and the names of lenders who participate in the Guaranty Export Revolving Line of Credit program.

International Trade Loan Program

Approximately, $30.2 million went to 48 recipients in 1993 for an average of $629,166 per International Trade Loan Program loan. Guarantees of up to $1 million for fixed assets and $250,000 for working capital (for a combined total of up to $1.25 million) are available from the SBA for exporters and businesses that have been hurt by imports. Loans may be used for working capital, acquisition, construction, renovation, modernization, improvement, or expansion of productive facilities or equipment in the United States for the production of goods and services destined for international trade. A maximum term of 25 years is available on fixed-asset loans and three years on working-capital loans. Rates range from prime plus 2.25 to 2.75 percent.

Small General Contractor Loans

Through this program, the SBA provides financing for small general contractors to finance construction or renovation of residential or commercial buildings that will be offered for resale. Not more than 20 percent of the total loan may be used for the purchase of vacant land, and not more than 5 percent may be used for streets, curbs, and other developmental costs that benefit properties other than the one being financed.

Guarantees of up to 85 percent are available on loans up to $750,000. Loans of less than $155,000 may qualify for a guarantee of up to 90 percent. Contractors must demonstrate successful experience in similar projects. Borrowers pay only interest during the building phase with principal due on sale of the project. The loan term cannot exceed 36 months plus a reasonable estimate of the time it takes to complete the construction and renovation. Loan rates range from prime plus 2.25 to 2.75 percent.

8(a) Loans

In 1993, $4.7 million went to 29 recipients, for an average of $162,069 per loan. The 8(a) program provides federal government contracts and other assistance to small companies owned by socially and economically disadvantaged persons. Once approved for and enrolled in the 8(a) program, participants may apply for 8(a) loans either from an SBA lender, or, as a last resort, from the SBA directly.

SPECIAL GOVERNMENT, QUASI-GOVERNMENT, AND PRIVATE INITIATIVES

A number of programs funded by federal, state, and local government agencies are aimed at promoting economic development. Program objectives often include the creation of jobs for low-income people, and the acquisition of fixed assets (land, buildings, and equipment) particularly in low-income, distressed, or economically disadvantaged communities. The number of new jobs that must be created, or in some cases retained, is based on the size of the loan. A typical formula is one job for every

$15,000 to $35,000 loaned. These programs tend to be more appropriate for manufacturers than for service or retail businesses, since the latter are less asset- and employee-intensive.

Most government-funded loan programs are *participatory lending programs,* meaning they'll fund some percentage of the project cost (usually 40%–50%), the owner must contribute some equity (usually 10%–25%), and another primary lender (typically a bank) funds the balance. Often, the government agency's portion of the loan is subordinated to that of the primary lender in order to encourage that first lender to do the deal.

Many of these special lending programs offer extremely low interest rates (often lower than the prime rate and in some cases as low as 2%), longer than normal repayment schedules, and flexible underwriting standards. Most require a great deal of paperwork, take several months to finalize, and have minimum loan request amounts of $25,000 to over $100,000.

Economic development programs are offered through a variety of federal, state, and local agencies; they're usually administered by various local organizations. To encourage programs that address local problems, a variety of organizations may exist in a single state to offer these loans. An apparel loan fund might be offered in a region where the apparel industry is important, a steel loan fund might be established in another area, and loans to companies in environmental businesses might be available in still another locale.

Community development programs are often aimed at assisting special interest groups such as the handicapped or disadvantaged businesses in distressed areas. Such programs are often less stringent than other economic development programs about the job creation or asset purchase criteria, and are thus more available to retail and service businesses. An example of such a program is the Enterprise Zone Loan Program. It's offered in various forms and under various names in distressed communities throughout the country as a way to encourage businesses to move into their areas. Such loans often bear extremely low interest rates with long-term repayment options.

Unfortunately, these programs come and go, and change their names and addresses, at the whim of local, state, and federal politicians. Since most are administered by local field offices, your best approach to tracking down these programs is to talk to your local librarian about recent directories of local loan programs. A good source is *The States and Small Business.*[2]

Other sources of information about programs like these include your local Economic Development Authority or Industrial Development Authority (they should be listed in your phone book), your local and state commerce departments, larger chambers of commerce (which often publish directories of local lenders and loan programs), university-based small business development centers, bankers, accountants, and other professional loan consultants.

Most (but not all) loan programs that use government funding are a paperwork and approval nightmare. Be prepared for several months or longer of false starts, false promises, last-minute changes, and lots of legal fees (which can total thousands of dollars). Your best bet to navigate your way through these programs is to enlist the help of someone who's been through the process before. Once you're involved, try to deal with the most senior and experienced program person around. Even program employees are often ill-informed about the realities of the process.

The biggest problem with many of these programs is that your request has to be considered and approved at a number of different levels. For example, before an Industrial Development Authority (IDA) loan can be approved at the local level, you have to submit a loan commitment from a bank for their portion of the loan. (The IDA will loan you 40 percent of the amount you need if you can find a bank to lend you another 40%; you'll provide the remaining 20%.) But naturally the bank can't approve its portion of the loan until the loan officers know the IDA's terms and conditions. You'll bounce back and forth between the IDA and the bank until the lender has enough information to take the request to its loan committee.

But you're not finished yet! The bank's loan committee meets, let's say, every Friday, and the IDA meets, let's say, on the third Thursday of each month. So when your request is approved by the bank on the second Friday of the month, they'll send a commitment letter to you for your IDA loan package. Naturally, you missed the IDA's deadline for submitting your request (which was several weeks before the meeting date) so you're bumped out to next month's meeting. In the meantime, however, the IDA's loan schedule for next month has already been booked, so it'll be several months before your deal is presented. But, wait, there's more.

When the IDA finally does review your package, they'll find that some "i's" weren't dotted and some "t's" weren't crossed, and they'll no doubt need some additional information. All of which will have to be presented before a preliminary approval can be granted. (*Preliminary Approval!* Holy moly, all this for a preliminary approval?) Anyway, assuming everything goes well at the second IDA meeting, your request will be forwarded to the state for its approval. And guess what? The state's committee doesn't meet until the second Thursday of the month, and here it is the third Thursday. But, let's assume when they finally do meet at the state level, you're approved. OK! Where's the check?

Not so fast, sometimes even with state approval, getting the money isn't as straight-forward as you might hope. It may be that it's the end of the fiscal year, and all the funds for this fiscal year have been spent. But, hey, your loan is *only* number 50 in next year's funding. Just one little problem. Federal politicians are talking about cutting back on your state's allocation. Now if you're really lucky, your bank might fund the whole loan, with the understanding that it will be partially replaced by the state's portion of the loan when that finally comes through. But if the bank has any suspicion that the state's ship won't come in, the loan officers are likely to tell you to forget the whole deal. Maybe, just maybe, if your company can carry all the debt at the bank's less favorable rates and terms, it will do the deal anyway (of course, that will require another bank committee approval and more delays).

Are we having fun yet? Well, if you think this scenario sounds bad, just imagine you're trying to buy a property with the proceeds. The deal will be dead (and you may be too) by the time the loan is funded. So why does anyone bother? Financing realities, actually. If you can land 2 percent financing over 25 years for the IDA portion of the loan, it's worth the sweat and frustration.

COMMERCIAL FACTORS

So-called *factoring* companies purchase your accounts receivable, either with or without recourse (meaning that they do or don't absorb the risk of bad debt), and immediately advance 50 percent to 80 percent of the face value of the receivables to you. The balance of the funds is released once the receivables are collected, less the factor's discount. This discount is how the factor makes money, and the discount can range from 1.5 to 5 percent of the face value of the receivables. This form of factoring is referred to as advance/reserve factoring. Factoring differs from accounts receivable lending because, unlike lenders, factors actually buy, and take possession of your accounts receivable and become operationally involved in collections as a value-added service.

Factoring, once common in the textile industry, has spread to other industries in recent years and is appropriate for businesses that are unable to obtain adequate working capital financing from conventional lenders. This includes young and fast-growing companies, companies involved in international trade, and other companies that do not qualify for conventional loans but that have a strong receivables base.

Once a factoring relationship is established, disbursements from the factor to the client are quick and sometimes even transparent to your customers. As long as your company continues to generate quality receivables, it has a built-in source of finance. In addition, since factors advance money on your receivables, they'll also help you determine the creditworthiness of prospective customers.

Factoring fees vary based on the volume factored, the number of days it takes to collect on invoices, the number of debtors, and other conditions. Discount rates start at 2 to 3 percent for invoices collected in 15 days. Increased discount rates of 1 to 3 percent for each additional 15 days are common. Exhibit 3.6 shows how factoring fees work.

Based on an 80 percent advance and the collection of all accounts in 30 days, the factor's discount in Exhibit 3.6 is the equivalent to finance charges of 60 percent per year. Here's the math: If you paid $4,000 to have $80,000 advanced for 30 days, $4,000 is 5% of $80,000; on an annual basis that's 60% (5% × 12 months). While that may seem high, remember that the factor is assuming a level of risk that other lenders wouldn't.

Obviously, factoring is more expensive (OK, much more expensive) than traditional sources of finance, but it may be the only viable alternative when nothing else is available. Before entering into this kind of relationship, just be sure the factoring fees don't absorb all your profits. Alternative pricing techniques used by factors include the following methods.

Flat-fee Plus Interest Factoring

With flat-fee plus interest pricing, the factor charges a flat fee of around 1 percent of the face value of factored receivables. The company can draw against up to 90 percent of the face value of factored receivables paying interest on the amount advanced. As receivables are collected by the factor, the unadvanced balance of the factored receivables is remitted to the company (less the factor's fees).

EXHIBIT 3.6   Rate Schedule for Advance/Reserve Factoring Provided by the Edward Directory of American Factors

Face Value of Invoices	$100,000			
Initial Funds Advanced (80%)	$80,000			
Reserve Balance (20%)	$20,000			
If payment is collected in:	Factoring Fees To Client	Discount Rate To Client	Reserve Rebated	Balance of Loan To Client
1—15 days	$2,000	2%	$18,000	$98,000
31—45 days	$6,000	6%	$14,000	$94,000
45—60 days	$8,000	8%	$12,000	$92,000
62—75 days	$10,000	10%	$10,000	$90,000
76—90 days	$12,000	12%	$8,000	$88,000

Maturity Factoring

Similar to credit insurance, maturity factoring allows companies to establish a predictable cash flow at a relatively low cost by offering what amounts to a slow payment insurance policy. The maturity factor guarantees payment of a company's accounts receivable such that if collections slow, the factor will advance funds on unpaid invoices for which they collect a fee (typically 1% of the face value of the invoice).

Most factors prefer to establish a continuing relationship with a company rather than factoring on a one-time basis, but about half the companies are willing to spot factor, as it's called in the trade. Most professional factors will help you negotiate with your bank if your receivables are already pledged on loans. With their experience, they can be very helpful in this regard.

The "Edwards Directory of American Factors,"[3] published annually, includes a listing of over 200 factoring firms around the country. According to the Directory, small and mid-sized factoring firms account for less than 20 percent of the nation's annual factoring volume, but they comprise more than 90 percent of all factoring companies in the United States. In 1993 the top 13 factors accounted for almost 81 percent of the $62 billion in U.S. factoring volume. Large factors tend to focus on financing needs exceeding several hundred thousand dollars a month. Smaller factors are more interested in the financing needs of entrepreneurial businesses, including those with financing needs as little as $1,000 per month.

During 1993, Edwards Research Group conducted an extensive study of U.S. factoring company preferences. Exhibit 3.7 is a summary of their findings.

Lest you think that factoring is only something to be tried when things are going bad, consider the following success story offered by Dave Clark, owner of Riviera Finance, a well-respected factor that specializes in helping entrepreneurial companies.

The personal credit histories of both owners of a start-up Chicago-based trucking company were, shall we say, weak; and as a new business the company had no financial history. Obviously, their deal would be tough to finance conventionally, if at all. Riviera Finance factored the start-up's $15,000 in receivables, which were from strong corporate customers. Four years later, the company is still factoring with Riviera Finance, but now at a volume of $800,000 per month.

Riviera Finance's nonrecourse factoring offers an immediate advance of 91 percent of receivables less its discount. Riviera does all the company's credit approvals prior to accepting new customers, which substantially mitigates the risk of bad debt. While some who contemplate the use of a factor may fear loss of business as a result of notification of

EXHIBIT 3.7   Factoring Company Preferences

- *Industry Preference.* 59% of respondents indicated no industry preference although only a few factors reported a willingness to factor construction, third-party medical, or foreign debtor receivables.
- *Aging Preference.* The majority were flexible about the age of the receivables factored.
- *Spot Factoring.* Respondents were just about evenly divided on their willingness to purchase receivables on a one-time basis rather than through a continuing relationship.
- *Transaction Structure.* Most respondents (51%) preferred the advance/reserve structure.
- *Recourse vs. Nonrecourse Factoring.* 38% of respondents practiced non-recourse factoring, 28% practiced recourse factoring, and 29% practiced both.
- *Maturity Factoring.* Only 16% of factors surveyed offered maturity factoring.
- *Notification.* More than two thirds of respondents notify their client's debtors that their invoices have been assigned.
- *Client Receipt of Factored Proceeds.* 69% of surveyed factors do not permit their clients to collect factored receivables. Instead payments are generally mailed to a post office box controlled by the factor.
- *Contract Term.* 66% of respondents do not impose minimum term lengths.
- *Collateral Security.* 37% require all receivables (factored or not) as collateral; 23% require only factored receivables; and 8% require all company assets.
- *Personal Guarantees.* 40% of factors require a personal guarantee against all factoring losses; 18% require a personal guarantee against all factoring losses except those caused by debtor insolvency; 15% require a personal guarantee to cover client misrepresentation; and only 8% say they require no guarantee.
- *Verification of Accounts Receivable.* 72% of factors surveyed contact account debtors prior to advancing funds in order to verify the validity of invoices.
- *Verification Methods.* 60% verify invoices by telephone; 22% require written confirmation from debtors; and 61% verify invoices through shipping documents.
- *On-Site Client Audits.* 42% of respondents require period on-site audits of clients.
- *Purchase Order Financing.* Only 11% of respondents gave an unequivocal "yes" to their willingness to factor purchase orders. 25% said that they would offer such financing to existing factoring clients only; 53% gave an unequivocal "no" to the question.

customers that their accounts are being factored, Mr. Clark points out that most don't even realize that anything's changed because the accounts payable department is notified, not the buyer.

A final word on factors. There's relatively little regulation of the factoring industry and not all factors operate reputably. Be sure to check a prospective factor's references, and its reputation among bankers, accountants, and others before using their services.

VENTURE CAPITAL FUNDS

In 1993, the venture capital industry raised $4.2 billion for 859 deals, an average of $4.9 million per deal according to Venture One, a San Francisco-based research firm. Venture One specializes in tracking the business progress and financing plans of thousands of privately held, venture backed companies. Their research provides valuable insights into the otherwise murky world of venture capital, and contributes extensively to this and later sections.

If you're trying to find money, attracting a venture fund is certainly one way to do it; but you, your product or service, and your company are going to have to be very special. Most venture firms focus on emerging technologies and are primarily interested in companies with proprietary products or services, although there are exceptions. Retail or consumer deals are of interest only if they offer strong national or international expansion potential. Venture One's summary of venture capital investments shown in Exhibit 3.8, shows that the majority of funding goes to emerging technologies in the computer, biotechnology, telecommunications, and health-care fields.

Details about raising money from venture capital sources are provided in Section Three but, in general, venture funds invest in companies that demonstrate the following qualifications:

- *Proprietary Products or Services.* Companies with proprietary products or services often enjoy a desirable "unfair" competitive advantage by virtue of the exclusivity of their products. Patents, trademarks, copyrights, exclusive distributorships, or other special rights may protect a company's unique position in the market. Sometimes, a nonprotected product or service with an exceptional headstart on potential competition can fit this criterion, as well. The point is that the company must have some significant advantage over existing or potential competitors so it can achieve and maintain a dominant position in its industry.

EXHIBIT 3.8   1993 Venture Capital Investments ($,000)

Industry	Number of Deals	Dollars Raised	Average Investment
Software and computer services	152	$496.1	$3.26
Biotechnology and pharmaceuticals	140	$806.5	$5.76
Communications and networking	139	$698.1	$5.02
Medical devices and equipment	90	$392.8	$4.36
Electronics and computer hardware	83	$293.9	$3.54
Retailing and consumer products	65	$473.3	$7.28
Health care services	44	$280.8	$6.38
Semiconductors and components	39	$189.2	$4.85
Environmental	11	$152.6	$13.87
Other	96	$646.7	$6.74
Total	859	$4,208.3	$4.90

Source: Information in this exhibit is taken from *Venture One 1993 Entrepreneurial Investment Report,* Venture One, San Francisco, CA, 1993. Used with permission.

- *Huge Market Potential.* Venture funded companies are expected to be able to grow to $30, $50, or even $100 million in five to seven years. This means that the industry has to be big enough to support such growth. But many venture proposals fail to adequately convince investors of the market potential while others naively project that they'll capture 10, 20, or even 50 percent market share in a very short period. When you're projecting potential market share, consider the fact that IBM achieved less than 8 percent market share in 1994 personal computer sales.

- *Proven Management Talent.* Management is the most important element in a venture capitalist's decision to invest in your company. Are you, and the others in your company, capable of building a $50 million business? Have you managed similar growth in the past? Do you have, or are you able to hire, the top people in your field? Venture capitalists will want to see real depth.

- *Extraordinary Returns.* Venture capitalists are looking for returns of 35 to 50 percent per year. A 50 percent return means that, if they invest $1 million, they want to wind up with $5 million in four years. Obviously, most businesses, even the highfliers, won't achieve that kind of return through profits. In fact, most will lose money in the early years. Therefore, you have to be willing and able to sell the company or go public in three to seven years.

While the venture community is known for its incubation of start-up businesses, the majority of their funds (almost 60% in 1993) go to more established companies. According to Venture One's research, the typical venture-backed company, when financed, was three years old with 42 employees. They also reported that a total of only 65 start-up companies in the whole country, for the whole year of 1993, won seed financing. This figure represents less than 2 percent of all venture investments that year. What's more, an average of just $2.4 million was raised for each start-up, far lower than the average venture investment of $4.9 million.

The average venture capital investment has grown since 1991, reflecting the industry's emphasis on higher quality, later stage deals. These later stage deals are more in vogue right now. This, however, is a pendulum that swings with changes in the economy, the initial public offering (IPO) market, and the portfolio mix within the venture industry.

In any case, the competition for venture capital is fierce. Venture firms fund fewer than one in a hundred of the business plans they receive, and they expect only one in ten of those businesses to provide a home run. Less than half of their investments, they figure, will even make it to first base.

Investments are, for the most part, proportional to the fund's size, but few will look at deals of less than $250,000—it's just as much work to do a small deal as it is a large one.

While some venture firms seek majority interests in the firms they finance, most take a minority position. Regardless of their ownership, some venture sources will want to take an active role in your business, and some will be passive investors. As you can see from Exhibit 3.9, more experienced companies give up less ownership and control than early-stage ventures in first-round financing.

EXHIBIT 3.9   First Round Investment as a Percentage of Company Valuation

Startup	44.0%
Restart	30.0%
Product Development	28.9%
In Beta Testing	22.1%
Shipping Products	18.8%
Profitable	18.2%

Source: Information in this exhibit is taken from *Venture One 1993 Entrepreneurial Investment Report,* Venture One, San Francisco, CA, 1993. Used with permission.

Finding the right venture capitalist for your situation, and negotiating a good deal, is quite an art. Informed professionals can make the process go much smoother, but in the end the venture capitalist is investing in you, not your advisors. Section Three is a must-read if you're planning to go this route. It offers plenty of insider secrets about how investors evaluate proposals and structure their investments.

INTERNATIONAL FINANCE

More and more companies are exploring international markets for business expansion. But exporting is complicated and potentially risky business. One of the biggest risks in exporting is the risk of not getting paid. That risk has two components, company risk, which involves the creditworthiness of foreign buyers, and country risk, which involves the political and economic stability of country in which the company resides. Fortunately, bankers and other lenders have developed special loan products to help you mitigate these risks. In addition, a number of government programs offer both assistance and financing for businesses involved in international trade. The SBA's export programs were described earlier in this chapter in the section on SBA loans. Other international financing programs are available from Ex-Im Bank and OPIC.

Export-Import Bank of the United States (Ex-Im Bank)

Ex-Im Bank is a small, independent agency of the federal government. Its mission is to create U.S. jobs by financing and facilitating export of U.S. goods and services. Established in 1933, it helped finance the building of the Burma Road and the Pan American Highway, assisted in the reconstruction of post-World War II Europe, and underwrote the first overseas sales of U.S. commercial jet aircraft. It does not compete with commercial lenders, but assumes risks they will not accept. Ex-Im Bank small-business activity in 1993 totaled $1.8 billion representing 12 percent of its operation.

Export Credit Insurance

Ex-Im Bank will insure short-term credit sales for small business export products with at least 51 percent U.S. content. Single or multibuyer insurance programs are available. This insurance protects U.S. small business exporters against political risks (up to

Ex-Im Bank's 1993 Loan Volumes					
	1992		1993		
	#	$	#	$	Average
Program ($ Millions)					
Export Credit Insurance	713	$1,234	994	$1,238	$1,245
Working Capital Guarantees	130	$ 143	126	$ 149	$1,182
Guarantees	106	$ 516	49	$ 356	$7,265
Loans	50	$ 170	13	$ 24	$1,846
Total	999	$2,063	1,182	$1,767	

100% coverage), as well as commercial risks (up to 95% coverage), and thus enhances the financeability of accounts receivable from foreign customers. Eligible products and services include consumables, raw materials, spare parts, agricultural commodities, capital goods, consumer durables, equipment leases, and services. Some insurance programs are also available from the time the sales contract is executed rather than from the date of shipment, which is important to companies that have to invest long lead times in production of their products.

Ex-Im Bank Working Capital Guarantees

The Working Capital Guarantee program guarantees up to 90 percent of the principal and interest that commercial lenders extend to creditworthy borrowers for export-related working capital loans. These loans require 100 percent collateral. Funds must be used to directly assist in the export of U.S. products and services. Exporters should apply to Ex-Im Bank for a preliminary commitment and then contact a commercial lender.

Ex-Im Bank Foreign Buyer Guarantees

Ex-Im Bank provides loan guarantees to domestic and foreign lenders. These guarantees cover up to 100 percent of principal and interest on fixed or floating rate loans to foreign buyers of U.S. capital equipment and services. These guarantees are intended to facilitate a foreign buyer's purchase of U.S. goods.

Ex-Im Bank Foreign Buyer Direct Loans

Ex-Im Bank provides loans to foreign buyers of U.S. capital equipment and services. Two- to seven-year favorable fixed-rate financing can be arranged for up to 85 percent of the sale price of exported goods thus facilitating purchase by foreign buyers.

Additional information about Ex-Im Bank's lending programs can be obtained by calling Ex-Im Bank's hotline at 800-565-EXIM (800-565-3946).

Overseas Private Investment Corporation (OPIC)

OPIC is a self-sustaining agency of the U.S. government that serves to promote economic growth in developing countries by encouraging U.S. private investment in those nations. OPIC services include direct loans, loan guarantees, equity investments, and political risk insurance. OPIC's assistance is available for new ventures and existing businesses providing that they are commercially viable. OPIC projects must have a positive effect on U.S. employment and must assist in the social and economic development of the host country. The following programs are available.

Finance Program

Loans and loan guarantees from OPIC are available for U.S. businesses that are commercially and financially stable, have demonstrated management competence and success, and have significant equity participation from owners. Direct loans ranging from $2 million to $10 million are available to small businesses. Loan guarantees ranging from $10 million to $200 million are available for larger projects. Some equity investments are also available, but OPIC is extremely selective.

Political Risk Insurance

OPIC offers investment insurance covering the risk of expropriation, currency inconvertibility, and political violence for certain types of U.S. investment in developing countries.

Additional information about the programs and services is available by calling OPIC at 202-336-8400.

Many states also offer assistance to exporting businesses. A good place to start your search for these programs is with your State

Department of Commerce. Also try the U.S. Department of Commerce's International Trade Administration and the Bureau of Export Administration. These government agencies offer assistance in a variety of nonfinancial matters that will be useful to you as you begin to explore the world of exporting.

MORTGAGE BANKERS

Mortgage bankers make (or, as they would call it, *originate*) real-estate secured loans that are either held for their own portfolio or sold to other lending institutions. Mortgage bankers often retain the servicing component (sending bills and collecting payments) of the loan even after the actual loan is sold. Many mortgage bankers are actually correspondents or agents of other financial institutions such as life insurance companies, commercial banks, and thrift institutions.

Mortgage bankers maintain relationships with a large number of local and national lenders so they can offer a wide variety of real estate secured products. Some specialize in investment or business properties. Their rates and fees are competitive with bank lenders, although some offer a higher-priced alternative for marginal loans or difficult properties that banks wouldn't touch at any price.

INSURANCE COMPANIES AND PENSION FUNDS

Life insurance companies and pension funds often invest a portion of their money in real-estate-secured loans and venture capital. Their money is more frequently allocated to venture funds than to individual businesses. Their activities as a direct lender may include long-term financing for real estate, but they tend to focus on very high quality income-producing properties. Minimum loan size is $1 million and higher. Rates and fees tend to be lower than those of commercial banks, and loan terms are generally 20 to 30 years. Insurance company financing is a good choice for large, top-quality real estate projects (including office buildings or shopping centers) in locations that have proven cash flow.

PUBLIC STOCK OFFERING

A public stock offering or, going public, as it's called, isn't a common form of finance for new and emerging companies due to the cost, the temperamental nature of the market for initial public offerings (IPOs), and the mountains of red tape. Only 120 businesses with assets less than $10 million went public in 1991 raising on average, $11.7 million each.

Don't even think about going public unless you can make a very good case for how you're going to manage the public's money, unless you can prove that you'll provide a high rate of return on investment, and unless you're willing to risk over $500,000 to fund the IPO process. (Believe it or not, just the printing bill for an IPO will run you into six figures!) And just because you spent the time and money preparing for the IPO, you have *no* guarantee your offering will be successful.

On the other hand, if your company has a strong earnings history, tremendous growth prospects on a quarter-by-quarter basis, a strong and well-rounded management team, excellent information systems, well-respected advisors, a clean background for all owners and managers, a balance sheet and income statement that it isn't jumbled up with a lot of insider transactions and strange equity structures—and you personally have a great deal of patience—going public *might* pay off. When you decide to go this route, you'll need accounting, legal, and banking advisors with strong reputations, who can demonstrate a successful track record in taking companies public. Best to put these folks on your team years before you intend to make your first public offering.

Be sure to read more about alternatives to going public such as private placements in Section Three.

JOINT VENTURES, CO-OPS, AND STRATEGIC ALLIANCES

Often the resources of two companies, sometimes of similar size (or sometimes more akin to Fay Ray meets King Kong), can be brought together to offer a unique approach to solving financial, technical, and strategic problems.

Alliances often result in the formation of a separate entity born out of the needs of the participating companies, but focused on a solving a specific problem. A joint venture might take the form of one company's investment in another. A cooperative venture might begin based on the complementary technological interests of several companies. Whatever the form, these types of venture can, and often do, create increased opportunity for all participants. Such activities are growing at a dramatic rate, and even rivals like IBM and Apple are shedding their competitive armor and cooperating on projects of significant importance.

Joint ventures, co-ops, and strategic alliances are covered in more detail in Section Three.

GRANTS

Grants are available from a wide variety of sources for nonprofit organizations, but some programs are open to for-profit companies as well.
    Federal grants for technology-related ventures that address spe-
cific needs of the government are available from the Small Business
Innovation Research Award Program or SBIR Program. In 1992, a total
of 3,475 SBIR awards were granted to small businesses for a total of
$508.4 million.
    SBIR grants are awarded in two phases:

1. Phase I grants are available to evaluate the scientific merit and fea-
    sibility of an idea. Awards are for periods of up to six months in
    amounts of up to $100,000.
2. Phase II grants are available to expand on the results and further
    pursue the development of the Phase I project awardees. Awards are
    for periods of up to two years in amounts of up to $750,000.

The following agencies participate in the SBIR Grant Program:

Department of Agriculture.
Department of Commerce.
Department of Defense.
Department of Education.
Department of Energy.
Department of Health and Human Services.
Department of Transportation.
Environmental Protection Agency.
National Aeronautics and Space Administration.
National Science Foundation.
Nuclear Regulatory Agency.

    Each agency solicits proposals from small businesses that address
its own specific problems. Some agencies will also accept unsolicited
proposals. A brief description of upcoming solicitations is published
quarterly in the SBA Office of Technology SBIR Pre-Solicitation Announcement. Firms interested in submitting proposals can contact the
appropriate agency for their solicitation package. Each agency solicits
proposals at least once a year, approximately three months prior to the
deadline for proposal submission.
    A proposal preparation handbook is available from the SBA. To
order the handbook or to be included on the Pre-Solicitation

Announcement mailing list, call the SBA Small Business Answer Desk at 800-827-5722.

In addition to federal grants, many states have programs aimed at fostering the development of technology or solving local social or economic problems. Also, some private foundations support social causes such as education, the environment, and the arts through their own grant programs.

Grants are often made only on a matching basis. That means you'll have to find a source for one-to-one (one dollar in grant money for every dollar you raise). Some grants require greater than one-to-one matching. Grant approval processes are often lengthy (three months to a year) and paper intensive, and the competition for grant dollars can be fierce.

CREDIT ENHANCEMENTS

While they're not directly a place to find money, a credit enhancement, as the name implies, can help a marginal company over the edge of financeability. The following are examples of credit enhancements that might do the trick for you.

Accounts Receivable Insurance

You may want to consider insuring your accounts receivable both for your own financial well-being and to improve their loan collateral value. According to Mike Cushinsky, president of American Credit Indemnity (ACI), a subsidiary of Dun & Bradstreet and the oldest and largest business credit insurer in the United States, about 20 percent of their customers use their credit insurance policy to obtain or improve conventional financing.

Many businesses use credit insurance as a halfway house between a factoring relationship and conventional financing. Companies with credit insurance may find it easier to obtain conventional accounts receivable financing because lenders can be named as a beneficiary in the event of bad debt—greatly reducing their risk.

ACI and other credit insurers offer a variety of coverage options for both domestic and foreign business receivables including coverage of all receivables, certain receivables, some risk, or all risk. Credit insurance covers risks arising from insolvency, bankruptcy, or any other bad debt except for those arising from disputed bills. Companies selecting coverage for all receivables will also benefit from the insurer's expertise in making credit decisions. According to Cushinsky, the credit insurer acts as your own credit department. Since they'll be insuring the risk, they'll want to make sure you're selling to credit-worthy customers, and they'll even help you collect from the ones that do go bad. ACI's small business credit insurance rates range from 0.2% to 0.4% of total sales, with a minimum annual fee of $5,000.

Letters of Credit

A letter of credit, issued by your customer's bank on your behalf, is essentially a promise from the bank that your customer can and will pay. Letters of credit are described more fully in Section Two, but for now consider them another way to make your accounts receivable, and even your purchase orders, more financeable.

On a large contract, you could have your customer's bank issue a letter of credit that promises payment at various stages of project completion. If you take that letter of credit to your bank as evidence of a future receivable, they should be willing to lend against it—if you can convince them you'll successfully fulfill your contract.

CREATIVE FINANCING

If all else fails, entrepreneurs often rely on their cunning and creativity to solve financial problems. A number of cash flow secrets are described in Section Four, but here are a few more:

- Barter (I'll trade some of mine for some of yours). Call the Barter Advantage at 212-534-7500 for a free copy of their quick how-to called *Barter Basics*.[4]

- Credit cards, which you should apply for before you start your business, while you're still employed so you won't have to check that revealing little block on the credit applications that says "Check here if self-employed."

- Cash surrender of that old whole life insurance policy that you bought years ago.

- Loans or investments from local religious organizations, some of which have established programs for lending to businesses.

By now, you've probably begun to figure out which kind of lender or investor is most likely to help you find the money you need. But how do you make sure that your request jumps to the top of the pile and sails through the approval process? Section Two will give you the inside scoop on what makes lenders say yes, and Section Three will show you how to dazzle investors.

SECTION TWO

FINDING MONEY FROM LENDERS

Once you've decided to borrow the money you need, or at least some of it, knowing what lenders will think when they review your loan proposal will help you win them over. Keep in mind that many, many people who apply for loans are turned down not because they didn't deserve the loan, but because they didn't know how to anticipate and answer the lender's questions. If you're gonna play the game, ya gotta know the rules.

HOW LENDERS EVALUATE YOUR LOAN REQUEST

For decades, lenders have evaluated loan requests using a method called the *Five C's of Credit.*

❏ Secret

Recently, a trend toward a system called *credit scoring* has emerged. Experts disagree on when, and even whether, credit scoring will actually replace the traditional Five C's approach, but it's apparent that economic and regulatory pressures are creating a great deal of interest in this new approach to commercial loan decisions.

While it seems likely that credit scoring will play a significant role in the future of commercial lending, the Five C's of Credit are, at the time of this writing, still the de facto standard. Regardless of the use of credit scoring in the future, you need to understand the Five C's since many of the principles underlying this traditional approach to loan decisions create the basis for credit scoring. Credit scoring is discussed in more detail at the end of this chapter.

Lenders are taught to evaluate you and your company based on Character, Capacity, Collateral, Capital, and Conditions—the Five C's of Credit. What they really want to know is: Will you pay? Can you pay? What if you don't pay? How much do you have at risk? And what might happen to your company, to the economy, or to your industry that might impede your ability to repay your loan? Here's an insider's look at how they do it.

THE HAIRY EYEBALL TEST

When your loan proposal first hits a lender's desk, it will receive what we call the "Hairy Eyeball Test." Essentially, a lender will quickly assess:

- How much are you looking for?
- Are you profitable enough and do you have enough cash flow to carry the requested debt?
- Do you have enough collateral to cover the loan?
- Does your company have a reasonable balance between debt and equity?

That's it; in five minutes or less, the lender will determine if your deal has half a chance. If it does, the assessment will move on to the Five C's of Credit.

CHARACTER: WILL YOU PAY?

Your character is, by far, the most important criterion in a lender's decision to be involved with you and your business. Fundamentally, the lender wants to know are you the kind of person whose word can be trusted . . . especially, will you repay this loan? If a lender doesn't believe that you'll treat your obligation honorably, the deal will never happen, no matter how good your numbers look. So, how do lenders decide about your character?

Credit Checks

Once lenders determine that your loan request looks doable, the very first thing they'll do is run credit checks on you, your business, and any prior businesses. Their best indicator that you'll pay your bills in the future is whether you've satisfied your obligations in the past. They'll also look for indications of your lifestyle from your credit report. Heavy consumer debt, overdrawn accounts, or missed payments indicate a lifestyle and character that probably will carry over to your business.

Since credit checks are so vital to a lender's decision-making process, it's imperative that you know what your credit reports say about you. Even if you think that you have a spotless credit record, and especially if you know you don't, obtain a copy of your reports from TransUnion, TRW, and Equifax. (See Exhibit 4.1.) Also order a copy of your business report from Dun & Bradstreet. Credit reports can include someone else's credit information under your name, billing disputes that may have been resolved, liens on property that were satisfied years ago, loans that were paid off but still show as outstanding, and endless other black marks. Because different lenders use different credit agencies, look at reports from each agency because some creditors and associated mistakes may appear on one report but not on the others.

❑ **Secret**

> If you can't have a disputed or adverse entry removed from your credit report, you can and should add a statement correcting misleading information or explaining the issue from your point of view. You may also submit a voluntary statement at any time explaining any personal or business problems that may have damaged your credit history. A divorce, disaster, or extended illness would be worth noting, but don't try, "The dog ate my checkbook."

There are companies that claim they can fix or repair your bad credit. They use, and in some cases abuse, the laws of the Fair Credit Reporting Act to make credit bureaus remove incorrect and adverse

EXHIBIT 4.1   Credit Report Sources

TRW*	TransUnion*	Equifax*	Dun & Bradstreet
Box 2350	Box 7000	Box 105873	899 Eaton Avenue
Chatsworth CA 91313	N. Olmstead OH 44070	Atlanta GA 30348	Bethlehem PA 18025
800-392-1122	714-738-3800	800-685-1111	800-333-0505

* Include your name, address, years there, previous address, telephone number, Social Security number, date of birth, and a copy of current utility bill as proof of address. Spouse's name, Social Security number, and signature should be included for joint credit reports. Call each company before you mail your request because nominal fees ($7–$15) may apply. Thanks to the Fair Credit Reporting Act the personal credit reports are free if you've been denied credit in the past 60 days.

credit information. By law, consumer credit agencies are required to remove any information that cannot be verified or that's found to be inaccurate. Therefore, if you submit a dispute letter, and they can't verify that the information submitted by the creditor is valid, they must remove the entry from your report. At your request, the credit bureau will also notify creditors who have recently received your credit report that the entry's been deleted.

The key to convincing lenders that you're a good credit risk, whether you have a good credit record or not, is to *avoid surprises*. Nothing will scare lenders away quicker than the feeling or knowledge that you're hiding something. If you're aware of mistakes or legitimate problems, be sure to address them with your lender before they become an issue.

As a good example of the kind of credit nightmare you can encounter, consider the plight of a paper recycler who applied for a $100,000 loan from his local bank. When the bank received his credit report, it showed that he'd purchased an airplane some years ago and had defaulted on the loan. The owner was shocked to learn of the problem since he'd never even thought about buying an airplane—in fact, he didn't even like to fly. He tried to resolve the problem on his own, but couldn't. So he hired a lawyer who eventually tracked down a person with the same name as the owner, who had purchased the airplane and subsequently reneged on the loan. The business credit reporting company still wouldn't remove the black mark (business credit reporting agencies are not bound by the same rules as consumer agencies). Even after pounds of paperwork and hundreds of dollars in legal fees, the company owner still didn't have a clean credit record. But, by submitting all the paperwork to the bank, the lender was willing to ignore the issue and continue with the loan.

The moral of the story: Know thine own credit report and document any inaccuracies or extenuating circumstances.

Background Checks

Beyond credit checks, lenders will be interested in your education and your background—what you've done in the past, whether you've been successful in this or other businesses, and what people think of you. They'll derive much of this information from what you supply; from talking to your customers, suppliers, and professional advisors; from your historical financial performance; and from references obtained through other banks.

❑ Secret

Most banks *will* share information with other banks about your average account balances, borrowing and payment history, collateralization, and if your accounts have been overdrawn (which *is* a major issue from the bank's point of view). As we said before, the key is to avoid surprises that could cause anyone at the bank to question your personal and fiscal integrity.

Lien and Encumbrance Searches

Banks *will* do a lien search if they're taking any property or other assets as collateral. Liens and encumbrances can haunt you if you don't know what's on your record. Liens on property and other assets (personal and commercial) placed by lenders, credit companies, or taxing authorities are often quick to be filed but slow to be released. As with credit reports, it pays to do your own searches, or have an attorney do them before unexpected liens or encumbrances surprise you and your prospective lender.

CAPACITY: CAN YOU PAY?

While lenders are establishing whether they trust and believe in you, they'll begin evaluating your financial statements and/or tax returns. Past financial performance will be weighted much more heavily than projected growth in any decision to lend you money. Let's take a look at what lenders want to see and what they'll be thinking about.

Historical and Projected Performance

Lenders prefer slow, steady, controlled growth over rapid growth because they perceive less risk in the former. In general, they want to see that:

- The past two to three years have been financially successful with steady growth in revenue and profits, and relative stability in direct and operating expenses.
- Profits have been retained in the business rather than fully distributed to investors and owners.

- Cash flow is sufficient to meet your company's obligations and provide an adequate living.
- Your company maintains a reasonable balance between debt and equity.
- Projections for future performance are realistic and provide sufficient cash flow to cover the payments on proposed debt (called debt service).
- Future financing needs are anticipated and well documented.

The first thing lenders will do with your financial statements is ship them off to the credit department to be entered into their computerized credit analysis system. This system will convert your balance sheet, income statement, cash flow, and projections into a standardized set of reports for analysis by your lender.

One of the more popular software programs used by many of the country's largest banks, as well as other finance professionals, is called STAN by Baker Hill Corporation. Exhibit 4.2 provides a copy of STAN Highlights report to give you an insider's look at the information lenders consider important. Once your financial data have been crunched into the lenders' standard *spreads* (lender lingo for the reports they generate from your financial statements), your original financial statements are rarely used.

Since the lender's decision will be based on your spreads, they can make or break your loan request. Thus it's vital that *you* understand what they report. The old saying "garbage in, garbage out" applies. Your financial statements won't tell all there is to know about your business, but if you know how lenders interpret your financial information, you'll be able to prevent them from drawing incorrect conclusions. We're not talking about cheating on your taxes or lying on your financial statement here—we're talking about dealing with the basic deficiencies inherent in even the best financial reports.

So here are some of the procedures lenders will use to evaluate your company's financial performance, along with suggestions on how to make sure they draw the correct conclusions.

Ratio Analysis Lenders will use ratios derived from data on your fiscal-year-end balance sheets and income statements to evaluate your company's past and projected performance. Like it or not, lenders are numbers types. And, like it or not, if you want their money, you have to play the game by their rules. Fortunately, a lender's financial analysis of your company is not all that complicated; and, as we've said before, you don't have to understand accounting to understand ratios. You *do*,

EXHIBIT 4.2

Surgical Products Company September 26, 1994 Statement in Thousands $	Jun. 30 1990	Jun. 30 1991	Jun. 30 1992	Jun. 30 1993	RMA 1993 SIC 3841
Highlights					
INCOME STATEMENT:					
Sales	404	981	1,368	1,440	1,440
Gross Margin	222	490	646	684	615
Operating Expenses	244	425	567	598	514
NPBT	(22)	65	79	68	73
NPAT	(22)	52	55	47	NA
Cash Dividends	0	0	0	0	NA
BALANCE SHEET:					
Total Current Assets	47	131	217	357	360
Net Fixed Assets	0	0	0	120	99
Total Assets	47	131	217	477	477
Short Term Obligations	0	0	0	50	57
Total Current Liabilities	17	49	80	158	171
Long Term Debt	0	0	0	135	77
Total Liabilities	17	49	80	293	NA
Net Worth	30	82	137	184	219
RATIOS:					
Sales Growth		142.82%	39.45%	5.26%	NA
Gross Margin	54.95%	49.95%	47.22%	47.50%	42.70%
Profit Margin	(5.45)%	5.30%	4.02%	3.26%	NA
Current Ratio	2.76	2.67	2.71	2.26	2.00
Quick Ratio	2.12	1.96	1.83	1.72	1.20
Working Capital	30	82	137	199	NA
Age of Receivables	28	33	37	56	44
Days Supply in Inventory	22	26	36	41	48
Age of Payables	34	36	40	52	26
Debt/Tangible Net Worth	0.57	0.60	0.58	1.59	1.40
Breakeven Sales - Cash Basis		977	1,363	1,353	NA
Actual Sales/Breakeven Sales		1.00	1.00	1.06	NA
CASH FLOW: Incr (Decr) in Cash					
Cash From Sales		923	1,320	1,356	NA
Cash From Trading		440	593	614	NA
Net Cash After Operations		2	2	55	NA
Cash After Financing Costs		2	2	37	NA
Cash After Debt Amortization		2	2	37	NA
Capital Expenditures				(180)	NA
Financing Surplus (Requirement)		2	2	(143)	NA

Reprinted with permission, copyright Baker Hill, 1994

however, have to understand what numbers lenders look at, what they're looking for, and how the numbers on your financial statements could lead them to draw the wrong conclusions about your company.

Ratios and other rules of thumb, when used without proper explanation, can be very misleading. However, when used to compare your performance from year to year, and to compare it with that of your industry peers, ratios can be quite informative. Most bankers belong to trade organizations and use service bureaus that supply industry ratios against which they'll compare your numbers. You can (and should) obtain a copy of a report that summarizes your industry norms.

❏ Secret

The source that most bankers use is *Annual Statement Studies*[1] by Robert Morris Associates (RMA). RMA is the largest trade association for lenders and finance professionals. Exhibit 4.3 shows a sample report. These studies are a valuable tool for both you and your lender to compare your company's financial performance with others in your industry. Many bankers now use computer programs, including STAN, that automatically compute and print your ratios next to those provided by RMA.

Be sure to provide lenders with your correct Standard Industrial Classification Code (SIC code) so that they don't compare you to the wrong group of peers. And be sure to point out any reasons why your business may be substantially different than others in that SIC. We found, for example, that one tire wholesaler's ratios were way out of whack with those of that industry because the business included a substantial retail component. Had the wholesaler not pointed this out to lenders, they might have concluded that the company's profit margins were too thin, the inventory moved too slow, and the fixed expenses were too high.

In some cases, trade associations can provide industry ratios that are more fine-tuned than those reported by RMA. If more representative ratios are available from your trade association, include them in your loan proposal.

Now, let's look at the five areas that are of concern to lenders, the ratios they use to evaluate each, and the potential lies they can tell about your company's financial health and creditworthiness.

The ratio calculations will be based on the financial statements from a fictitious company, A Typical Photo Lab, Inc. (ATP Labs), shown in

EXHIBIT 4.3   RMA Statement Study: Services-Photofinishing Laboratories

Current Data Sorted By Assets							Comparative Historical Data	
2	1	2		2		# Postretirement Benefits		
						Type of Statement		
	2	3	2			Unqualified	13	4
1	9	7				Reviewed	19	16
11	9	1				Compiled	32	26
8	1	1				Tax Returns		1
2	8	4			1	Other	20	25
	23(4/1-9/30/93)			47(10/1/93-3/31/94)			6/30/89- 3/31/90	4/1/90- 3/31/91
0-500M	500M-2MM	2-10MM	10-50MM	50-100MM	100-250MM		ALL	ALL
22	29	16	2	1		NUMBER OF STATEMENTS	84	72

0-500M	500M-2MM	2-10MM	10-50MM	50-100MM	100-250MM		6/30/89-3/31/90 ALL	4/1/90-3/31/91 ALL
%	%	%	%	%	%	**ASSETS**	%	%
14.1	13.8	4.5				Cash & Equivalents	9.2	9.6
13.5	25.5	24.1				Trade Receivables - (net)	21.1	23.2
15.1	9.9	9.9				Inventory	13.2	12.4
.9	.8	1.4				All Other Current	2.4	1.4
43.6	50.0	39.9				Total Current	45.8	46.6
46.8	44.2	50.6				Fixed Assets (net)	43.6	44.5
5.7	1.2	.4				Intangibles (net)	4.6	3.2
3.9	4.7	9.2				All Other Non-Current	5.9	5.7
100.0	100.0	100.0				Total	100.0	100.0
						LIABILITIES		
8.5	4.1	7.5				Notes Payable-Short Term	7.8	6.8
7.5	8.1	10.5				Cur. Mat.-L/T/D	7.9	9.3
12.7	15.0	8.6				Trade Payables	13.7	13.3
1.2	.1	.4				Income Taxes Payable	.4	.7
5.9	8.3	7.6				All Other Current	8.1	7.3
35.7	35.6	34.6				Total Current	37.9	37.3
37.2	26.1	23.4				Long Term Debt	30.0	30.5
.4	.5	1.2				Deferred Taxes	1.0	.5
6.2	1.3	1.6				All Other Non-Current	1.6	2.7
20.4	36.6	39.3				Net Worth	29.5	29.0
100.0	100.0	100.0				Total Liabilities & Net Worth	100.0	100.0
						INCOME DATA		
100.0	100.0	100.0				Net Sales	100.0	100.0
65.4	48.4	44.1				Gross Profit	48.6	48.8
58.9	43.8	40.3				Operating Expenses	43.9	44.8
6.5	4.6	3.8				Operating Profit	4.8	3.8
2.1	1.3	1.1				All Other Expenses (net)	1.9	2.0
4.5	3.4	2.8				Profit Before Taxes	2.9	1.8
						RATIOS		
1.9	2.1	1.7				Current	2.0	1.9
1.4	1.6	1.1					1.2	1.3
.8	1.2	.9					.8	.9
1.4	1.7	1.4				Quick	1.3	1.4
.9	1.2	.8					.9	.8
.4	.8	.6					.5	.6
5 76.7	25 14.4	36 10.2				Sales/Receivables	15 24.0	16 22.3
12 29.5	46 8.0	42 8.6					35 10.5	39 9.4
19 19.7	53 6.9	58 6.3					53 6.6	51 7.1
20 17.9	10 35.2	20 18.3				Cost of Sales/Inventory	20 18.4	14 26.6
45 8.1	20 18.4	26 13.8					34 10.8	26 13.9
81 4.5	39 9.3	60 6.1					56 6.5	51 7.2
17 20.9	20 18.7	11 32.4				Cost of Sales/Payables	23 16.2	19 19.1
33 10.9	33 10.9	23 16.1					34 10.8	33 11.1
52 7.0	58 6.3	37 9.8					65 5.6	64 5.7
15.7	8.4	12.0				Sales/Working Capital	9.3	9.8
45.3	12.6	54.0					26.3	26.1
−41.0	37.4	−88.5					−23.6	−37.5
9.9	6.1	1.9				EBIT/Interest	3.6	3.8
(21) 3.2	(27) 2.5	(14) 1.4					(76) 2.3	(67) 2.0
.5	1.7	−1.6					1.1	.7
	2.7					Net Profit + Depr., Dep., Amort./Cur. Mat. L/T/D	3.5	3.1
	(14) 1.7						(45) 1.9	(45) 1.6
	1.2						1.0	.6
.9	.8	1.0				Fixed/Worth	.8	.8
1.7	1.2	1.7					1.6	1.5
−33.3	1.8	2.0					4.9	5.1
1.4	.9	.8				Debt/Worth	1.2	1.1
2.6	1.6	1.7					2.4	2.6
−85.4	4.6	2.8					9.7	12.5
144.0	24.9	14.0				% Profit Before Taxes/Tangible Net Worth	40.6	36.9
(16) 47.5	(27) 13.7	(15) 2.8					(67) 16.6	(57) 17.8
−3.2	3.3	−20.8					5.5	.8
31.3	10.6	5.5				% Profit Before Taxes/Total Assets	12.8	12.0
13.2	5.0	1.9					5.2	5.3
−3.0	1.4	−7.3					.3	−1.3
10.4	9.0	5.9				Sales/Net Fixed Assets	9.9	9.6
7.2	5.2	3.5					4.8	5.3
3.2	3.5	3.1					3.4	3.2
4.7	3.1	2.2				Sales/Total Assets	2.8	3.0
3.2	2.4	2.0					2.1	2.3
1.6	1.8	1.6					1.5	1.8
4.6	2.7	3.8				% Depr., Dep., Amort./Sales	3.3	3.0
(19) 6.2	(28) 4.6	4.1					(78) 5.2	(65) 5.0
9.1	5.8	6.6					8.4	7.4
4.2	4.4					% Officers', Directors', Owners' Comp/Sales	3.5	5.1
(11) 8.5	(16) 5.7						(34) 6.0	(28) 7.5
13.7	7.4						10.2	9.5
12200M	86837M	102895M	81387M	131782M		Net Sales ($)	416532M	232827M
4221M	31221M	54292M	42588M	69911M		Total Assets ($)	230320M	102506M

M = $thousand   MM = $million

Reprinted with permission, copyright Robert Morris Associates 1994

EXHIBIT 4.3 *(Continued)*

	Comparative Historical Data					Current Data Sorted By Sales				
	1		**5**		**0-1MM**	**1-3MM**	**3-5MM**	**5-10MM**	**10-25MM**	**25MM & OVER**
# Postretirement Benefits					2	1				2
Type of Statement										
Unqualified	9	6	7		1	1		2	1	2
Reviewed	23	18	17		10	1		6		
Compiled	34	24	21		1.1 / 5	4		1		
Tax Returns	4	3	10		8 / 1			1		
Other	21	12	15		2 / 4	3	4		1	1
	4/1/91-3/31/92	4/1/92-3/31/93	4/1/93-3/31/94		23(4/1-9/30/93)			47(10/1/93-3/31/94)		
	ALL	ALL	ALL							
NUMBER OF STATEMENTS	91	63	70		21	21	9	14	2	3
ASSETS	%	%	%		%	%	%	%	%	%
Cash & Equivalents	10.8	12.9	11.9		14.7	14.8		6.3		
Trade Receivables - (net)	20.3	21.0	21.0		13.4	22.6		26.2		
Inventory	11.4	10.6	11.5		14.5	8.3		10.9		
All Other Current	1.3	1.9	1.2		.2	1.4		1.1		
Total Current	43.8	46.4	45.6		42.8	47.1		44.4		
Fixed Assets (net)	45.5	43.6	45.6		47.2	46.5		47.0		
Intangibles (net)	3.4	3.6	3.4		6.6	.8		.3		
All Other Non-Current	7.3	6.4	5.5		3.4	5.6		8.3		
Total	100.0	100.0	100.0		100.0	100.0		100.0		
LIABILITIES										
Notes Payable-Short Term	9.1	7.8	6.1		7.6	7.0		6.6		
Cur. Mat.-L/T/D	8.2	10.6	8.3		8.8	9.2		7.7		
Trade Payables	12.8	10.9	13.1		12.1	11.6		8.5		
Income Taxes Payable	.6	.5	.6		.2	1.2		.5		
All Other Current	10.5	6.5	7.3		5.8	-5.5		7.7		
Total Current	41.2	36.2	35.5		34.5	34.7		30.9		
Long Term Debt	28.2	27.6	28.7		43.3	19.5		26.4		
Deferred Taxes	.6	1.2	.6		.0	.9		.6		
All Other Non-Current	2.8	1.3	3.0		6.1	1.6		1.5		
Net Worth	27.3	33.6	32.2		16.1	43.3		40.6		
Total Liabilities & Net Worth	100.0	100.0	100.0		100.0	100.0		100.0		
INCOME DATA										
Net Sales	100.0	100.0	100.0		100.0	100.0		100.0		
Gross Profit	49.8	49.9	52.3		65.5	52.1		44.8		
Operating Expenses	45.5	43.8	47.1		58.9	47.6		39.3		
Operating Profit	4.2	6.1	5.1		6.6	4.5		5.5		
All Other Expenses (net)	1.4	1.4	1.5		2.6	.5		1.0		
Profit Before Taxes	2.8	4.7	3.7		3.9	4.0		4.5		
RATIOS										
Current	1.8	2.4	1.9		1.9	2.2		2.0		
	1.2	1.3	1.3		1.3	1.6		1.1		
	.8	.9	.9		.8	1.2		.9		
Quick	1.4	1.9	1.6		1.5	1.9		1.8		
	.8	1.0	1.0		.9	1.4		.8		
	.4	.7	.6		.4	.9		.6		
Sales/Receivables	14 26.4	21 17.6	14 25.2		6 58.6	25 14.4		36 10.2		
	30 12.1	37 9.9	36 10.2		14 26.3	43 8.4		42 8.6		
	50 7.3	49 7.5	49 7.4		23 15.9	53 6.9		61 6.0		
Cost of Sales/Inventory	11 34.0	13 28.6	14 25.4		24 15.1	7 53.5		20 18.1		
	25 14.6	24 15.2	26 13.9		48 7.6	24 15.3		30 12.3		
	42 8.7	53 6.9	51 7.1		83 4.4	41 9.0		54 6.7		
Cost of Sales/Payables	20 18.6	17 21.9	18 20.3		21 17.3	11 34.3		14 26.1		
	30 12.0	31 11.9	33 11.2		35 10.5	28 13.0		23 16.1		
	56 6.5	47 7.7	52 7.0		56 6.5	78 4.7		37 9.9		
Sales/Working Capital	11.1	10.2	9.4		12.3	8.0		9.1		
	43.4	22.1	26.7		55.6	15.5		54.0		
	-24.2	-67.8	-107.2		-31.2	33.1		-75.4		
EBIT/Interest	4.5	5.9	5.9		9.4	6.4		2.8		
	(84) 2.3	(57) 2.5	(65) 2.4		(20) 2.5	(19) 3.0		(12) 1.8		
	1.3	1.4	.7		.5	1.7		.5		
Net Profit + Depr., Dep., Amort./Cur. Mat. L/T/D	2.4	2.7	2.2							
	(38) 1.7	(26) 1.9	(29) 1.3							
	.9	1.2	.6							
Fixed/Worth	.8	.7	.7		1.1	.7		.7		
	1.6	1.6	1.4		4.9	1.1		1.6		
	11.1	4.5	4.4		-3.1	1.5		2.1		
Debt/Worth	1.1	.9	1.0		1.6	.6		1.1		
	2.5	1.9	1.9		8.3	1.2		1.7		
	23.1	8.0	6.0		-6.1	2.6		3.1		
% Profit Before Taxes/Tangible Net Worth	49.8	45.5	40.0		146.4	20.6		34.4		
	(73) 20.3	(52) 22.7	(59) 14.0		(14) 47.5	(20) 15.1		11.4		
	7.4	5.5	-3.3		1.9	3.9		-7.4		
% Profit Before Taxes/Total Assets	14.3	20.0	16.1		32.4	11.0		15.3		
	7.5	6.8	5.2		13.1	5.5		3.5		
	1.2	2.3	-1.4		-3.1	2.0		-2.0		
Sales/Net Fixed Assets	9.5	9.9	9.3		9.5	7.8		7.0		
	5.5	5.6	5.3		5.5	5.0		3.9		
	3.3	3.6	3.2		2.9	3.2		3.2		
Sales/Total Assets	3.1	3.0	3.1		4.5	2.9		2.3		
	2.3	2.3	2.2		2.7	2.3		2.1		
	1.8	1.8	1.7		1.5	1.6		1.8		
% Depr., Dep., Amort./Sales	2.9	2.4	3.5		5.1	3.8		2.3		
	(85) 4.5	(60) 4.5	(65) 4.7		(18) 6.8	(20) 4.7		4.0		
	6.3	7.4	6.8		11.0	6.2		6.0		
% Officers', Directors', Owners' Comp/Sales	3.8	4.3	4.3		4.2	3.8				
	(43) 7.4	(23) 7.7	(32) 6.2		(11) 7.3	(12) 5.7				
	13.7	12.7	8.4		11.5	7.5				
Net Sales ($)	380364M	294119M	415101M		9474M	38712M	35090M	88069M	30587M	213189M
Total Assets ($)	247371M	103618M	202233M		4604M	19518M	13496M	44343M	7773M	112499M

M = $thousand   MM = $million

EXHIBIT 4.4 A Typical Photo Lab, Inc., (ATP Labs) Balance Sheet and Income Statement

ATP Labs BALANCE SHEET				ATP Labs INCOME STATEMENT		
(,000 omitted)	Year 1	Year 2			Year 1	Year 2
Assets				**Sales**	$1,200	$1,600
Cash	$30	$40		Cost of Goods Sold (COGS)	$700	$1,000
Accounts Receivable (A/R)	$100	$140		Gross Profit	$500	$600
Inventory	$50	$90				
Current Assets	$180	$270		Operating Expenses	$400	$450
				Operating Profit	$100	$150
Fixed Assets	$90	$90				
Total Assets	$270	$360		Interest	$10	$30
				Net Profit before Taxes	$90	$120
Liabilities						
Accounts Payable (A/P)	$55	$95		Taxes	$30	$40
Current Maturities of LTD	$40	$40		**Net Profit**	$60	$80
Current Liabilities	$95	$135				
Long-Term Debt (LTD)	$90	$90				
Total Liabilities	$185	$225				
Net Worth						
Owner's Capital	$25	$25				
Retained Earnings	$60	$110				
Total Net Worth (NW)	$85	$135				
Total Net Worth & Liabs	$270	$360				

Exhibit 4.4. The RMA data for SIC code 7384, Photo Finishing Laboratories, shown in Exhibit 4.3 were used for comparison.

Liquidity Ratios Liquidity ratios indicate whether you have a comfortable balance between liabilities that will require cash in the near term (such as bills and loan payments) and assets that will contribute cash in the near term (such as cash accounts, receivables, and inventory). If cash requirements continually exceed cash resources, your long-term survival is obviously threatened. Lenders measure liquidity with two primary balance sheet ratios: current ratio and quick ratio.

Current Ratio. Lenders want this ratio to be 2:1 or higher, meaning that you have twice as much cash likely to come in within a short period as you do uses for that cash.

Current Ratio = Current Assets ÷ Current Liabilities

ATP Labs Current Ratio

Year 1: $180/$95 =	1.89:1
Year 2: $270/$135 =	2.00:1
RMA Industry Comparison	1.30:1

Interpretation: Liquidity is improving, largely due to increased accounts receivable and inventory. The company is more liquid than its industry peers.

Quick Ratios. This ratio should be 1:1 or higher. The Quick Ratio is more conservative than the Current Ratio because it recognizes that inventory cannot always be sold (liquidated) quickly.

Quick Ratio = (Current Assets − Inventory) ÷ Current Liabilities

ATP Labs Quick Ratio

Year 1: $130/$95 =	1.37:1
Year 2: $180/$135 =	1.33:1
RMA Industry Comparison	.9:1

Interpretation: This ratio is declining very slightly due to heavier inventory balances, and they're somewhat higher than the industry average. Lenders might be concerned about excess or stale inventory.

❏ Secret

One-time large purchases, such as buying in quantity at year end before prices go up, can have a negative impact on this ratio because it inflates the value of inventory beyond your normal business level. Be sure to explain any events that cause unusually high year-end receivables, inventory, or payables. Offer a more typical number if the year-end value is unusually high or unusually low.

Leverage Ratio Lenders use a debt-to-worth ratio to measure a company's leverage. Leverage represents the level of capital contributed by creditors to owners' capital contributions. Generally, higher leverage leads to higher risk for the company and, therefore, for the lender.

Debt-to-Worth Ratio. Lenders want this ratio to be 3:1 or lower. In other words, they want to be sure that your company has financed its assets with at least one dollar of your own contributed or accumulated funds for every three dollars of borrowed money.

Debt-to-Worth Ratio aka Debt-to-Equity Ratio =
Total Debt ÷ Net Worth, or Equity

❑ Secret

(1) Highly depreciated assets, or assets owned by related entities such as a real estate partnership can make this ratio look worse than it is; (2) be sure to point out any friendly debt that could be subordinated to (paid after) other loans. If you point out such circumstances, the lender will usually add subordinated debt to equity for the purpose of calculating this ratio.

ATP Labs Debt-to-Worth Ratio

Year 1: $185/$85 =	2.18:1
Year 2: $225/$135 =	1.67:1
RMA Industry Average	1.2:1

Interpretation: Leverage actually declined from last year and is only slightly higher than industry peers. If the company's $90,000 in long-term debt was actually a loan from the owner that could be subordinated to bank debt, a lender would calculate the Year 2 debt-to-worth ratio as ($225 − $90) ÷ ($135 + $90), which would improve the firm's leverage to a very low .6:1.

Performance or Productivity Calculations   These calculations tell the lender how well you're managing the *things* (assets) that are supposed to eventually generate cash flow for your company as well as how well you're controlling your costs. Primary calculations used are:

Net Profit as a Percent of Sales aka Profit Margin =
(Sales − All Pretax Expenses) ÷ Sales

Profit Margin. This percentage should be stable or increasing from year to year. Since it's the primary measure of your firm's profitability, any decline in this figure may cause the lender to be concerned about your company's financial health.

Anything that understates your company's profitability should be explained.

❑ **Secret**

The following events as well as other factors can skew this and all other income-statement-based figures:

- An unusual one-time expense.
- A one-time contract that overinflated income last year (and thus makes it look like this year's income declined).
- Accounting changes.
- Discretionary expenses such as a company car for the owner, home office deductions.
- Other owner perks.

ATP Labs: Pretax Profit %

Year 1: $90/$1,200 =	.075 or 7.5%
Year 2: $120/$1,600 =	.075 or 7.5%
RMA Industry Average	4%

Interpretation: To the company's credit (literally), net profit margin stayed the same in spite of a large increase in sales, and it's doing substantially better than the industry average. Most growing companies have a hard time keeping expenses in line with sales growth.

Gross Margin. This ratio should be stable or increasing from year to year. Dips in gross margin will cause lenders to wonder if prices are falling or direct costs are increasing.

Gross Profit as a Percentage of Sales aka Gross Margin =
(Sales − Cost of Goods Sold) ÷ Sale

❑ **Secret**

The following events can skew this indicator:

- Inconsistent year-to-year classification of direct and operating expenses.
- A change in sales mix toward low margin items.
- Sloppy accounting for sales and costs.
- One-time sales that are priced with unusually high or low margins.

ATP Labs: Gross Profit Margin

Year 1: $500/$1,200 =   .416 or 41.6%

Year 2: $600/$1,600 =   .375 or 37.5%

RMA Industry Average   52.1%

Interpretation: The company's gross margin declined substantially from the prior year and is significantly lower than that of its peers. Obviously, since their net profit margin is strong, they must be operating more efficiently. Some lenders, however, may be concerned that the company's operating expenses are unsustainably low and are likely to grow substantially in future years. The company should have a good reason for the year-to-year changes and for the contrast with their peer group. A plausible explanation, for example, would be that the company specializes in a particular type of lower margin business, such as mail order photo processing, that allows them to have lower than average overhead. They can afford the lower margin because they can make do with less elaborate facilities than a photo processor doing a wider range of work from a storefront.

Operating Expense as a Percentage of Sales. This percentage should be stable or decreasing from year to year. A steady increase will suggest that your expenses are growing out of control. Often businesses allow their expenses (particularly salaries, rent, telephone, office expense, and advertising) to grow in anticipation of sales. If the expected sales never come, or they come more slowly than anticipated, the extra expenses eat away at the company's profit and cash flow. Lenders will pay close attention to any trends that indicate growth in your company's expenses is disproportionate to your growth in sales.

Operating Expense as a Percentage of Sales =
Operating Expenses ÷ Sales

❑ Secret

One-time expenses such as office renovations, product development expense, and changes in your accounting methods can skew this percentage.

ATP Labs: Operating Expense

Year 1: $400 ÷ $1,200 =   .33 or 33%

Year 2: $450 ÷ $1,600 =   .28 or 28%

RMA Industry Average   47.6%

Interpretation: The fact that this percentage is declining may reflect good management or indicate that the company is "over the hump," and can now earn more money with the same fixed expenses. Normally, a lender would see this trend as a good sign. However, because ATP Labs' expenses are so much lower than the industry average, the lender might suspect, as mentioned earlier, that this company enjoys lower overhead because of something in the nature of its particular business. Another reason for the disparity may be that this company classifies some expense differently from most of the industry. For example, if most companies classify rent as an operating expense, and this company shows it as a production expense, that would explain both the lower than average gross profit margin and the lower than average operating expense margin.

Accounts Receivable Turnover. This number indicates how effectively your company manages its accounts receivable. If the result of the calculation is equal to 12, then you're collecting your accounts receivable approximately every 30 days (365 days in a year/12). If A/R turnover days grow from year to year, or if they exceed your stated payment terms, your credit policies and procedures may have deteriorated, which will cause lenders to suspect that some receivables are uncollectable.

Accounts Receivable Turnover = Sales ÷ Accounts Receivable

A/R Turnover (Days) = 365 ÷ (Sales ÷ A/R)

❑ Secret

As with any balance sheet calculation, one-time year-end events may skew the result. For example, if you made a very large sale at year end, the balance sheet value for accounts receivable may look unusually high. In addition, if your sales mix changes from one year to the next and this year you're selling to businesses that require longer payment terms, or you're selling to fewer cash customers, you need to explain the change so it won't be interpreted as a problem.

ATP Labs: Accounts Receivable Turnover (Days)

Year 1: 365 ÷ ($1,200/100) =   30 days
Year 2: 365 ÷ ($1,600/140) =   32 days
RMA Industry Average   43 days

Interpretation: The company is collecting its account receivable roughly every 30 days. If they're selling on 30-day terms, they're doing a great job of collection, even better than their industry peers.

Inventory Turnover. This number measures a company's ability to purchase and utilize inventory effectively. If the value is equal to 12, then your company is selling, or *turning*, its inventory approximately every 30 days (365/12). If inventory days grow from year to year, a lender will be wary that some inventory might be stale or, at the very least, that your business has slowed.

$$\text{Inventory Turnover} = \text{Cost of Goods Sold} \div \text{Inventory}$$

$$\text{Inventory Turnover (Days)} = 365 \div (\text{COGS} \div \text{Inventory})$$

❑ **Secret**

Again, year-end events, such as buying in quantity before prices go up, will skew this figure, so explain if necessary.

ATP Labs: Inventory Turnover (Days)

Year 1: 365 ÷ ($700/50) =   26 days
Year 2: 365 ÷ ($1,000/90) =   33 days
RMA Industry Comparison   24 days

Interpretation: The company is turning its inventory slightly slower than it was last year and slower than the industry average. The company should have a reason for the change, but since that inventory represents a fairly minor asset in this company, the change probably won't draw too much attention.

Sales to Fixed Assets. This ratio provides an indication of a company's effectiveness in purchasing useful fixed assets. An increase in this ratio from year to year might indicate that your company is investing in equipment that's not productively employed in the business and thus is draining its resources.

$$\text{Sales to Fixed Assets} = \text{Sales} \div \text{Fixed Assets}$$

❑ **Secret**

If a company does not add to its fixed assets as it grows, this ratio will decline. Also off-balance-sheet assets such as leases or buildings owned in personal names will not be reflected.

ATP Labs: Sales to Fixed Assets

Year 1: $1,200/90 =	13.33:1
Year 2: $1,600/90 =	17.78:1
RMA Industry Comparison	5:1

Interpretation: This company seems to leverage more out of its fixed assets than its peers. The improvement from year to year is the result of increasing sales on stable assets. While all this seems positive, lenders might wonder if the company is keeping up with technology or if it is pushing old equipment to its limits with a possible future decline in quality.

Accounts Payable Turnover. This number indicates how you pay your bills. If the cost of goods sold (COGS, your direct production expenses) entry is twelve times payables, then you're probably paying your bills every 30 days (365/12). This number should be in line with your vendor's payment terms. If payable days are increasing from year to year, which indicates that you're paying your bills slower, the lender will worry about your relationship with your vendors.

$$\text{Accounts Payable Turnover} = \text{Cost of Goods Sold} \div \text{Accounts Payable}$$

$$\text{A/P Turnover (Days)} = 365 \div (\text{Cost of Goods Sold} \div \text{Accounts Payable})$$

ATP Labs: A/P Turnover (Days)

Year 1: 365 ÷ ($700/55) =	29 days
Year 2: 365 ÷ ($1,000/95) =	35 days
RMA Industry Comparison	28 days

Interpretation: The company seems to be paying its bills a little slower than it was last year, but it is close to the industry average and only a few days off of typical 30-day payment terms. No cause for alarm on this point.

Z-Score. This value, developed by Professor Edward Altman of New York University, has proven to be a useful indicator of future insolvency or bankruptcy. Private companies with a score of less than 1.23 indicate potential bankruptcy within two to three years. Scores of over 2.90 indicate the likelihood of continued operations.

$$\text{Z-Score} = (.7 \times \text{Working Capital} \div \text{Total Assets}) + (.8 \times \text{Retained Earnings} \div \text{Total Assets}) + (3.1 \times \text{Earnings before Interest and Taxes} \div \text{Total Assets}) + (.4 \times \text{Book Value of Equity} \div \text{Total Liabilities}) + (1 \times \text{Sales} \div \text{Total Assets})$$

❏ Secret

All the balance sheet and income statement issues mentioned earlier are potential problems in this score. Z-score is considered to be more reliable for companies with annual sales greater than $20 million.

ATP Labs: Z-Score

Year 2: $(.7 \times (\$270 - \$135) \div \$360) + (.8 \times \$110 \div \$360) + (3.1 \times \$120 \div \$360) + (.4 \times \$135 \div \$225) + (1 \times \$1,600 \div \$360) = 6.22$

Interpretation: According to this test, the company shows a low risk of insolvency or bankruptcy.

Cash Coverage Ratios   Cash coverage ratios provide lenders with a quick read on whether your firm can cover its present or proposed loan payments.

Cash Flow to Current Maturities of Long-Term Debt aka CMLTD = (Net Profit + Depreciation + Noncash Expenses) ÷ CMLTD

Lenders want to see that a comfortable margin exists between net cash generated by the business and cash needed to cover loan payments. Such assurance can be demonstrated through historical business performance and sometimes well-documented projections of future performance. In start-up situations, some lenders will temporarily consider other sources of income such as a working spouse or second job. They'll be comfortable with a ratio in excess of 1.2:1. A decline from year to year will obviously concern them.

❑ Secret

One-time and discretionary expenses should be added back to net profit for the purpose of this calculation.

ATP Labs: Cash Flow Coverage Ratio

Year 1: $60 ÷ $40 =   1.5:1

Year 2: $80 ÷ $40 =   2.0:1

Interpretation: The company appears to have a strong cash flow coverage of its debt and could likely handle additional borrowing.

❑ Secret

Cheating on your taxes will frustrate your ability to find money. No one likes to pay taxes, but don't expect any sympathy from your banker if your abuse of the system makes some of your ratios look out of whack. Some business owners (not you or anyone you know, of course) try to find ways to hide income from Uncle Sam by not booking a portion of their cash sales. Later, when they're trying to find money, they go to their banker claiming that their income is really higher than the tax returns show. Revelations like this definitely won't win you any character points from your banker. Your lawyers may be bound to keep anything you tell them confidential, but your banker isn't. Don't trying creating a second, better looking, version of your tax returns, either. The IRS and the bank will discover your little scheme, and you could land in jail. We don't have any secrets on how to find money from jail!

Ratio Analysis Summary   ATP Labs fared quite well in the ratio analysis. Their liquidity is good and improving. Their leverage shows additional capacity for debt. Their performance ratios are strong, though there could be a question about their continued ability to keep operating expenses low, and their gross profit margins don't leave much room for mistakes. Their accounts receivable and inventory management are good, and they appear to maintain good terms with their vendors. Their cash coverage ratio indicates that they can handle additional debt, but a lender will want to see a cash-flow projection as confirmation.

One final point, for emphasis. Don't expect lenders to find or even look for items on their own that may skew your ratio performance. Often junior lenders aren't aware of the kinds of things that can distort the numbers. A good loan request package will point out any substantial distortions in your balance sheet and income statement, and will calculate adjusted ratios for the lender.

To prove the point about the importance of teaching lenders your business, how would do you think a lender would feel about a company with the following ratios?

**Some Unknown Company in an
Unknown Industry
Ratio Analysis**

Current ratio	1:1
Quick ratio	.5:1
A/R turnover	180 days
Inventory turnover	360 days
A/P turnover	90 days
Debt/Worth	3:1
Gross profit margin	60%
Net profit margin	10%

Their liquidity ratios, the current and quick ratios, are well below where lenders would want them at 2:1 and 1:1, respectively. The management of receivables, inventory, and payables appears abysmal; they're only turning their inventory once a year. And they're already pushing a lender's comfort level on debt-to-worth. All they seem to have going for them is profitability.

And now for the rest of the story. Suppose the company we're looking at is a distributor of rock salt and other snow-removal products, and the preceding ratios are based on its December 31 year-end balance sheet. At the end of December, a rock salt distributor is probably holding its maximum annual inventory because the heaviest snow season is ahead. The inventory and payables are therefore higher than they'll be at any other point in the year. Recognizing this fact, suppliers offer the company seasonal payment terms, which are due at the end of the season. The receivables, a result of salt already distributed in October, are mostly due from local municipalities, which are notorious for slow payment. And naturally the debt-to-worth ratio is high; this is the firm's peak borrowing season. If you looked at its balance sheet in May, you'd see a much different picture.

All of which is to point out the importance of educating your lender about the idiosyncrasies of your business. If this had been your company, it wouldn't have received a second glance from a lender without an explanation of the unusual nature of your situation.

Common Size Analysis

In addition to ratios, lenders' handy-dandy computer spreads also supply a common size report that provides percentages for each category of income, expense, asset, liability, and so forth. This allows lenders to quickly spot year-to-year changes and to compare your business with others in your industry. Exhibit 4.5 shows a partial common size report for ATP Labs.

In common size analyses, lenders are looking for expenses or assets that grow out of proportion to sales, percentages that don't compare favorably with others in the industry, and any items that change substantially from year to year. For example, if most photo labs' inventory is about 8.3 percent of assets, and ATP Labs shows 25 percent of assets in inventory, a lender might suspect stale inventory. If the company spent 10 percent of income on advertising last year, and this year they're only spending 2 percent, a lender might worry that future sales are going to suffer. Common size analysis also allows lenders to quickly analyze how the company is financed and how that financing is used. For example, this company's long- and short-term debt was reduced from Year 1 because its profitability increased retained earnings.

Like ratios, lots of factors can cause common size analysis to be misleading. Changes in the classification of expenses, changes in accounting methods, one-time expenses, year-end aberrations, and any other potentially misleading items should be explained to your lender.

Financial Projections

These days, most lenders require that prospective borrowers submit two or three years of financial projections (balance sheet, income statement and cash flow) with their loan request. At one time, while most lenders required them, few paid much attention to your projections. Thanks to the S&L debacle, lenders not only pay more attention now, but many will actually hold you to them. If you've missed your projections when next year comes, at the very least you'll have some explaining to do, and you might find yourself shopping for a new lender. Obviously, they're

EXHIBIT 4.5   ATP Labs Common Size Analysis

Balance Sheet ($,000)

	1992 $	1992 %	1993 $	1993 %
Assets				
Cash	$30	11.11%	$40	11.11%
Accounts Receivable	$100	37.04%	$140	38.89%
Inventory	$50	18.52%	$90	25.00%
Current Assets	$180	66.67%	$270	75.00%
Fixed Assets	$90	33.33%	$90	25.00%
Total Assets	$270	100.00%	$360	100.00%
Liabilities:				
Accounts Payable	$55	20.37%	$95	26.39%
Current Maturities of LTD	$40	14.81%	$40	11.11%
Current Liabilities	$95	35.19%	$135	37.50%
Long-Term Debt (LTD)	$90	33.33%	$90	25.00%
Total Liabilities	$185	33.33%	$225	25.00%
Net Worth (NW)				
Owners Capital	$25	9.26%	$25	6.94%
Retained Earnings	$60	22.22%	$110	30.56%
Total Net Worth	$85	31.48%	$135	37.50%
Total NW and Liabs	$270	100.00%	$360	100.00%

Income Statement ($,000)

	1992 $	1992 %	1993 $	1993 %
Sales	$1,200	100.00%	$1,600	100.00%
Cost of Goods	$700	58.33%	$1,000	62.50%
Gross Profit	$500	41.67%	$600	37.50%
Operating Expenses	$400	33.33%	$450	28.13%
Operating Profit	$100	8.33%	$150	9.38%
Interest	$10	0.83%	$30	1.88%
Taxes	$30	2.50%	$40	2.50%
Net Profit	$60	5.00%	$80	5.00%

not going to hold you to the penny, but neither will they let you be too far off, particularly in a negative direction.

Lenders will often use your projections to set loan covenants and conditions. If you project net income of $100,000 or your projected balance sheet shows a current ratio of 2:1, those numbers may be written into your loan agreement. And missing them will be a condition of loan default. The point here is that you need to predict, as accurately as possible, what your financial future will hold. This is not the time to try to impress your lender with how wonderful tomorrow might be. Be honest and conservative, and both you and the lender will be a lot happier come next year's loan negotiations.

COLLATERAL: WHAT IF YOU DON'T PAY?

If for some reason you don't pay, lenders want to have something of value that they can sell to recoup some of their loss. Most small businesses loans are secured by both company and personal assets.

Setting collateral values on assets is always a source of contention between lenders and borrowers. Let's say you bought a piece of equipment with $75,000 of hard-earned cash yesterday, and today the lender wants to assign a collateral value of just $45,000. What gives? Well, the difference is due to the reality that, if the bank has to liquidate an asset (sell your equipment), it will rarely see 100 cents on the dollar. In fact, lenders are lucky if they see more than 10 cents on the dollar with some assets. The following rules of thumb will help you understand how lenders are likely to value your collateral:

Collateral Values

Accounts Receivable (A/R)	60%– 85%
Inventory	10%– 80%
Furniture and Equipment (F&E)	10%– 80%
Real Estate	50%– 90%
Cash	90%–100%

Accounts Receivable as Collateral (A/R)

Lenders will generally consider the collateral value of receivables to be 60 to 85 percent for those less than 60 to 90 days old unless the payment terms in your industry are longer than average (e.g., as might be the case if you're paid through Medicare proceeds). The collateral value of your A/R will be lower if:

- You historically write off a high percentage of A/R for collection problems.
- You sell to consumers versus businesses.
- You sell to small businesses versus large businesses.
- You sell to high-risk industries (e.g., restaurants).
- Your customers routinely dispute their bills (e.g., insurance companies).
- You sell to foreign customers.
- You sell to few rather than many businesses.
- You allow customers to pay slow (evidenced by your A/R Turnover ratio).
- You continue to sell to accounts that have past due balances.
- You lack formal credit policies and procedures.

Exhibit 4.6 shows how lenders will look at your A/R Aging Report to determine how much they'll lend against, or *advance* against your receivables. The formula they use to describe how much they'll lend is called the *advance formula*. A common advance formula is 75 to 80 percent of A/R less than 60 or 90 days old.

Exhibit 4.6 shows that if the lender was using a strict advance formula your company could only borrow $3,600 on receivables totaling $7,900. The reason for the big difference is that several of your receivables are ineligible for advance because a portion of the outstandings are too old. Unless you have a good reason for continuing to sell to a customer who has a past-due balance (such as a dispute over a single bill but a long track record of on-time payment), all amounts owed by that customer will be subtracted from the eligible receivables. Here again, you need to educate lenders about the details behind the numbers so that they don't draw the wrong conclusions.

Submitting an annotated A/R aging, explaining any slow payments, is a good way to ensure that lenders have the right picture. For example, a medical products company with average A/R in excess of 120 days was turned down by a lender. We helped the borrower prepare an extensive analysis of its history of collections showing that, while the company collected slow, it collected 99 percent of all accounts receivable. The lender reconsidered the proposal in light of the new information and extended the loan.

EXHIBIT 4.6   How Lenders Determine How Much You Can Borrow on Accounts Receivable

---

Aged Accounts Receivable Report

Customer	Balance	Age of Accounts Receivable			
		0-30	30-60	60-90	over 90
ABC Company	$2,000	$1,500	$500	$0	$0
DEF Company	$1,800	$200	$600	$1,000	$0
GHI Company	$700	$700	$0	$0	$0
JKL Company	$2,100	$1,100	$1,000	$0	$0
MNO Company	$1,300	$700	$0	$0	$600
Total A/R:	$7,900	$4,200	$2,100	$1,000	$600

Lender Advance Formula Calculation

Assumption: Bank Receivable Advance Formula is 75% of A/R less than 60 days old

	Elgible	Advance	Reason:
ABC Company	$2,000	$1,500	All A/R eligible for 75% advance.
DEF Company	$0	$0	Unless the company has a good reason for the $1,000 that's 60 days old, the whole customer balance will be excluded.
GHI Company	$700	$525	All A/R eligible for 75% advance.
JKL Company	$2,100	$1,575	All A/R eligible for 75% advance; if the balance slips out another month, the whole A/R may be excluded in next month's advance.
MNO Company	$0	$0	The over 90 day balance will cause the whole A/R to be excluded from advance.
	$4,800	$3,600	Your company can borrow up to $3,600, which represents only 46% of total A/R.

Inventory as Collateral

A lender will assign 10 to 60 percent of the balance sheet value of your inventory as collateral value. Inventory with any of the following characteristics will be assigned a lower value:

- Slow turning (as evidenced by the inventory turnover ratio).
- Distributed over many locations or located out of state.

- Located in a leased facility (unless a landlord's waiver is obtained).
- Heavily comprised of work-in-progress (unfinished stuff that the lender would have a hard time selling) versus finished goods.
- Built on spec. rather than on a purchase order basis.
- Highly technical.
- Hard for the lender to unload.
- Perishable, fashionable, or requiring special storage.
- Valued at substantially more than its balance sheet value (due to accounting and/or tax games).

At the risk of overemphasizing the point, be sure your lender understands everything behind your numbers when you submit them. Details about your inventory may be common knowledge to you because you deal with them every day, but you *must* assume they aren't obvious to a lender.

Consider the example of a manufacturer of specialty instruments who held more than $1 million in inventory, approximately half of which was raw material. A lender would advance 70 percent on finished goods (since they were built on a purchase order basis), but would advance only 10 percent on the raw materials portion of the inventory. At our suggestion, the manufacturer asked his supplier to submit a bid to buy back the raw material, which was actually specialty steel. The supplier, in fact, offered to buy it back at 95 cents on a dollar—essentially dollar for dollar, less a restocking charge. The supplier's offer convinced the lender that the raw materials would not be as hard to unload as previously thought and agreed to an advance of 60 percent. With $500,000 in raw materials in the inventory, the difference between a 10 percent advance and a 60 percent advance meant additional borrowing capacity for our client of $250,000.

Furniture and Equipment as Collateral

A range of collateral values from 10 to 80 percent will be assigned to your furniture and equipment (F&E). Lower values will be assigned where the equipment is:

- Very specialized.
- Of little value in the secondary market.
- Obsolete or fully depreciated.

- Located out of state or in a variety of locations.
- Located in a leased facility (unless a landlord's waiver is obtained).

Another example of why you have to educate your lenders comes from a transportation company we worked with. They owned over a hundred trailers that rode piggyback on freight trains. The trailers were almost fully depreciated over their assigned five-year life, so their balance sheet value was almost nil. When the bank wanted to give them zero collateral value on their rolling stock, we investigated and found that these trailers spent their entire life on a train and had very little wear. We felt that with a fresh coat of paint they could actually be sold at greater than their original purchase price, given recent favorable market demand. The bank requested that the owner obtain an appraisal on a representative sampling of the trailers. The appraisal proved our point, and a 30 percent advance was established. In fact, the advance might have been higher if the trailers were all stored in one place, but because they were all over the country it would have been a nightmare for the lender to find and collect them.

Real Estate as Collateral

You can figure 50 to 90 percent of the appraised value (less any liens or mortgages) for the collateral value of real estate. Your home and company properties will be considered more valuable on corporate loans than investment real estate, but probably not as valuable as you might hope.

Real estate will be valued lower if it is:

- Investment real estate.
- Subject to existing mortgages.
- Special-use property.
- Located in a distressed area.
- In a slow real estate market.

Recent regulations require that lenders order appraisals (which you'll pay for), so don't order an appraisal yourself until the bank gives you the go-ahead. You can present an appraisal from the very same place the bank sends you, but the one you have won't be acceptable because the bank didn't order it. This is supposed to protect lenders from getting a bogus appraisal done by an insider.

If there's any possibility of environmental contamination (either due to the property's historical use or its proximity to other known or suspected environmental problems), the bank will require that you conduct an environmental study before it will accept your real estate as collateral. As with appraisals, follow your lender's lead on ordering such a study. Be sure to budget for these appraisals as they can run thousands of dollars.

Cash as Collateral

We're talking collateral here, and we bring up cash? We're gonna give money to get money? Don't laugh! Even if you have access to cash that you could contribute to the business, you might opt instead to pledge it as collateral on a loan to help establish a credit record. Lenders *will* accept cash in the form of a certificate of deposit (CD) from their bank as collateral. But believe it or not, even a CD from their bank won't be given 100 percent collateralization value, much less one from another bank.

Other

Some lenders will accept stock, bonds, or other people's assets (real estate or certificates of deposit) as collateral. Some government lending programs, and occasionally conventional lenders, will even accept a contract or purchase order as collateral. The concern of lenders, however, in accepting purchase orders as collateral, is how they'll be paid if you don't perform—in most cases they won't easily be able to have someone else fulfill the order so they can collect the proceeds. If you can offer some solution to this problem, you might convince them to lend you money on a purchase order.

CAPITAL: HOW MUCH DO YOU RISK?

Business statistics and experience show that companies that carry a heavy debt load run a higher risk of financial trouble than those that carry less debt. In addition, lenders have observed that owners with a larger stake in their business are less likely to default on loans. For these reasons, lenders want you and your company to share with them in financing responsibilities. As we discussed, lenders become nervous at the point where total company debt is more than three times greater than the company's equity, in other words, at a debt-to-worth ratio over 3:1.

   If you're starting a business or taking on a project that will cost $100,000, lenders will want you to contribute approximately $25,000 of your funds before they'll supply the remaining $75,000 (debt of $75,000 ÷ equity of $25,000 = debt-to-equity ratio of 3:1). Sometimes they'll reduce or even waive this requirement for established profitable companies whose leverage, measured by their debt-to-worth ratio, is very low.

Unfortunately, as we saw earlier, the balance sheet from which your debt-to-worth ratio is calculated doesn't always reflect reality. Remember, be sure to point out anything that could help this ratio, such as friendly debt that can be subordinated to other loans and any highly depreciated assets.

A good case in point is a 30-year-old steel fabricating company's balance sheet, which showed a debt-to-worth ratio of 4.7:1. However, the company's buildings and equipment, valued at over $1 million were shown on the balance sheet at only $500,000 because (1) the equipment was almost fully depreciated; and (2) the building was owned personally by the company's owner and leased to the company. In addition, there was a loan of $700,000 shown simply as long-term debt on the balance sheet. When we investigated, we discovered the $700,000 loan was from the owner, had been on the books for many years, and was not being repaid. At 4.7:1, the debt-to-worth ratio was too high for the lender to consider financing. However, when the balance sheet was reconstructed to reflect the true value of the buildings and equipment (verified by appraisals) and the owner's debt was subordinated to proposed debt (which allowed it to be treated as equity), the picture changed dramatically. The impact of these changes on the company's debt-to-worth is shown in Exhibit 4.7.

Once these changes were made, instead of looking overleveraged, the company showed very low leverage of less than 1:1. After confirming that the property was not an environmental risk, the bank extended a loan of $1 million to this company. This still only brought the company's debt-to-worth ratio to .8:1 as shown in Exhibit 4.6.

The moral of the story (yes, we know you've heard this before, but this is a crucial point): It's up to you to be sure that lenders understand the true value of your assets and liabilities so that they don't overestimate your leverage.

CONDITIONS: WHAT ELSE MIGHT HAPPEN?

Assuming you pass the tests of character, capacity, collateral, and capital, lenders will still need to know what might happen in the economy, your industry, or your company that could impede your ability to repay your loan. But industry comparisons can be misleading in the same way

EXHIBIT 4.7   Adjusted Debt-to-Worth

Steel Fabricator, Inc.
Balance Sheet (,000 omitted)

1) Before Adjustments:

Assets:	$1,000	**Liabilities:**	$825

Including $500 in equipment.

Including $700 loan from Owner

Net Worth: $175

Debt-To-Worth Ratio:
$825 ÷ $175 = 4.7 : 1

2) Adjusted for Undervalued Assets and Owner Loan

Assets:	$1,500	**Liabilities:**	$125

Including an additional $500 in buildings and equipment.

Less the $700 loan from Owner.

Net Worth: $1,375

Plus subordinated owner loan and additional asset values.

Debt-To-Worth Ratio:
$125 ÷ $1,375 = .09 : 1

3) After New Debt:
Adjusted for Undervalued Assets and Owner Loan

Assets:	$2,500	**Liabilities:**	$1,125

Adjusted equipment values plus $1,000 in loan proceeds.

Plus the new $1,000 loan.

Net Worth $1,375

Reflecting new debt, adjusted asset values and the owner loan as subordinated debt.

Debt-To-Worth Ratio:
$1,125 ÷ $1,375 = .8 : 1

that ratios can be misleading. Again, you need to understand the lenders' process so that you can approach them armed with information about your industry and why you're different—or, if your industry is strong, why you're the same.

Lenders gather information about the health of your industry from a number of different sources including insider information about their own customers and prospects, annual reports from public companies, and public and private compilations of industry information.

A good example of the kind of misunderstanding that can occur comes from a $1 million commercial printer who approached a banker for a loan to expand facilities. Because the printing industry was having trouble at the time, several local banks had lost money when loans went bad and the used equipment market softened. Understandably, financing for new printing equipment was not high on their list of favorite loans. However, this company was unique as a printer of specialty labels for the pharmaceutical industry. That niche was very strong, and the firm was well entrenched with several large pharmaceutical houses. The company's sales and profits from this facet of the business had grown steadily in each of the preceding five years and were projected to expand.

To prove the point to the company's banker, we suggested having its five largest customers provide a projection of their label needs for the next two years. At the same time, the customers expressed their satisfaction with our printer's services and their intention to increase future purchases. In addition, we helped the company prepare a detailed breakdown of its profitability from various types of business, including the pharmaceutical line, and compared this with the typical profit margins of other nonspecialty printers (obtained from a print industry trade association). Our printer's margins were over 30 percent higher than those of their peers.

The analysis took some time, but as a result, the lender decided to do the deal. In spite of continued trouble in the printing industry, they've expanded the printer's credit every year since that first loan.

CREDIT SCORING

In the mid-1950s The Fair Isaac Company, Inc., pioneered the development of a system for applying risk scores to consumer credit. By the early 1980s, as a direct result of the widespread use of credit scoring, the mass market for consumer credit products was born. By simplifying and standardizing the method of evaluating consumer credit, credit card issuers and other consumer credit companies are able to quickly approve and even preapprove new customers.

While evaluating commercial loan risk is substantially more complex than evaluating consumer credit risks, the need for a commercial credit scoring system is being driven by a number of factors including:

1. Economic pressures that are causing lenders to search for more efficient methods of handling smaller loan requests and of training lenders.

2. Regulators that are pressuring lenders to ensure "fairness in lending" by consistent application of credit standards.

3. Recent changes in securities, banking, pension, and tax laws that are encouraging the development of an investment grade securities representing pooled small business loans. These securities will create a secondary market, similar to the secondary mortgage market, for small business loans. The development of such securities will require some uniform rating system for the risk of the pooled loans.

4. Financial institutions that need to standardize the underwriting criteria of their lenders.

5. Increased competition for quality small business loans that is driving the need for a preapproval process for marketing purposes.

According to Dan Morefield, Senior Vice President of First Interstate Bank of California, one of the nation's largest banks, "Within the next five years, credit scoring will become the method of choice for approval of loans under $250,000." Other industry experts agree that such systems will replace or augment traditional underwriting methods for loans under $100,000 for businesses with revenues of less than $5 million a year.

So what is credit scoring and how does it work? Essentially, lenders can assess a variety of personal and business information, and points are gained or lost for each factor to produce a score that measures the risk of lending to a small business applicant. According to Mark Zmiewski, Information Products Manager for Robert Morris Associates (RMA), "Using credit scoring, a lender can reduce the traditional 8- to 12-hour decision-making process to less than 30 minutes."

In early 1995, Fair Isaac and RMA released a credit scoring tool called the RMA/Fair Isaac Small Business Scoring Service (SBSS). According to Latimer Asch, Senior Manager at Fair Isaac and one of the pioneers of credit scoring, the SBSS system is based on small business credit scorecards that tabulate data on the applicant business, its principals, consumer and business credit reports, tax returns, financial statements, and the loan application. Unlike many other credit scorecards, the SBSS model is derived from the pooled credit experience and practices of many of the nation's largest banks. Other scoring systems are based on a lender's judgment of expected loan success or failure, rather than actual loan experience, and most are based on a single lender's credit experience, rather than the pooled experience of many lenders.

Credit scorecard factors vary from one model to the next but often are based on information such as personal credit history of the owner, whether or not the company is incorporated, the net worth of the owners, business credit history, business checking account balances, the nature of the business, and company financial performance.

What all this means for you as a small business owner looking for money is that in the future you can expect quicker loan decisions, a credit-approval process that offers a better appreciation for the financial realities of a closely held business, and perhaps new loan products such as preapproved lines of credit and even lines of credit that don't require annual renewal. Just imagine opening your business mail one day and finding a letter from a lender you never met saying:

Your Business Has Been Preapproved for a $100,000 Line of Credit

Dear Business Owner:

Because of your good credit history and other factors, you've been preapproved for a $100,000 line of credit.

Imagine what you could do with $100,000! Take advantage of early payment discounts from vendors, purchase new inventory, use quantity discounts, etc.

And, if you act now, we'll also include a gold card good for discounted travel to exciting destinations like the North Pole . . . the South Pole . . . the Equator . . . even the Bermuda Triangle.

Act now! Simply return the attached R.S.V.P. Certificate and we'll do the rest . . .

PUTTING IT ALL TOGETHER

Experience teaches lenders that they need to analyze different industries differently. At one level, they know that manufacturers and service businesses are prone to different problems. At another level, they know the risks in lending to a clothing manufacturer are different from the risks in lending to an electronics manufacturer. And, at still another level, lenders know simply to avoid certain types of business because of high failure rates and other risks—restaurants fall into this category.

So how do you know what they're really worried about?

❏ Secret

You can find out how lenders feel about your industry by contacting Robert Morris Associates (RMA). As a bank trade association, RMA publishes a variety of information aimed at helping its member banks. In addition to *Annual Statement Studies,* which we mentioned in Chapter 2, RMA also offers the following publications that provide real insight into how lenders feel about certain industries:

Credit Considerations (Volumes I, II and III), profiles the financial and credit aspects of lending to over a hundred types of businesses.

The Journal of Commercial Lending, a monthly publication, includes articles about lending to various industries.

Lending to Different Industries (Volumes 1, 2, and 3) includes a collection of articles from the *Journal of Commercial Lending.*

In addition to books and journals, RMA also offers an inexpensive information search service that will research its various publications for articles relevant to your business or other financing interest. An index or the full text of articles can be faxed to you for a nominal charge.

Written for lenders, but available to the public, RMA's publications offer valuable insight into what lenders worry about. If you want to know how they feel about lending to dentists, home health-care agencies, vineyards, barge operators, television stations, car dealers, funeral homes, magazine publishers, child-care centers, and dozens of other industries, just call RMA at 215-851-0585. Ask for a copy of its publications catalog or talk to the company's reference librarian.

With an understanding of how lenders evaluate loan requests, and a list of the specific concerns they'll have about your industry, you're almost ready to prepare a winning loan proposal. But first you need to know more about what types of loans are available and appropriate for your situation, and how loans are structured.

STRUCTURING DEBT

5

Debt can be structured in a wide variety of ways. Loans can be long term or short term; secured, unsecured, or partially secured; fixed or variable rate (or some combination); and that's just the beginning. There's a whole smorgasbord of terms and conditions that might be applied to your loan. Which you choose (or wind up with) is a function of the loan's purpose, your financial situation, and your lender's preferences and guidelines.

WHAT KIND OF LOANS ARE AVAILABLE AND APPROPRIATE?

Conventional term loans, while common, are only one of many ways to borrow money for your company. Lines of credit, swing loans, special loans for buying real estate or for construction, letters of credit, and leases, are all available depending on your business needs.

A fundamental concern of lenders is to match the type and term of the loan with the loan's purpose. In other words, they'll want to use a term loan to fund the purchase of assets that will expire of over some period. Assets with short useful lives should be matched with short-term loans, and assets with long useful lives should be funded with long-term loans. Similarly, lenders will want to use a line of credit for temporary cash flow needs that come and go with the cycles of your business.

Term Loans

Commercial term loans, which vary in length from 1 to 20 years, are used to finance furniture, fixtures, equipment, improvements, land, buildings, and long-term capital needs.

Term loans require monthly payments of principal and interest. But, unlike consumer mortgages, which also pay out over long periods, commercial term loans usually involve level monthly payments of principal with monthly interest calculated on the outstanding balance that month.

For example, a $72,000 five-year consumer loan with 10% interest will call for payments of approximately $1,530 per month. In the first month of the loan, most of the payment will be applied to interest, and very little will go to retire principal. By contrast, a commercial term loan monthly payment will be calculated by a commercial amortization schedule that takes the loan amount and divides it by the number of months over which the loan is amortized to arrive at just the principal portion of the loan payment. The interest portion is then calculated by applying the interest rate of 10 percent (per annum) to the balance of the loan, which declines every month.

In the first month, the commercial loan payment on a $72,000 five-year loan would be approximately $1,800, including $1,200 of principal and $600 of interest. The following month the principal portion of the payment will be $1,200 again, but the interest portion will be slightly lower because the principal was reduced by $1,200 last month. This way, the lender recoups the principal evenly throughout the life of the loan. While your initial payments will be higher than with a consumer loan, you'll be retiring principal more quickly so your interest charges and payments will be lower in later months.

Lines of Credit

Lines of credit are most often used to finance temporary needs for capital. In a perfect world, you'd collect cash from your customers at the same time you need it to pay your suppliers. But since the world doesn't work that way, lines of credit are often used to fill the gap that exists between the time when you have to pay cash for things like inventory and labor, and when you receive money back from customers through the sale of goods. Although your suppliers probably have offered extended payment terms, *you've* probably offered terms to *your* customers too, so you end up needing a cash-flow solution anyway.

Under most circumstances, you'll be cash poor just after purchasing raw materials or products, and cash rich just after you're paid. With a line of credit, you can borrow when you're cash poor and pay only interest based on the outstanding principal balance, and then repay the principal when you're cash rich. Lenders assure themselves that your situation is temporary, rather than permanent, by requiring that you *clean up* the line (reduce it to zero) for at least 30 days during the year.

Banks usually reaffirm lines annually, three to five months following the borrower's fiscal year end. However, most lines of credit to small businesses are really demand loans, meaning interest is payable monthly and principal is payable on demand. This means that the bank can actually require full payment on the loan at any time, not just annually. In most cases, lenders won't cancel prior to expiration, but it's important to recognize that if your business falls on tough times the bank can and *will* demand payment if its money seems to be at risk.

Temporary Lines of Credit

At some point, you might find yourself in need of more working capital than you originally anticipated due to a surge in business or some other temporary event.

❏ **Secret**

> If you truly believe the situation is temporary, talk to your lender about a temporary overage or temporary line of credit. Such an arrangement can often be handled outside full-blown approval channels if you already have a line of credit, and therefore can often be approved more quickly than a regular loan. This is particularly true if the new amount you need is less than 10 to 20 percent of the original line of credit.

Temporary lines of credit make a lot of sense if you're financing a special project or contract that falls outside your normal business volume. Let's say you have a $150,000 line of credit in place with your bank, and you just received a $100,000 order when most of your orders average $10,000 to $20,000. If you used your regular line of credit to finance the working capital needs of this new order, you'd practically exhaust the line and wouldn't have any financing for your regular business volume.

If you go to the bank in a panic after you've taken down all the cash in your line, loan officers will probably be less than understanding, thinking you should have anticipated this problem in the first place. If they do approve the loan increase, they'll probably increase the rate and fees on the whole line of credit too.

On the other hand, if you demonstrate good fiscal management by requesting a temporary line when you first receive the new contract, they'll probably establish a separate line for you. The new line will likely have higher rates and fees than the original line of credit, but they'll only apply to this one-time need.

Revolving Lines of Credit

Unlike demand loans, a revolving line of credit, or *Revolver,* as it's called, is extended for 12 to 36 months, and does not require annual cleanup. Following its initial period, a revolving line is usually converted to a term loan, or *termed out,* as it's called. During the period that the loan is a line of credit you can draw down as required, pay back principal as your cash flow allows, and pay interest monthly. Then the portion that has not been repaid during the initial credit period is converted to a term loan, and you'll pay monthly principal and interest over a term determined by the nature of the asset financed. This way both short- and long-term cash needs can be addressed.

Revolvers are commonly used in situations where a company needs to finance multiple asset purchases throughout a period or where the exact amount needed to finance growth can't be forecast. For example, an established Atlanta company needed to finance the opening of several satellite offices. The company projected total costs of $150,000 and anticipated that the offices would be self-supporting in two years. They obtained a revolving line of credit that would convert to a term loan in 36 months. The company drew down the whole line during the first two years. By the end of the third year, the satellite offices were contributing sufficient cash flow to allow the company to pay off $100,000 on the line of credit. At that time, the $50,000 balance was converted to a 36-month term loan.

Lenders, you should note, are reluctant to extend revolving credit lines to businesses that lack a substantial track record successfully managing growth and producing profits.

Undisclosed Lines of Credit

If your lender can anticipate your future borrowing needs, they might obtain internal preapproval for loans up to some dollar amount. The amount, and even the existence of the preapproved line of credit, may never be disclosed to you, but it will allow the lender to move more quickly when you request a loan. Such facilities are often used with companies that frequently buy small equipment, cars, or trucks. Such a facility is similar to a revolving line of credit, but since it's never formally disclosed to you, you don't have to pay fees to put or keep it in place.

❏ **Secret**

If you anticipate needing several small loans throughout the year, you might suggest that your lender obtain preapproval for those needs as a way to cut down on the lender's workload each time you need a small loan.

Swing Loans

Swing loans are used to finance a temporary need for capital that arises from a delay in closing a transaction. For example, you may need to close the deal on a new building by September 30, but closing on the sale of your existing property isn't scheduled until October 31. In some cases, a lender will extend a swing loan to cover you in the one-month period between the closings. Such loans, however, can be difficult to arrange unless you have a long-standing relationship with the lender, sufficient cash flow to cover both properties if the deal falls through, or a contract with a rock-solid, fully-funded settlement and no contingencies.

Real Estate Purchase Loans

Due to the complex and dynamic nature of the real estate market, lenders handle real estate loan requests (or at least monitor them) through a special division that verifies real estate values, considers environmental issues, and analyzes projected cash flows. If you're trying to find money for company-occupied real estate such as an office building, plant, or warehouse, the real estate division will look to the cash flow from your business to support the debt. For investment real estate, they'll review historical and projected rent rolls, evaluate existing and prospective tenant's creditworthiness, evaluate property competitiveness and marketability, review signed leases, and test cash flow assumptions including rental rates, vacancy projections, maintenance reserves, and expense assumptions.

Construction Loans

Like real estate loans, construction loans are usually administered by a special real estate division or lender. These loans are structured as a line of credit, with a schedule of takedowns, or draws against the line that are set to match certain benchmarks in construction such as completion of foundation, framing, plumbing and electric, interior, and certificate of occupancy. The lender's inspectors will visit the construction site at each stage of construction to verify the progress of the work.

These loans are usually granted contingent on an as-improved appraisal that shows what the property will be worth once constructed, and contingent on a permanent financing commitment or a signed agreement of sale that will pay off the construction loan. Often the same lender will handle both construction and permanent portions of the loan. Due to the cost of administration, both the rates and fees for construction loans are priced 1 to 3 percent higher than conventional loans.

Letters of Credit

Often used in international finance, documentary letters of credit (L/C) are issued by your bank, on your behalf, as surety for payment of goods or services. You might use a letter of credit to assure vendors that your bank will immediately issue payment when they ship goods to you, or some other named event. On the other hand, you might request a letter of credit from a customer—actually, from your customer's bank—before you begin to work on an order so that you know funds are available to pay you.

Irrevocable letters of credit, as the name implies, are irrevocable as long as all the terms and conditions are met (e.g., goods are delivered by a specified date and pass inspection). When requesting letters of credit from your international customers, remember that they're only as good as the bank that issues them, so check with the international lending divisions of major banks, which maintain lists of approved issuers.

Standby letters of credit, whose structure resembles that of documentary letters of credit, are not actually expected to be cashed. They're issued as guarantees of payment by promising that if you don't pay, the bank will. Bankers issue Standby L/Cs, as they're called, as though they could be cashed; so the loan approval process is similar to that of regular loans. Fees on irrevocable letters of credit typically range from 0.5 percent to 1.5 percent of the value of the L/C.

How Long a Term Can I (Should I) Expect?

The number of months or years over which a loan is repaid is based on the useful life of the asset being financed. Short-term loans with less than 12-month repayment schedules are used to finance high turnover assets such as inventory and accounts receivable. Intermediate-term loans with 1- to 5-year repayment schedules are used to fund assets such as vehicles, equipment, and leasehold improvements. Long-term loans with 5- to 20- (and occasionally 30) year repayment schedules are used to finance real-estate-related assets and some specialized equipment.

Balloon Payments

Lenders favor short-term loans over long-term loans because shorter terms enable them to monitor a company's progress, to reset rates and terms more frequently, and to limit their risk. Borrowers, on the other hand, favor long terms over short terms because lower payments on long-term loans free up cash. Among conventional lenders, loan terms in excess of 15 years are rare. Three-, five-, and seven-year terms are much more typical. To keep borrowers within these shorter time frames, lenders will often base payments on a long (10- to 15-year) or intermediate (5- to 7-year) repayment schedule, but set the loan term for a shorter period. Since the loan won't be paid off by the end of the term, a *balloon* payment is required at the end of the term.

For example, a loan on a piece of equipment costing $84,000 that has a seven-year life might be structured with a seven-year repayment schedule, but a term of only three years (referred to as a *three-seven loan*). In this way you'd make payments as though it was a seven-year loan for the first 36 months paying roughly $1,000 per month plus interest ($84,000/84 months). Then, at the end of three years, you'd owe the full remaining balance of approximately $48,000. If you performed well on the first loan, a second loan can often be established to pay off the balloon on the first, but new rates and fees will be involved.

Interest-Only Periods

Equipment and other assets that you purchase usually take some time to begin paying their way.

❑ **Secret**

> Lenders can, and often will, include an initial period of a few
> months to a year of interest-only payments, followed by the reg-
> ular principal-plus-interest schedule. This can really help your
> cash flow, but don't expect the lender to offer this feature to
> you, you'll have to ask for it.

HOW MUCH WILL IT COST?

When you borrow money, you'll pay for the use of it through interest
on the principal, through up-front fees, and sometimes through so-
called compensating balances in company accounts. The interest rates
and fees associated with a loan are negotiable if you know what's possible, know enough to ask, and have a good rationale when you do.

Interest Rates

Interest rates are set by lenders based on their cost of funds, internal
profit goals, and perceived loan risk. But they also take into consideration your relationship profitability, meaning the profit they make on all
your deposit accounts and other services you buy from them. If you have
several hundred thousand dollars on deposit with a bank, they'll price
your loan differently than they would if your balance totaled up to a
few less digits.

Fixed and Floating Loans   Rates can be either fixed (where they
stay at the original level throughout the life of the loan) or floating
(where they are set to vary with the prime rate of interest—also known
as Wall Street prime, which is the rate published daily in *The Wall Street
Journal* and reflects the rate charged by the largest banks to their best
customers). You may also find loans where the interest rates are some
combination—fixed for some period and then floating.

During periods of rising rates, a premium is placed on fixed-rate financing due to your lender's risk that tomorrow's rates will be higher
than today's. Therefore you might be offered a rate of prime plus 1.5
percent floating, or a fixed rate that equals today's prime plus 2 percent. A fee of 0.5 to 1.5 percent might apply to the floating-rate deal and
a fee of 1 to 2 percent may apply to the fixed-rate option.

Lenders sometimes talk about rates in terms of *basis points* where 10 basis points equal one-tenth of a percent. Small business lending by banks is usually priced in the range of prime plus 0 percent to prime plus 3 percent. A typical formula used by banks for setting interest rates on small business loans is to start at prime plus 0.75 or 1 percent (75 or 100 basis points), and then add or subtract to reflect risk, anticipated relationship profitability, and competitive factors.

❏ Secret

During periods of exceptionally low rates, some banks will establish their own prime rate rather than use the more customary Wall Street prime. Thus if your bank's prime rate is defined as Wall Street prime plus 2 percent, your bank's prime plus 1 percent could really be equal to Wall Street prime plus 3 percent. Be sure to ask whether your rate is based on Wall Street prime or the bank's own prime rate when comparing loan costs.

Caps and Floors Some lenders offer maximum rates or *caps* and minimum rates or *floors* on variable rate loans. While rare in small-business lending, such features may be negotiable in areas where there is heavy competition between lenders. Again, you'll have to ask for what you want.

Loan Fees

Most lenders charge fees on term loans, and some charge them annually on lines of credit as well. Loan fees, like consumer mortgage points, are usually 0.25 to 3 percent of the loan amount and are payable when the loan is granted (sometimes they are payable 50% at the time of the lender's commitment and 50% at loan closing). A 2 percent fee on a $100,000 loan is $2,000, so on a cash flow basis, you're actually only getting $98,000 rather than the full $100,000—although the check will be for $100,000. Also keep in mind that if your interest rate is 10 percent, you'll be paying the $2,000 fee plus $10,000 in loan interest to use $98,000. So the effective interest rate is actually 12.25 percent (($2,000 + $10,000) ÷ $98,000).

Some lenders also charge fees on the portion of a line of credit that you don't use. The logic here is that it costs the lender something to maintain the facility on your behalf. What they worry about is that you'll never use your line of credit, so they'll never collect any interest from you—lenders call these *ego lines*. Rates and fees for lines like these may be set at, say, prime plus 2 percent (let's assume that adds up to 10% for the purpose of this example) with a 0.5 percent fee up front and a 1 percent fee on the unused portion of the line. If you only use $45,000 of the line, you'll pay $500 for the up-front fee, $4,500 in interest on the $45,000 you borrowed, and at the end of the year another $550 on the $55,000 you didn't use.

Fees, like interest rates, are generally higher on fixed rate loans (something like 1%–3%) than they are on variable rate loans (0%–1.5%).

Compensating Balances

Compensating balances, or minimum balances that must be maintained in your company's accounts, are simply another way that lenders extract income from your relationship since they use your money free of charge. On a $200,000 loan, the lender might require $25,000 in compensating balances. In other words, you need to keep a minimum of $25,000 in your checking account. This means that you're effectively getting to use only $175,000 of the $200,000 line. If your loan rate is 10 percent, you'll pay $20,000 in interest over the period of a year ($200,000 × 10%). The effective rate, however, will be 11.43 percent because you're paying $20,000 to use $175,000.

Compensating balance requirements aren't as common as they once were because business owners are more aware of money market funds and other interest-bearing account options.

❏ **Secret**

If you happen to have a good business reason to maintain high average checking account balances anyway, ask for a lower loan rate based on the money the bank will make on your compensating balances.

A point worth mentioning: Many business owners confuse *free balances,* the funds that stay in your checking account, with the cash that passes through it. Don't expect the $1 million that passes through your checking account every year to excite lenders. What they make money from are balances that stay put.

Relationship Profitability

Many banks use the income that they derive from your free balances to offset their standard checking account fees. While it may seem nice to not have to pay a fee for every check and every deposit, you might find that you're better off paying the fees and investing your idle cash more wisely. If you've negotiated with your banker to waive checking account charges (either because you're a good customer or because of the free balances you maintain), recognize that your relationship profitability will decline and that can impact your loan rate.

Most banks can produce monthly account analysis statements that show them the profitability of their accounts. Some even produce sophisticated customer profitability statements (including loans, fees, cash management, trust, and other bank services, less the bank's cost of maintaining the accounts).

❏ **Secret**

Ask your bank for a copy of your account analysis or customer profitability statement—lenders are usually willing to share this information. Make sure that it includes all of your accounts and services and use the information to negotiate a lower loan rate.

Prepayment Penalties

Many fixed-rate loans carry a penalty for early payment. In setting a fixed rate, lenders take a risk that tomorrow's rates will be higher than today's, so in exchange they want to encourage you to keep the loan if rates decline. A penalty of 1 to 2 percent is commonly applied to the remaining balance if a loan is prepaid.

❏ **Secret**

Such penalty fees are often negotiable both at the signing of the loan and even sometimes at the time of prepayment, particularly if you're planning to maintain a relationship with the lender.

Other Penalty Fees

In an effort to enforce loan covenants, and conditions (described later in this chapter) and in an effort to make more money, lenders are becoming increasing aggressive with penalty fees. Fees of between 25 and 100 basis points (0.25%–1%) may be charged for failure to clean up a line of credit, missing a debt-to-worth covenant, missing a net income covenant, missing a current ratio covenant, failure to submit timely financial statements, and so forth. These fees may be negotiable both at loan closing, and occasionally at the time they're due. However, you're always better off to negotiate from a position of strength; it'll be a lot harder to negotiate penalty fees when you've just turned in a poorer than expected performance.

NEGOTIATING RATES AND FEES

Rates may be more negotiable than fees, or vice versa, depending on your lender's own financial position. In recent years, lenders have become more aggressive with loan fees because they provide a more stable and predictable cash flow than the money they make on the difference between the rate you pay them for money and their own cost of the money. Remember that your total loan cost includes both fees and interest. In consumer lending, this cost is disclosed as annual percentage rate or APR, but no such disclosures are required in commercial lending so you'll have to figure out the effective pricing on your own.

❏ **Secret**

Deciding whether to negotiate on rates, fees, compensating balances, prepayment penalty fees, other penalty fees, checking account fees, or all the preceding costs requires some strategic thinking on your part. Certainly, you ought to try to figure out which is more important to your lender, but first you ought to figure out which is more important to you. For example, assume you're negotiating a $100,000 line of credit, but you only anticipate using $25,000 to $50,000 of it for most of the year, and the full amount only at the peak of your season. You probably ought to negotiate harder on the fee that will be based on the full $100,000 whether you use it or not, than on the rate, which will only be based on the amount that you use. Conversely, if you expect to use all of the line, you probably ought to focus on the rate rather than the fee.

❏ Secret

Most people think lenders' rates are carved in stone; after all, you wouldn't try to negotiate the rate a bank pays you on your savings account. In fact, rates are often negotiable within 25 to 75 basis points (0.25%–0.75%), and sometimes more. Whether this is your first loan negotiation, or an annual rate discussion with your lender, if you think there's some fat in their pricing, try countering with pricing that's 50 to 100 basis points (0.5%–1%) lower than the bank's original offer. Then you can compromise on a rate that's 25 to 75 basis points lower than the one you were first offered. With loan fees, you might want to start the negotiations at 50 to 75 basis points below the bank's offer and plan to settle at 25 to 50 off. And by the way, don't be afraid to split hairs. If you can't make them to budge a quarter of a percent, try an eighth. After all, they ought to admire your frugality—and the worst they can say is no!

If you've used your best negotiating approach and they still won't move on price, at least try to have them explain the conditions under which they'll lower their rates or fees. (See Exhibit 5.1.) "If I work my debt-to-worth ratio down to 2.5:1 next year and report a net income of at least $50,000, will you lower my rate by 50 basis points?" It's highly doubtful that they'll agree to anything like this in writing, but they won't be around very long if they don't keep their word. In any event, just in case you have a new loan officer next year, you might want to follow up such a conversation with a letter summarizing what was discussed. Just be careful not to put words in the lender's mouth when you do so.

A 10-year-old company that sold lighting fixtures wholesale is a good example of how relationship profitability can affect negotiations. The owner approached a lender for a $150,000 line of credit. The business showed a small profit every year on roughly the same level of sales. It was neither growing or declining so it was hard for the lender to understand why the firm suddenly needed a line of credit. The company appeared to have sufficient cash flow to carry the requested debt, but if its volume slipped at all, it might run into trouble. The lender offered the company a $100,000 line at prime plus 2 percent with a 1 percent annual fee.

The business owner wasn't happy with the offer and engaged our help. We encouraged her to emphasize how valuable she was to the bank. She was a long-time customer of the bank's trust department, which managed her $2 million dollar trust account—something that the lender missed on the owner's personal financial statement since she

EXHIBIT 5.1   Business Characteristics That Affect Rates

You'll Be Given the Lowest Rates and/or Fees If:

- Your company is a good credit risk.
- You're a long time customer of the bank.
- Another bank is competing for your business.
- You've just completed a good year.
- Your company's financial statement and ratio performance have improved.
- You bring them, or could bring them, significant other business such as trust services, cash management services, credit card merchant services, or customer referrals.
- You maintain significant balances in non-interest bearing accounts.
- You were referred to the lender by someone who refers them other business.
- Your personal friends with one or more of the lender's senior muck-a-mucks.

Expect Higher Rates and/or Fees If:

- Your performance has deteriorated recently.
- You've missed your financial covenants.
- You're maintaining lower average free balances.
- You need the money in a hurry.
- You barely use the line that you have.
- You fail to clean up your line of credit.
- You need to renegotiate the original loan payment terms because you can't meet the current payments.
- You're a trouble-maker, or a constant complainer, and your lender would be just as happy if you found another bank.
- Your friend, the senior muck-a-muck, was just asked to retire early.

didn't name the trust manager. She was also the president of a condominium association comprising a large number of influential people who were prospects for the bank. In addition, the association maintained substantial escrow account balances at various banks, which she was willing to move.

All of a sudden, the profitability side of the equation shifted because she represented substantial business for the bank. The rate dropped to prime plus 0.5% and the fee was dropped altogether (although a 0.5% fee was imposed on the unused portion of the loan).

In this case, the lender goofed by not gaining a full understanding of the potential value of the owner's relationship. The owner goofed by not blowing her own horn a little louder and a little earlier. The moral of the story: Loan negotiations are no time for modesty!

❑ Secret

While we've just encouraged you to negotiate rates and fees, in the end pricing shouldn't be the deciding factor in your choice of lender. In the long term, developing a relationship with a banker that you can trust, grow with, and even like is far more important than paying the lowest possible rate. A strong relationship with a lender can make or break you if you run into financial trouble down the line. Hopping from bank to bank for the lowest rate is not a good way to build a relationship. Therefore, given a choice between a bank and banker you like, but who wants to charge you 25 basis points more than another lender you don't like, you're better off to go with the former. After all, 0.25 percent on a $100,000 loan only amounts to $250 a year.

COLLATERAL AND SECURITY STRUCTURE

Most small-business loans, particularly to businesses with less than five years of successful financial history, are secured or partially secured. Wide differences exist, however, in the degree of security required.

Blanket Liens versus Specific Liens

The most encompassing and common type of lien is a *blanket lien* on all assets. The language of such a lien goes something like this: "This loan is secured by all existing and future accounts receivable, inventory, furniture, fixtures, improvements, equipment, and real estate." Note that lenders with blanket liens are usually willing to allow you to separately finance specific equipment as long as you ask their permission first.

Since having a lien doesn't mean much unless the rest of the world knows it, lenders file their liens with authorities that vary from locale to locale so that they have legal rights to your assets in the eyes of the court (called *perfecting* a lien). Once perfected, lenders have legal evidence of first rights to the assets specified. In part, the liens are filed to prevent you from pledging the same assets all over town, and thus creating a burdensome level of debt for you and worthless collateral for them.

Be sure to not inadvertently violate your collateral agreements by pledging assets that are already pledged elsewhere.

Advance Formulas and Collateral Monitoring

For high-risk lending, advance formulas are often set specifying, say, that "loan value shall not exceed 75% of accounts receivable less than ninety days old." Collateral monitoring and verification procedures may also be established to increase the bank's comfort with the loan. Advance formulas can be informal, where it's understood between the lender and the borrower that loan values will be *in formula* with the bank's loan limits; or formal, where quarterly, monthly, or even daily borrowing limits are set based on collateral reports that are submitted by the borrower. Collateral monitoring can range from informal monitoring, based on reports submitted by the borrower, to formal monitoring where, at the extreme, the borrower's assets are physically controlled by the bank.

Lending that involves strict formula advances and asset monitoring is known as *asset-based lending*. The borrower's customers are instructed to pay through a post office box that's actually owned by the lender, inventory may be maintained in a public warehouse that the lender controls, and frequent collateral audits (for which the borrower may pay thousands of dollars) are conducted by the lender's auditors. It's an expensive form of finance, often priced at prime plus 3 percent or higher with two to three points in fees, but it may be the only option for a struggling business.

GUARANTEES

Business owners, understandably, hate guarantees, but lenders understandably, love them and require them. So most small-business owners, whether they run a sole proprietorship, partnership, or corporation are, at some point in their history, required to personally guarantee company debt and pledge personal assets. That's because small-business lending is done based on the philosophy that the business is the owner, and the owner is the business. Your lender is really betting on you more than on your business.

Recent court cases have made it difficult for bankers to request a spousal guarantee, but the issue is really only a technicality since they probably won't approve your loan without it. One exception may exist to this rule, though. If you own substantial assets in your own name, you may be able to negotiate a single-signature guarantee. Otherwise, at the point in the conversation where the banker says bank can't do the loan because all your assets are jointly owned with your spouse, that's your cue to offer up your spouse. But don't worry, lenders will usually make sure that you don't miss your cue, even if they may not be able to come right out and ask for the second signature.

Personal guarantees are usually structured as *joint and several* meaning that each guarantor is wholly responsible for the loan. So even a 20 percent owner/guarantor is responsible for the whole loan not just 20 percent of it. It also means that lenders may try to collect from any and all guarantors in any order they choose. So if you happen to have the deepest pockets, chances are they'll be knocking on your door first.

The lender's theory on personal guarantees is that if you're not willing to put yourself and your personal assets on the line, why should they? Keep in mind that as your equity grows through investment and profitable performance, you may be able to negotiate for the release of your guarantees and personal collateral. If you can't convince your lender to release a guarantee, ask what targets you'll have to reach before the bank will let them go.

COVENANTS AND CONDITIONS

Loan covenants and conditions will spell out things that you can and can't do, and set financial targets such as minimum net worth, profit or cash flow targets, maximum debt-to-worth ratios, and penalties for violating these covenants. The most common small-business nonfinancial loan covenants and conditions include:

- No senior management or ownership changes without approval.
- Maintenance of key person insurance.

- Financial statements to be submitted (quarterly, semiannually, or annually; management-prepared or accountant-prepared compilation, review, or audit certification).
- Negative borrowing covenants (you can't borrow from any one else).
- Negative collateral pledge (you can't allow other lenders to place subsequent liens on collateral).
- Deposit accounts must be maintained with the lending institution.

Financial loan covenants have become increasingly popular since the S&L crisis. If included in your loan agreement, they are based on the areas of your business that are of greatest concern to your lender. The following are typical financial covenants.

- Maximum debt-to-worth covenant.
- Minimum current or quick ratio.
- Minimum level of net income.
- Minimum level of cash flow.
- Minimum gross profit margin.
- Cap on owner withdrawals or compensation.
- Cap on research and development expenses.
- Cap on capital expenditures.

Covenants and conditions are often negotiable within reason; but, once set, be very careful to keep your promises. Failure to do so could result in penalty fees or could constitute a loan default, and you'll be asked to pay back the whole loan immediately. And remember, your financial covenants will probably be based on information you provide the bank as part of your financing proposal, so make sure your forecasts are realistic and not wishful thinking. Before you sign on the dotted line, be sure to have your accountant review the tax implications of covenants. And be sure that you've included the effect of taxes in your pro formas. In case you missed the point: Be *very* sure financial covenants are achievable!

The significance of loan covenants is shown by the experience of a $10 million wholesaler of industrial products. The company maintained a number of loans with its bank, and after a buyout of a former owner, which the bank financed, the company's debt-to-worth ratio was fairly high at 4.5:1. Financial covenants were set to give the lender comfort that the company would hit its financial projections. A debt-to-worth target of 4:1 was set for the end of the first year, 3.5:1 at the end of the second year, and so forth. In addition, a minimum net income covenant was set at $200,000, the owner's salary was capped at $100,000, and owner withdrawals or loans to owners were prohibited. Shortly after the loan was booked, the bank was acquired in a merger by another bank with stricter policies.

At the end of the first year, the owner called us both proud and worried. The way he figured it, his company would meet all but its debt-to-worth covenant. But he asked for our help dealing with the bank, because *on paper* it didn't look that way. He'd discovered, for example, that while they'd made $15,000 more than the $200,000 covenant stipulated, they'd forgotten to apply appropriate accelerated depreciation to certain assets on the pro formas they'd originally submitted. Therefore, the company's tax returns were going to show less than the $200,000 required.

In addition, he'd learned that he could save substantially on taxes by bonusing out some of the profits to key employees, but the covenants prohibited that. And worst of all, he realized that because his company was an "S" corporation he'd have to pay taxes on the company's profits, but loan covenants capped his salary and other withdrawals. With those constraints, he couldn't begin to cover his personal expenses and his taxes. He wanted us to help make the point to his lender that he actually *had* achieved most of the goals that were set, and so the bank ought to allow him to do what was in their collective cash flow interest. Namely, he thought the lender should let him use every legitimate tax savings opportunity to save the company money.

He also asked us to see if the bank would release his soon-to-be ex-wife from her personal guarantees. Knowing what we knew about his bank, the banking environment, and his situation, we suggested he worry about that little problem later. Kenny Rogers was right when he sang "Ya gotta know when to hold 'em. Know when to fold 'em. Know when to walk away, and know when to run."[1]

What we realized that the owner didn't, was that he was very close to having his loans called altogether. In the midst of the S&L crisis, the new bank was taking a very conservative approach to a highly leveraged company's loan covenants and missed projections. While he considered the missed debt-to-worth covenant to be a minor faux pas, we knew the lender would take it as a serious violation of the loan terms.

Here's how the lender saw the situation. If the owner declared all $215,000 in profit, the company would still show a debt-to-worth ratio of 4.1:1 (vs. the covenant of 4:1). And, if they let him maximize the company's potential tax savings and report a lower net income, that ratio would barely change from its prior level of 4.5:1. Period. Nothing personal. But the numbers weren't where they were supposed to be.

The owner couldn't realistically change banks because a new lender wouldn't accept his high debt-to-worth ratio either. And even if a new bank would take him on, it would be a whole lot more expensive.

We suggested scheduling a meeting with the lender and the lender's boss so we could present the situation and the debt-to-worth problem. After a lot of explanations, arguments, figuring, proposals, and counterproposals, the lender agreed to allow the owner to withdraw funds from the company to cover his taxes.

Bonuses, however, in spite of the potential savings, were not allowed. A $2,000 penalty was charged for missing the covenants, and the loan rate was increased from prime plus 0.75 percent to prime plus 1.25 percent. The next year's covenants were unchanged, which meant that the company would have to work harder this year to make up for already being behind.

There's a lot to be learned from this situation. The borrower, unfortunately, underestimated the lender's concern about the debt-to-worth ratio. In fact, the lender had already been stretching to do the deal the prior year, it turned out; and the terms that were granted under the circumstances were actually quite good. To make matters worse, the borrower didn't realize the company's projections would be used to establish financial covenants or he would have made sure they were prepared more carefully. And no one thought to consider the tax impact that a profitable S corporation has on the owner's personal taxes (a common problem).

The lender wasn't blameless either. The bank had given the owner a false sense of security by allowing him to miss covenants in the past and hadn't considered the personal tax problems that the covenants would create. On top of it all, because of the merger and several changes in account officers, no one at the bank had kept up with the company's interim progress and reinforced the necessity for the company to meet its covenants.

Finally, lest the federal government go unscathed, it was also partially to blame because this whole situation occurred when banks were running scared of federal regulators as a result of the S&L debacle and perhaps overreacting.

The moral of the story, which fortunately had an acceptable, if not happy, ending: Take your covenants very seriously, know where you stand with your lender, know your financing options, and know when it's time to negotiate and when it's best to accept what you're offered.

FINDING A LENDER | 6

Now that you know what's possible in terms of loan structure, and what's likely in terms of how a lender will evaluate your deal, it's time to look for a lender, develop your loan request package, meet with the lender, and navigate your way through their loan approval process.

Simply choosing the bank with the closest branch is shortsighted. Even if you don't intend to borrow money right away, you ought to begin thinking in terms of finding a lender that you can grow with, like, and trust.

WHAT SHOULD YOU LOOK FOR IN A LENDER?

If you could place an order from a catalog for the perfect lender, you'd search for one with these characteristics:

- Aggressive lending policies.
- Genuinely interested in your size business.
- Flexible policies and procedures.
- Interested in, and perhaps even familiar with, your type of business (or at the very least not turned off by it because of a bad experience in your industry).
- Actively seeking new loans.
- Creative in its approach to structuring loans.
- Properly staffed and organized to approve and service loans like yours.
- Capable of servicing larger financial needs as your business grows.

- Able to service your noncredit needs (e.g., checking and savings accounts, payroll, international services, cash management, coin and currency services, trust services, personal banking services, etc.).
- Financially stable and in good stead with the federal regulators.
- Not likely to be acquired any time soon.

So how do you find one that fits the specs? Is it the biggest lender? The smallest lender? And, not so incidentally, how do you know if a lender is financially sound?

REFERRALS

By far, the best way to find a lender is to ask business owners in your area who they use. Accountants, attorneys, and other advisors can also be a good source; they can help refer you to someone on the inside. A referral from a trusted professional always gets a little extra attention because the lender stands to receive additional business in that way.

A referral from a senior executive from within the lending institution will guarantee you even more attention. This is no time to be shy about dropping names. If you met the president of a bank at a ball game (perhaps when a drink was spilled on you during a cheer), call that executive and ask who is the best person to talk to about a loan. You can be sure that lenders will spend a whole lot more time declining a loan from someone who's referred by the president of the bank, than they will a loan that simply wandered in off the street.

Ideas for Finding a Good Lender

- Ask for a referral from others in your industry (their lenders will already have some understanding of your business).
- Order Dun & Bradstreet reports for your competitors (which often report liens and the name of the lender).
- Call your local SBA office for the names of the most active small-business lenders.
- Keep your ear to the ground for the names of lenders who are most active in your community.

BANK SIZE

Is a small lender better than a large lender? Maybe, but not necessarily. Small lenders, almost by definition, tend to focus on small loans. Their loan approval processes are often simpler than larger banks, but don't expect their credit criteria to be lax. With smaller portfolios, they sometimes need to be extra careful about marginal deals. Some small lenders still make loans largely, though not exclusively, based on the character of the borrower. At some small banks, for example, you might find that the bank president is involved in every loan decision and personally meets with every borrower.

When dealing with a small bank, be sure it will be able to service your future borrowing and other relationship needs. Some are severely limited in the size loans they can make, but most maintain relationships with other lenders that allow them to handle larger requests.

To compete with more flexible local lenders, some large banks have distributed their small-business lending practices to regional levels. While CoreStates Bank is one of the largest East Coast small business lenders, their lenders and regional managers are given lending authority that allows them to act like small independent banks. Thus they can offer the services of a large bank with the flexibility of a small one.

BANK RATINGS

These days, it's a good idea to check out the financial strength of your lender. Weak lenders are under pressure from federal regulators to eliminate marginal deals. If yours happens to be one of them, you'll be hard pressed to find another lender after the one you're with gives you the boot. Stronger lenders, on the other hand, can better afford a few marginal deals in their portfolios.

While financial analysis of banks is a complicated business, in general there are two figures you can look at as rough tests of financial strength.

The first figure compares the bank's level of capital to its level of risk-rated assets such as loans. The more of its own capital the bank has to cushion any future loan losses the better. Specifically, banks with a relationship of what's called Tier 1 capital to risk-rated assets of at least 6 percent and total capital to risk-rated assets of at least 10 percent are considered strong. The second measure of a bank's strength is return on assets, where at least 1 percent is desirable.

These figures are available from the reporting agencies such as Thompson BankWatch, Standard & Poor's, and Moody's. Or, ask your lender directly about their numbers; after all, they ask about all of yours.

GETTING TOGETHER

Once you find a lending institution, an individual lender will be assigned to your request based on the size of your business, its location, and the size and nature of your desired loan. When you talk to the lender, briefly describe your request and offer to send the person your loan request package for consideration. The lender may want to come out to see you first, but most will appreciate being able to review your information before meeting you.

If your request passes the *hairy eyeball test*, the lender will want to meet to learn more about you. If you're already in business, bank representatives will probably want to meet at your office or plant so that they can kick the tires.

PREPARATIONS

Don't be insulted by some of our advice in this chapter. You'd be amazed at some obvious mistakes business owners make in this first, all-important meeting. You'll be judged, formally and informally, on how you conduct yourself, how well you know your business, how good a manager you are, how you interact with others in your organization, how financially astute you are, what impression your office or plant creates, how busy your business looks, and so forth.

It's perfectly OK if you're not the expert in all areas. Feel free to include your accountant, financial manager, sales manager, or other co-workers in the meeting if you think they can help. After all, knowing what you don't know is a sign of good management.

Try to think in your prospective lender's terms during this meeting. Often enthusiastic owners want to show off their neat product or technology, and barely address the lender's issues.

Start out with an office tour, but be sure to give your employees a heads-up a day or so ahead of time so that they can remove any politically incorrect materials from their walls, hide any final notice bills that are laying on their desks, and curtail any screaming at nonperforming vendors. Try to look like the proverbial calm, cool, and collected duck when the bank visitors arrive, even if you're collectively paddling like crazy under the water. No real need to dress up for the meeting, you re the boss on your turf. On the other hand, if you go to the lender's office, best to play the bank's dress-up game. If your clothes look like the lender's, you won't lose any points, but you might if you go in starving artist, rock star, or motorcycle mama costume no matter how proud you may be of your occupation. When in Rome . . . .

THE VISIT

Lenders like to see friendly rapport between you and your employees. Introduce your visitors to your key players, or even to everyone in the office if the company is small. Take the opportunity to brag about your team, how well qualified they are, what a good job they do, and so forth. Make sure your people are busy. If they look idle, your lender might wonder how active your business really is. In fact, invite them at your busiest time of day so they can see the place in action, not at a slow time, even though that might be more convenient for you.

As the bank representatives tour your office, building, or plant, don't forget that they'll be sizing up the collateral value of your assets. They'll be disturbed by idle equipment, dusty or poorly organized inventory, or a sloppy bookkeeping area. If you're applying for an expansion or equipment loan, be sure to point out how the new device or facility will improve your operation (e.g., lower costs, speed up production, increase revenue).

THE MEETING

Now go back to your office to talk about things in more detail. If your office isn't quiet or private, find some place that is. (We once met with the owner of slaughterhouse who's office—without going into details—was much too close to operations.) If possible, have all but your most important calls held so that you can focus on the meeting. If the lender asks a question that you can't answer, admit it and offer to find the answer from someone else. If you aren't really running the business, make sure whoever is attends the meeting . . . and let that person do the talking. If your accountant and financial consultants can't join you for the meeting (and what could be more important?), at least have them available to answer telephone questions. Offer to have your accountant call the lender directly to discuss any open issues afterward. Make sure lenders feel that you're eager to provide whatever information they want; never let them think that you're unwilling or withholding something.

THE REAL ISSUES

The lender's reason for wanting this meeting is to learn as much as possible about your company's management, staffing, business, industry, strategies, financial performance, future projections, borrowing needs, and collateral options. Most, if not all of this information should have been in the loan proposal you sent the bank earlier. Nevertheless, you'll want to be sure the lender leaves the meeting with the answers to anything that might create a problem.

Management Issues

- Is management capable?
- Is there depth or redundancy in management or are you the only one who knows what's going on?
- What plans do you have for management succession?
- Do you recognize your management strengths and weaknesses?
- How much cash and sweat do you have invested in the business?
- If partners are involved, do you work well together; in any event is there a buy-sell agreement?
- If you're a husband and wife team, what will happen in the event of a divorce?
- Are you or the business involved in any lawsuits or other legal actions?
- What forms of business insurance do you carry?
- Do you have key-person life insurance?

Employment Issues

- Are your employees happy?
- Is there a lot of employee turnover?
- Are labor unions involved in your business?
- If so, what's your experience with them, and when is your next contract negotiation?
- Is there an available labor pool for the type of employees you need?
- Are your salaries, benefits, and other compensation plans in line with those of your competitors?

- Are you up-to-date on all employee taxes and other legal responsibilities?
- Do your policies comply with all relevant regulations?

Plant and Equipment

- Do you have a detailed list of assets and their location?
- Is your equipment adequately insured?
- Is your equipment subject to any liens?
- Is there a resale market for your equipment?
- What's it worth at resale?
- Do you own or rent your building?
- If you rent, what are the terms of the lease?
- What rent increases are expected?
- How much do you spend each year for new equipment?
- What are your future equipment needs?
- Is any equipment leased? What are the terms of the leases?
- How long can you operate in your present facility? with your present equipment?

Products and Services

- What do you make or do?
- Are your products or services likely to become obsolete?
- Are your products or services seasonal? If so, when are the peaks and valleys?
- What's your product or service pricing mix?

Marketing

- How big is your market?
- What's your market share? Are you gaining or losing?
- How much of the market do you think you can capture?
- How do you market your business?
- How do you establish your prices?
- What are your selling terms?

- How do you distribute your products?
- Who are your competitors?
- How do you differentiate yourself from your competitors?
- What's your market niche?

Customers

- Do you sell to a few large customers or many small customers?
- Do any customers account for more than 10 percent of your sales?
- If so, what do you know about their financial health?
- How much of your volume is the result of repeat business?
- Do you survey your customers to find out if they are happy?
- Are your customers mostly large businesses, small businesses, new businesses, established businesses, end users, distributors, retailers, consumers?
- Are customers local, regional, national, or international?

Industry

- What industry are you in (SIC code)?
- How does your business differ from others in your industry?
- Does your industry trade organization offer any financial statistics?
- Where is your industry in its life cycle?
- Is the industry subject to periods of boom and bust?
- What's the outlook for your industry?

Financial Management

- Do you regularly evaluate your financial performance?
- Do you prepare and use a budget?
- Do you maintain checks and balances to protect against fraud or theft?
- Do you adequately evaluate the creditworthiness of customers?
- What's your bad debt and slow pay history?
- Do any customers enjoy special payment terms?
- Do you pay your bills on time?

- Do you take advantage of early payment discounts?
- Do you have a bookkeeper, controller, chief financial officer?
- If so, what are their qualifications?
- How long have you been with your present accounting firm?
- If you've changed firms recently, why?

Income Statements

- Were there any unusual income or expenses in the statements submitted?
- Have there been any significant changes in accounting methods?
- What salary and other benefits do you draw from the company?
- Are there any hidden perks in the expenses?
- What's your break-even point?
- What's your burn rate (monthly minimum level of expense)?
- If you have a number of different products, what's their relative contribution to gross profit?
- What's the reason for any significant changes in income or expense (on a category-by-category basis)?

Balance Sheets

- Are there any off-balance sheet items?
- Are the asset and liability values on the statement representative of typical levels?
- What are the peak levels for A/R, inventory, and A/P?
- What are the terms on all existing debt (original amount/date, payment terms, collateral, guarantees, date due)?
- Are any assets significantly undervalued on the balance sheet?
- What's included in "Other Assets" and "Other Liabilities"?
- What are your ratios and financial test figures, and how do they compare to others in your industry?

Projections

- What are the assumptions behind the projections?
- What are the assumptions behind the assumptions?

- What are the assumptions behind the assumptions behind the assumptions?

WHERE DO YOU STAND?

When you finish answering all the questions at this meeting, you'll probably be exhausted, you'll understand better what the Inquisition was all about, and you may begin to wonder if you really need the bank's stupid old money anyway.

Well, before you show your visitors out, it's perfectly reasonable to ask about *their* organization and what they think of the deal. Ask them about their bank's lending preferences. Ask them about their approval process. Ask for the name and title of your lender's boss and the boss's boss. Encourage, maybe even insist (nicely), on meeting some of the others who'll be involved in the loan decision. Ask about the bank's financial health, and find out whether there are any merger and acquisition plans. Ask for customer references. Ask about the bank's other products and services. Lending isn't an esoteric science or art, so ask your lender to give you some read on your chances of qualifying. Ask what rates, terms, and structure are being considered. Particularly ask what the bank's primary concerns are at this point in the process. And finally, ask when you can expect to hear from your lender.

YOUR LOAN PROPOSAL

Even if you've done a brilliant job of convincing a lender that you're a good credit risk, your efforts may be in vain if the lender doesn't do an equally good job of convincing others in the organization of the same. The fact of the matter is that you may never have a chance to meet the rest of the people who will be involved in approving or, heaven forbid, declining your loan. Obviously, if you could meet them, they'd be equally impressed with your brilliance, wit, charm, and business acumen. But more likely, all those other faceless, nameless folks will rely on the measly notes the lender scribbled in the margin of your loan proposal. And, there's a good chance that the lender you spent so much time with completely forgot (or worse yet misunderstood) some percentage of what you said in the meeting anyway.

The point is, you need a written loan request package that will allow you to communicate directly to the ultimate decision makers. You already know from reading about the Five C's of Credit what concerns such a package needs to address, and now we'll help you pull it all together.

The real purpose of your loan request package, in addition to the obvious one of giving your lenders all the information that they need to make a favorable decision, is to make their job of approving your loan as easy as possible. A loan proposal packaging approach we've seen used all too often is the *shopping bag and shovel approach*, where you give them every piece of paper you've ever created in your business in no particular order, and let them figure it out (sorta the way some people handle an IRS agent). Another less commonly used method, but one that's far more popular with lenders and therefore more successful, is to prepare a knock-their-socks-off loan proposal that communicates everything they need to know about you, your business, and why you're a good credit risk.

From a busy lender's perspective, it's a lot easier to reject a messy deal than a clean one because the former takes too much energy to consider. A good loan request package doesn't have to be a professionally bound work of art (in fact, lenders would prefer unbound presentations so they can make copies more easily), it just has to be organized and complete.

SUMMARY OF THE LOAN REQUEST

This section is the *Cliffs Notes®* for your loan request. Your lender should be able to read this two- to four-page summary and quickly understand:

- How much you're looking to borrow.
- What type of loan you want (term loan versus line of credit).
- What the funds will be used for.
- Over what term they'll be repaid.
- What the source of repayment will be.
- What collateral and guarantees are available.
- A summary of your historical, current, and projected financial performance and ratios.

What you propose should look remarkably similar to how the lenders would have structured the deal on their own. This alone should impress the heck out of your prospective lenders because they're used to getting pie-in-the-sky proposals for loans that don't have a chance of being approved (from business owners who obviously didn't read this book).

HISTORICAL BALANCE SHEET AND INCOME STATEMENTS

Historical balance sheet and income statements must be included, but understand that all financial statements are not created equal. A lender's confidence in the numbers you provide will depend on the reputation of the accounting firm that prepared the statements, the thoroughness of the statements (meaning the level of detail provided about your income and expenses, assets and liabilities), the quality and level of detail in the financial notes, and the level of certification that the preparer applied to their preparation. Businesses with over a few hundred thousand dollars in revenue should have their financial statements prepared by a certified public accountant (CPA), although smaller businesses can usually make it by with tax returns.

Financial Statements

According to Don Sontag of Sontag & Associates, a regional CPA firm specializing in the accounting and financial management needs of small and medium-size businesses, CPAs can provide three levels of financial statement preparation. As you might suspect, the price will vary with the level of verification performed, how good your financial documentation is to begin with, the size of your company, and the complexity of your statements.

An audited financial statement will be reviewed independent of your company's management and whoever prepared your financial statements. Auditors form their opinion of your financial statements based on selective testing directed toward discovery of any material misstatements. Their opinions are just that, an opinion of your organization's financial statements as a whole, not a statement of certainty about the accuracy of every item. Finally, auditors are concerned with the financial presentation and not the financial quality of your company, the wisdom of your management decisions, or the risk of doing business with you.

For most small companies, the level of assurance provided by audited financial statements is unnecessary and prohibitively expensive anyway. If your company has loans totaling less than $1 million or sales less then $5 million, you'll probably engage CPAs to review or simply compile your financial statements.

The objective of a review is to provide limited assurance that no material modifications are necessary for your financial statements to conform to GAAP or other comprehensive basis for accounting. This objective differs significantly from an audit because it does not provide sufficient background for an opinion on the financial statements; only limited assurance is provided.

The objective of a compilation service is to present information supplied by your company in the form of financial statements. Technically, accountants are not required to express an assurance about whether the statements conform with generally accepted accounting principles (GAAP) or with another comprehensive basis for accounting; but in practice they will undertake at least a minimum level of review to ensure they understand how you're keeping your books.

In any case, if your accountants don't use GAAP to prepare your financial statements, they might use the income tax basis, cash, modified cash, or regulatory basis, which are considered to be comprehensive and acceptable for preparing financial statements. Auditors may express opinions of statements prepared on these bases, but they'll reword their report to recognize the basis for accounting used, will explain that the statements are not intended to conform with GAAP, and will refer to notes describing the basis your accountants used and how they differ from GAAP.

Lenders will often request an increase in the level of your financial statement as your sales and/or loan balance increase, if your company's financial performance deteriorates, or if they have any reason to want greater assurance that your company is performing as reported. Policies vary from one lender to the next, but you can expect a conversation about providing review-basis statements when your sales exceed about $5 million or when your loans reach $1 million.

❑ Secret

Higher levels of certification require more cash out of your pocket for accounting services (which, by the way, comes out of the same cash flow you have to use for your loan payments) so it's reasonable to argue against such a request for as long as possible. As a compromise, you might offer to switch to an accounting firm that the lender knows and trusts. Sometimes a compilation from a known and trusted firm is considered equally credible as review-basis statement from an unknown CPA. The lender scores brownie points with the firm that gets your business, by the way, so you may get some benefit back on that over time.

Interim Financial Statements

If your financial statements are more than three months old, an internally prepared balance sheet and income statement should be included. Lenders may require a CPA compilation of this information before they fund the loan. Companies with sales of over $1 million will probably be expected to supply quarterly CPA-prepared financial statements.

Notes/Explanation to Financial Statements

In addition to the standard accounting notes that accompany your financial statements, you should include a side letter about any balance sheet or income statement items that might misrepresent your financial performance including:

- Reasons for significant expense increases/decreases.
- Significant accounting changes.
- Unusually high or low year-end balance sheet values.
- One-time expenses.
- Owner perks.
- Loans from owners or other friendly debt.
- Off-balance sheet assets.
- Highly depreciated assets.

Also, be sure that your financial statement notes include a detailed breakdown of any existing debt on your balance sheet (including the date and original amount of the debt, the interest rate and payment terms, any balloon payments, and the present balance).

PROJECTED BALANCE SHEET, INCOME STATEMENT, AND CASH FLOW

When you include your projected balance sheet, income statement, and cash flows in your loan proposal, make sure they're realistic and achievable. Include two to three years of projections. The income statements and cash flows should be monthly for the first projected year and quarterly thereafter. Even more important than the financial statements are the assumptions that accompany them. Be sure to document all assumptions and footnote any significant changes from historical performance. And don't forget, you may be held to your projections, and the lender may build in covenants and conditions that require you to meet ratios that are calculated from your projections.

SUMMARY OF FINANCIAL PERFORMANCE

Make your lender's job easier. Rather than making loan officers leaf through piles of financial statements and projections, put the highlights on a nice, tidy summary page that even includes the ratios you know they'll want to see. This would be another good place to footnote any information that could be misinterpreted.

ACCOUNTS RECEIVABLE AGINGS

An accounts receivable aging report will help your lender determine the collateral value of your accounts receivable. Don't forget to explain any slow payment accounts or other accounts that are over 60 days old.

ACCOUNTS PAYABLE AGINGS

An accounts payable aging report, similar to the A/R aging report, will help the lender determine the status of your relationship with your vendors. Be sure to explain any past-due balances or special payment terms. Also be sure to point out the savings you'd receive by having access to a loan that would allow you to pay within your vendor's discount periods.

BREAKDOWN OF INVENTORY

Companies whose inventory represents a significant asset should provide lenders with a summary of the inventory's balance sheet and market value. Manufacturers should break down inventory by raw materials, work-in-progress, and finished goods. Any information that might convince a lender of the market value of the inventory should be included in the loan request.

SCHEDULE OF FIXED ASSETS

A schedule of fixed assets should point out the market value (versus the balance sheet value) of your furniture, fixtures, equipment, buildings, or intangible assets. Any supporting documents (such as appraisals, ads for similar used equipment, or other information that would verify the market value you've assigned) should be included.

PROPERTY APPRAISALS

If you happen to have a recent appraisal for a potential collateral property, it can't hurt to include it but don't order a new appraisal until the lender tells you to do so. Post-S&L debacle regulations stipulate that the lender must be involved in choosing the appraisal firm.

SUMMARY OF COLLATERAL VALUES

To make the lender's job easier, summarize the market value of collateral offered, together with an appropriate advance percentage (which you learned about in Chapter 4) to arrive at the lender's collateral value.

❑ **Secret**

This allows you to subtly *influence* the value that lenders will assign. If you say your inventory should be valued at 70 cents on the dollar and they think it should be valued at 30 cents, they may just compromise to 50 cents. They might not, but it doesn't hurt to try!

PERSONAL FINANCIAL STATEMENTS

Personal financial statements should be submitted for any individual who owns more than 20 percent of your company and for any guarantors. Statements should be prepared on a joint basis if you're married, and both of you should sign and date the statement.

BUSINESS AND PERSONAL TAX RETURNS

Copies of tax returns for the past three years for the company, any related entities, and all guarantors will be required before the loan is approved. If you're applying for an SBA loan, the SBA may make the point that it doesn't require tax returns, but you can be sure your lender will.

SUMMARY OF THE BUSINESS AND INDUSTRY

A full business plan is highly recommended, but at the very least your loan request should include information about how long you've been in business, what you do, how you do it, who you and your key employees are, why you're qualified to run this business, and the nature of the industry in which you operate. A complete business plan is usually required by a lender for new businesses.

OTHER INFORMATION

In addition to the standard information already described, you may want to include, or a lender may request, some of the following:

- Product samples (as appropriate).
- Sample advertisements (as appropriate).
- Customer testimonials (as appropriate).
- Relevant articles (if available).
- Environmental studies of collateral properties (as requested).
- Articles of incorporation (as requested).
- Partnership agreements (as requested).
- Fictitious name filings (as requested).
- Copies of significant contracts, agreements, or leases (as requested).
- Copies of key-person insurance policies (as requested).

While preparing your loan request, keep in mind that this may be your only chance to convince someone you may never meet that you're a good risk. The professionalism exhibited by your package, and your a priori demonstrated understanding of the bank's financing guidelines, will go a long way toward making your case. On the flip side, approaching a lender with a sloppy and incomplete package for a totally unrealistic loan will alert the lender that you don't know what you're doing.

A final note on packaging your loan request. According to lenders, the biggest reason for loan approval delays is the lack of required information. So if you need the money ASAP, make sure you give them what they'll need to arrive at a speedy decision.

LOAN APPROVALS: BEHIND CLOSED DOORS

8

So you put together a terrific loan request package, you spent hours teaching the lender about your business, you shook hands, and the bank representatives left. Now what?

CALL REPORT

Unless they walk off scratching their heads wondering why in the world they came to see you at all, they'll go back to their office and write a call report; summarizing the visit. If they liked you, trusted you, believed in you, and thought that your deal has a snowball's chance in Haiti, they'll begin selling the deal up their organization.

❑ **Secrets**

Your lender is working for you at this point, as your salesperson with the rest of the organization. Think of the lender as such and treat him or her accordingly.

The longer it takes the bank to make a decision, the more likely it is favorably considering your request. "No's" usually come much quicker than "yes's." If your lender calls you for lots of additional information, it's a good sign! At least your request is still under consideration.

Since its important to stay on good terms with your lender, try to be patient with the approval process. Bugging the loan officer for a decision isn't in your best interest. There's a fine line between being assertive and obnoxious. Besides, you don't want to look desperate.

Spreads

With large lenders, your package including the call report will go to a central credit department that will take your financial statements and spread them into a standard computerized format that will include the required ratio and cash flow analysis. In smaller organizations, the *spreads* will be created by your loan officer. Based on the spreads and the credit department's industry research, they'll write a report that highlights any concerns about your loan application.

Meanwhile, the lender will have ordered a Dun & Bradstreet report on your company and personal credit reports for all owners and likely guarantors. Once the financial spreads are done, the lender will call you to clarify any open issues. It's very easy for someone to decline a marginal loan if the person's never met you, so you ought to really start pushing to meet everyone else in the organization who will be involved in your loan decision. Invite them to visit you and take them to lunch (nothing lavish . . . you don't want them to think you'll waste their money, do you?). Remember, *character* is the most important factor in their Five C's decision-making process, and the best way you can communicate your character is through a face-to-face meeting.

At about this point, your loan proposal will be subjected to its first real test. If you have any skewed or misleading ratios, you better have explained why. In some cases, they'll issue a credit rating on a scale of one to five that will follow your request throughout the organization. While the lender may have some say in that rating, some organizations require that the credit department apply the rating without the bias of having met charming ol' you.

LOAN COMMITTEE

Most lending decisions are made by at least two people and often by a credit committee. For example, a lender together with his or her boss might be able to approve loans of up to $150,000. Together with the approval of the next senior level executive, they could approve loans of up to $500,000. Larger loans would require committee approval.

❑ **Secret**

> Ask your lender about the bank's approval policies. Because committee approval is more complicated (and often intimidating to junior lenders), it may be better to stay below the committee minimum if you can.

Your lender/salesperson will probably suggest an appropriate structure and pricing for the deal, and others involved in the decision will either approve, decline, or suggest further follow-up. Since loan committees usually meet once a week, a day's delay in getting information to your lender can cause a week's delay in their decision.

APPROVAL (sigh)

If your loan is approved, the lender will issue a formal or informal commitment letter that spells out the pricing and structure of the loan. If you choose to negotiate, your lender will probably have to go back to some or all of the people who approved the initial deal, and obtain their permission to make changes. Be sure to negotiate all of the items that concern you at one time. That way, your lender can secure all the necessary approvals in one shot. Changing your mind or repeatedly coming up with new points for negotiation could label you a problem child for your lender, who might turn on you. Remember, you want your lender working for you, not against you.

Once the deal is done, the paperwork will be processed and a closing date will be set. Last-minute changes, especially at loan closing, are not a good idea so be sure to request copies of the documents in advance so that you have a chance to review them. If there are mistakes or they contain something different from what you expected, you'll want to work out the kinks before you go to the closing table.

REJECTION (gasp)

If your loan is declined, be sure to ask for reasons and for suggestions on how your request could have been stronger. At least you'll have learned something about how to strengthen your pitch for the next lender. Sometimes you and the lender will be able to come up with a creative solution to the bank's concerns such as adding a guarantor or additional collateral, but a reversal is rare.

One final point, bank-hoppers and loan-shoppers aren't appreciated in lender circles. It's OK to talk to more than one lender, but submitting requests to everyone around town only makes you look desperate. And they *will* all know you're shopping because a notation is made at the credit bureau each time someone checks your credit report.

9 DOTTING THE I'S AND CROSSING THE T'S

With some exceptions, lenders will use standard loan agreements for loans of less than a million dollars. Those agreements will contain a number of obscurely worded clauses that will give the lenders all kinds of rights to call the loan whenever they feel insecure about their ability to be paid. A good business lawyer will be able to help determine what's negotiable and what isn't. Notice that we said a "good business lawyer." That means one who knows what to expect in bank documents. A inexperienced lawyer will run up your legal bill trying to change language that the lender simply will not change. By the way, in addition to your own legal bills, you'll also be charged for the bank's legal fees if its own attorneys are involved. In the end, you'll be poorer, but no more secure.

Unless you're an attorney, you probably find reading legal documents about as much fun as watching paint dry but not nearly as straightforward. Nevertheless, you need to understand the terms and conditions so that you don't inadvertently trigger a default. While loan documents will vary from lender to lender, the issues are typically the same. CFI ProServices, Inc., is one of the leading providers of bank loan documentation software. Their Laser Pro® Closing Program is used by 20 percent of all U.S. Commercial Banks. Here are some of the more commonly misunderstood, though fairly standard, clauses you'll find in CFI and other bank loan documents:

- *Principal payable on demand* means just what it says, you owe payment of the money when the bank demands it. Most lines of credit are structured in this manner so that to the letter of the agreement, the bank can demand its money back at any time even though the renewal date is set for sometime next year.

- *Right of setoff* allows the lender to collect money owed by withdrawing funds directly from your accounts (whether single or joint with others) without notice to you. This includes accounts in place at the time the loan was signed or any opened later.

- *Material adverse change* clause, allows lenders to deny advances on established loans or to accelerate payment of your loans if your business performance deteriorates.

- *Continuity of operations* requires the lenders consent before a borrower may substantially change the nature of the business or its ownership.

- *Negative borrowing* clause requires the lender's consent prior to taking on any new debt.

- *Negative loans, acquisitions, or guarantees* clause requires that the lender grant permission before any loans are made to other entities, other businesses are acquired, or other indebtedness is guaranteed.

- *Lender insecurity* clause allows a lender to declare a loan default if the lender deems itself insecure (a nice little catchall).

- *Cross-collateralization* clause means that the collateral on this loan can also be applied to all other past and future loans to your company regardless of the specific collateral named on those loans.

- *Cross default* clause means that any default under this loan will constitute a default under any other loans to your company whether now in place or added in the future.

- *Confession of judgment* allows the lender to obtain judgments on you and your assets without notifying you. Essentially this allows the bank to seize your pledged assets without notice.

- *Right to collect on guarantees and liquidate collateral in any order* means they can take your house before your business assets if they feel it would be easier to liquidate. (Still sure you want to start a new business?)

- *Unlimited personal guarantees* are often written to apply to this and any future indebtedness even if you don't specifically guarantee the future loans. Such guarantees often set no maximum so even as your loan is repaid, your guarantee stays at an unlimited level.

- *Joint and several guarantees* allow the lender to proceed against any and all guarantees for the full amount of the loan plus interest, penalties, and collection costs (whoever has the deepest pockets will be tapped first).

While the lender might allow minor changes to standard clauses, don't expect much. If you're a long-time customer of the bank, and

Finding Money from Lenders: Do's and Don'ts

Do:

Find the right type of lender for your particular situation.
Understand why lenders lend.
Ask for what you need, no more, no less.
Prepare a written loan package and/or business plan.
Address lender's concerns in your plan and your presentation.
Plan an appropriate presentation.
Make your presentation to the decision makers.
Understand the approval process.
Understand appropriate loan structures.
Teach lenders as much as you can about your business.
Go in with your best shot the first time.
Understand loan terms and conditions.
Expect to personally guarantee debt.
Expect the loan to be secured.
Keep your credit record clean.
Involve appropriate advisors at the appropriate time.
Ask for reasons if you are declined.

Don't:

Lie, misrepresent, or exaggerate anything.
Wait until the last minute to request financing.
Allow any surprises to creep up in the approval process.
Supply unrealistic projections.
Play accounting or tax games.
Overestimate the value of your collateral.
Mismatch short-term debt with long-term needs.
Forget to document both a primary and secondary source of repayment.
Assume, or let the lender assume, anything.
Shop your deal to every lender in town.
Push the lender for a quick decision.
Expect money to solve your problems.

your company is financially strong, you might encourage the lender to limit personal guarantees to just this loan (and not all future borrowings), you might ask for a stated amount on the guarantee (versus making it unlimited), and you might request amending the cross-collateralization clause on any new loans that are well secured by new assets (such as an equipment loan).

Rather than focusing on the standard language, your time will be better spent negotiating the covenants and conditions that have been customized for your business. These may include financial benchmarks and financial reporting requirements (such as how often, how quickly, and in what form you need to submit financial statements).

❑ Secret

Be careful about the date you choose for a line of credit renewal. It should be set for at least a couple of months after you expect to receive your year-end financial statements. If your fiscal year ends on 12/31 and your financial reports are finished in March, the renewal date on a line of credit ought to be set for sometime in late April or May so that your lender has enough time to digest your information, meet with you to discuss your needs for the coming year, develop your renewal request, and have it approved. If it looks as if your financial statements are going to be late, be sure to let your lender know as early as possible so the bank can temporarily extend your line.

---

10 | THE GOOD, THE BAD, AND THE UGLY

Once you've found a lender, don't blow it. As with personal relationships, banking relationships aren't built on one-time interactions, they require continual work. If things don't go exactly as you plan somewhere down the road, a strong relationship with your lender can save your bacon. And a poor relationship will quickly seal your fate.

THE GOOD: YOU'RE APPROVED

Don't think the game's over just because you found the money you needed. Who knows, you may need more sometime down the road. So here are some tips for strengthening your relationship:

- Keep your lender informed of your progress.
- Send the lender relevant articles about your business or industry.
- Continually educate your lender about your business and industry.
- Anticipate future borrowing needs and begin to lay the seeds early.
- Borrow before you need it.
- Know your lender's co-workers, support staff, and management.
- Be the kind of person that people want to help.
- Pay your bills on time.
- Don't overdraw your account.
- Take care not to inadvertently violate loan terms and conditions.
- Try to understand your lender's perspective, needs, and wants.
- Don't be overly rate sensitive—the relationship is more valuable.

- Don't be a bank-hopper. Show loyalty if you expect it in return.
- Understand how your lender's performance is evaluated and help that person look good to senior management.
- Know the market so you'll know if you're being treated fairly.
- Don't misuse your loan proceeds (such as buying a truck with a line of credit).
- Refer other business owners to your lender.
- Keep abreast of news regarding potential mergers or shake-ups at your lending institution.
- Don't let your lender hear bad news about your business from someone other than you.

THE BAD: YOU'RE DECLINED

If your loan request is declined, immediately shift into detective (not defensive) mode so that you can learn where you went wrong. Dan Morefield, Senior Vice President and Manager of the Commercial Services Division of First Interstate Bank of California, one of the nation's largest banks, offers his top five biggest mistakes made by prospective business borrowers:

1. Not paying attention to personal finances and credit history. If you can't manage your own money, how can you manage a business?
2. Refusing to guarantee bank debt. If you aren't willing to put your assets on the line for your own company, why should the bank?
3. Not having a complete financial package for the banker to review. If we can't see where you've been, how can we tell where you are?
4. Not having a business plan. If you don't know where you're going, how will you know when you're there?
5. Not obtaining the legal and financial expertise required. If you want to dance, you need to pay the piper.

Here are some common reasons why banks decline a loan:

- Too much debt.
- Too little equity.
- Insufficient cash flow and/or profits to carry proposed debt.
- Insufficient collateral.

- Unprofessional financial statements.
- Underreporting income on tax returns and other financial statement games.
- Insufficient history in business.
- Poor planning.
- Evidence of poor management.
- Lack of trust in management.

If you're going to be declined, for some reason the bad news usually comes from lenders on Friday afternoon. Maybe it's because lenders want to have it out of the way so they can enjoy their weekend—in spite of the fact that they've ruined yours. So now that you have the bad news, what do you do?

FIND OUT WHY YOU WERE DECLINED

Finding out why you were declined may not be as straightforward as you'd expect. They'll probably say something obscure like "it just didn't meet our underwriting standards." Declining a loan certainly isn't the best part of a lender's job so the person may want to hang up as quickly as possible.

If you want lenders to help you figure out how to improve your package, it's important to avoid arguing about the decline or, for that matter, trying to change their mind. Short of some creative solution that dramatically lowers their risk, lenders almost never change their minds. Asking them to consider a smaller amount doesn't play well either because it will cause them to doubt the validity of your first request.

If you can establish a nonthreatening rapport with the lender, ask the following questions:

- What were the major and minor reasons for the decline?
- How could your loan proposal package have been stronger?
- How could your meeting with them have been better?
- What do they see as problems in your financial performance and ratios?
- Would an additional guarantor or additional collateral make a difference?
- What's been their experience in your industry?
- Did they consider an SBA guaranteed loan (if they don't do them, ask for a suggestion of a lender that does)?

- Do they think you have a chance with any other lenders? If so, who would they suggest?
- Are they willing to entertain your request at a later time? If so, under what conditions?
- Do they have any other suggestions?

A word of caution about a lender's suggestion of other lenders. Not all lenders are informed about the broad range of financing alternatives, and they may be naive about the lenders and programs they suggest. Their suggestions may be based more on who dropped off a business card last, or who sent them their last deal, rather than any real knowledge of the company's programs or reputation. If you're already a depositor, the loan officer may in fact, be reluctant to suggest another lender that also offers deposit accounts. And finally, a few bad apples actually collect commissions (also known in less polite circles as kickbacks) for referring you to loan brokers. While one philosophy says "Who cares, as long as you receive the money you need" the fact is you may not be getting the best deal. So don't overestimate the value of a lender's suggestion; follow up on suggestions, but proceed with caution.

CONSIDER PROFESSIONAL HELP

If your loan proposal is declined, consider professional help. We're not talking medical help or 1-900-PSYCHIC here, although you may be depressed and desperate. Desperate people often do desperate things, and later regret their actions. We mean professional financial help. Rather than running the risk of making matters worse, it might be time to call in the professionals.

Sadly, finding good professional financial help may not be as straightforward as you'd like. There's lots of bad advice and some very bad advisors out there. Some are simply naive; some are misinformed; some are specialists in just one kind of financing (and therefore that's the one they'll point you toward); others are downright incompetent; some will refer you to whoever pays the highest commissions; and still others are out-and-out scam artists who are out to rip you off.

Fortunately, some good professionals also are available to help companies just like yours. The good ones:

- Have had personal experience with most of the financing alternatives.
- Know lenders by name and thus can offer a personal introduction.

- Are respected by their peers so their referral carries some weight with potential lenders.

- Have a keen sense of what works and what doesn't, and can quickly hone in on the possible homes for your deal.

- Have seen a wide variety of creative solutions to problems just like yours.

- Have valuable industry contacts that allow them to run your deal past potential lenders without formally submitting it.

- Can remove themselves from the personal side of a loan decline.

- Can shepherd the deal for you so you can go back to running your business.

So who are these miracle workers and how do you find them? Professional financing consultants might be accountants, attorneys, exbankers or other exfinanciers, investment bankers, or merchant bankers. However, not all accountants, attorneys, or even exbankers fit the bill. In general, you should be looking for someone who has both experience in doing deals with a wide variety of money sources and someone who can offer a personal introduction to those sources. Your consultant's independence from the process is important. If they receive commissions or other consideration (like return business) for their referrals they may have a hard time acting in your best interests.

As for fees, accountants and attorneys will usually charge their standard hourly rates to help you find money. Full-time financing consultants, investment bankers or merchant bankers will probably charge a fee based on the percentage of the amount raised (typically 2 to 5 percent on debt and 3 to 10 percent on equity). Good consultants will review your financing proposal before requesting any significant fees. If they believe they can do the deal, they'll ask you for a retainer. A fee of $500 to $1,000 is typical, and should be at least partially refundable if they're unsuccessful. In addition, if a complete business plan is required (either because you don't have one or need a better one), consultants will typically charge between 5 and 15 thousand dollars.

Most consultants will request the exclusive right to represent you for some period so that you or someone else won't undermine their efforts. If you already have a good business plan (including well-documented financial statements and projections), the majority of the fees will probably be collected when, and if, they successfully place your deal. Be sure to obtain a list of whom they send the deal to so you know who's seen your package.

By the way, if your deal is successfully placed, but you decide not to go through with it, you'll still owe the consultant their fee. So be sure your agreement with your consultant stipulates the amount, rates, fees, and other costs, and any other financing terms you'll accept.

❑ **Secret**

Some unscrupulous loan brokers will shop your deal to every lender in town, often without your authorization to do so. Then, when the financing professional you actually do hire begins to circulate your deal they find that everyone has already seen it. A low-life broker will use this approach to place "first dibbies" on any referral fees that lenders might pay.

How do you sniff out the scam artists? Well first use your common sense. If they seem sleazy, they probably are. The Better Business Bureau may be some help, but the real "artists" change their names and addresses frequently. Here are some clues for finding the scum bags:

- They advertise heavily with ads that encourage you to "act now."
- They claim to have thousands of lenders who are just dying to do your deal (this usually means they are using a software program to blitz the world).
- They promise they can find you financing even before they see your package.
- They promise they can find you financing, period (the deal isn't done 'til you've got the cash, anyone who promises anything different is showing their ignorance).
- They require a large up-front, nonrefundable deposit to even consider your deal.
- They claim they can have the money you need in a matter of days.
- Their company goes by the name AAA Ace Financing or Acme something.
- They claim to be a government lender, but your local SBA office hasn't seen a deal from them in years.
- They "shop" your deal without your permission.
- They claim to be a direct lender, but then quickly shift into broker mode.
- They suggest you lie, fib, exaggerate, or misrepresent something on your loan application to make it look better.
- They claim to have a unique offshore lender and describe an elaborate process for how the funds flow through a bank in Haiti.

- They propose a deal and insist it's the best you're going to be offered, even though the rates and fees will put you out of business.
- They suggest "unique" ways of circumventing federal and state securities laws and tell you that "everyone does it."
- They suggest that you pay their fees "under the table."
- They're unable or unwilling to provide you with any credentials that demonstrate their expertise in financing.

In general, if it sounds too good to be true, it probably is!

A good advisor can make the difference for you, but we can't overemphasize the need to find someone you can trust. Once you do, don't blow it by forgetting to mention any skeletons that may be lurking in your closet. Like doctors and lawyers, advisors can't help you if you don't let them.

TRY OTHER LENDERS

Whether you choose to go it alone or you've teamed up with a good advisor, it's time to look around for other lenders because it's not at all unusual to be declined by several lenders and approved by several others. Even if you've been declined by one SBA lender, you may be approved by another.

Based on feedback received from the first lender, try to figure out which kind of lender you should approach next. If the explanation for your decline seemed like you were right on the hairy edge of approval, try other similar lenders. If the decline was delivered quickly and didn't seem to have any chance at all with that lender, try a different type of lender (go back to Section One to review your options).

Don't make the situation worse by shopping the deal to everyone in town because your credit report will show that a number of lenders have already looked at the deal. A new lender will have to wonder why all the others declined you and may not even try to do the deal. Or, for that matter, other lenders will assume you're window shopping and won't want the expend the energy to consider your request.

❏ **Secret**

Target a handful of likely lenders and approach them all at the same time. And don't offer information about your decline to other lenders. Let them draw their own conclusions. If they ask, however, be honest—you don't want to blow your credibility.

SHARPEN YOUR LOAN PROPOSAL

Be sure to sharpen your loan proposal based on the feedback from the first lender. If something was misunderstood, chances are the next lender will misunderstand it as well. If you're going to approach a different kind of lender, your new proposal may want to emphasize that kind of lender's concerns.

RECONSIDER INVESTMENT CAPITAL

Since you went for debt in the first place, you probably felt either that you couldn't attract equity capital or that you weren't willing to pay the price. Either way, it may be time to reconsider your strategy. If straight investment capital isn't in the cards, perhaps a quasi-investor could guarantee or pledge collateral on your loan request.

RECONSIDER YOUR NEED

Consider whether you really need the money right now or whether another approach might allow you to borrow less. A word of caution, however, don't just chop your loan request down or tweak your financial projections to make it look as if you need less money. Borrowing less than you need is often worse than not borrowing at all—it just prolongs the agony.

GO BACK TO BOOTSTRAPPING

Section Four offers a number of strategies for improving your internal cash flow. Think Lean and Mean. This is survival we're talking about. Survival mode is different from growth mode. Chop out every ounce of fat you can from your operation. Business owners often refuse to consider chopping certain expenses because, well, they just can't. But there are no sacred cows if you're dying of hunger.

 If you still believe you can make your business work, fill out every credit card application you can find (*Money Magazine* regularly reports companies with the lowest credit card rates and fees in the country). Submit your applications all at once so their credit checks all hit your credit report at the same time. Look for a part-time job. Get angry, get inspired, get moving!

Many of life's failures
are people who did not realize
how close they were to success
when they gave up.

Thomas Edison

GIVE IT UP

If you've done everything you can to borrow money, raise money, save money, or make more money and it's still not working, you need to sit yourself down and honestly decide whether you can continue without additional capital. If every month you're going deeper and deeper in the hole, living off cash flow, and paying your bills later and later, your personal credit will suffer permanent damage. You're at risk of financial ruin, so better to act sooner rather than later. If you're already up to your ears in debt and other obligations, maybe it's time to talk to your attorney about formal or informal bankruptcy.

Our society places a huge stigma on failure, so often we'll keep at it long after we should have quit just to avoid admitting defeat. Fact of the matter is, most successful people can point to at least one failure in their life. Failure builds character. If you don't fail at least once in your life, you're probably not pushing the edge of the envelope. Pull yourself together, learn from your mistakes, and move on!

only those who will risk going too far
can possibly find out how far one can go.

T.S. Eliot

THE UGLY: WHEN THINGS GO SOUR

Sooner or later, your plans may not go exactly as you expected. What then? How do you handle your banker? Well, in a word, *carefully*. First of all, you need to understand what lenders consider to be a problem because their definition might not be as liberal as yours. Here are some red flags that will make your lender nervous:

- Net losses.
- Substantially lower profits.
- Decline in gross revenue.

- Decline in collateral values.
- Any violation of loan terms or covenants (even if your lender has allowed them in the past).
- Poor industry-wide performance.
- Slower A/R, inventory, or A/P turnover.
- Reduction in prices.
- Increased bad debt.
- Frequent overdrafts.
- Declining deposit balances.
- Borrowing from another lender without permission.
- Liens from taxing authorities found on their annual lien searches.
- Any subsequent liens without their permission.
- Changes in ownership.
- Reduced account activity.
- Delinquent loan payments.
- Idle assets during plant tours.
- Excessive employee turnover.
- Frequent calls from your vendors verifying funds' availability.
- Loss of a major contract.
- Slow payment of taxes.
- Failure to clean up or substantially reduce the line of credit.
- High profile business failures in your industry.
- Unfavorable media exposure for you or your industry.
- Excessive salary draws and loans to officers.
- Numerous recent credit searches in your personal credit report.
- Increased consumer debt.
- Reduction in your involvement in the business.
- Excessive vacations.
- Reluctance to meet with or return phone calls from lenders.
- Reluctance to provide requested financial information.
- Legal actions against your company.

A company with two consecutive years of reported income statement losses (even if they were solely attributable to noncash depreciation losses) is a candidate for being considered a performing, nonperformer. Regulators are breathing heavily down the necks of lenders to classify performing, nonperformers as bad debt, and to proceed with immediate workout. While some lenders are more rational than others regarding loans in this condition, some have been known to demand immediate payoff forcing some companies into liquidation as a result. Be on your toes if you're getting ready to report a loss for the second year in a row, and start investigating your financing alternatives before your bank pulls the rug out from under you.

❏ **Secret**

> One of the little gems brought to us by the S&L bailout is a new classification for a loan, the "performing, nonperforming" loan. (Only federal regulators could come up with such a name.) This is a borrower that may have never missed a loan payment, but *per the company's financial statements,* may be at risk of default. (As we pointed out earlier in Section Two, your financial statements don't always show the whole picture.)

So what do you do if you're having financial problems? You start by being honest and open. Depending on the severity of the bad news, you might want to explore alternative financing options before the conversation with your lender, just so you know how hard you should bargain.

A phone call is probably sufficient if the problem is relatively minor and temporary. A face-to-face meeting is best if you're delivering poor year-end numbers, or if the problem is severe. Don't underestimate the importance of this meeting.

❏ **Secret**

> How the news is delivered is almost as important as the news itself in determining how your lender will respond. Some lenders are very levelheaded about problems, others border on irrational. Either way, prepare for the worst.

Assuming that you meet face-to-face, here's how that meeting ought to go. You should prepare whatever analysis is necessary to explain the nature of the problem, its impact on your past performance and future outlook, and the steps you've already taken to address the situation. Your presentation should:

- Show that you understand the problem.

- Demonstrate you're taking it seriously.

- Describe the steps you've already taken to correct the problem (e.g., layoffs, pay cuts, expense cuts, tighter policies, trade concessions).

- Explain the steps you plan to take in the future if the situation doesn't improve and what events will trigger those plans.

- Remind them why you continue to be a good credit risk.

- Demonstrate any recent improvements (interim performance, evidence of backlog).

In spite of the nature of the news, you need to try to be as positive, upbeat, and in control as possible. Your positive attitude will go a long way toward calming your lender's fears as long as you demonstrate that you understand the gravity of the situation and have viable solutions.

Your lender may request new projections and frequent updates on your financial performance. *Be conservative* with any projections you make at this point. And, if you promised or even suggested that you were going to do something, be sure you do it. Don't do anything that might lead the lender to mistrust or disbelieve you.

Depending on the bank's level of concern, it may tighten up on your loan structure or even transfer the loan to the asset-based lending group. Either way, you can probably expect a change in loan terms and pricing. If the lender doesn't already have your personal guarantee or home as collateral, these will almost certainly be required now. If you have an open line of credit, the lender may seal off further draws on the line. And, as you make payments on the line, the bank may not allow you to borrow that money back again. If it's unavoidable, you might request the restructure of your loans to lighten up on the cash flow drain. If you have to go to that extreme, however, the lender will be very nervous.

Lenders walk a fine line in situations like these. If they overreact, by calling the loan or refusing to allow you room to maneuver, or if they're too intimately involved in your management decisions, they run the risk of a lender liability suit. Such a suit could result in a finding that the bank is actually an investor and not a lender, and it could lose priority over other lenders and investors. Expect the bank's handling of you to be very formal and by the book.

If lenders think you may not be able to pay them, they'll put their loan workout group to work, only you probably won't be told that directly.

❑ **Secret**

> You can read the writing on the wall if they tell you they're bringing out a new loan officer to meet you, and your old lender won't take your phone calls. This new lender will be much more in-your-face than your first lender, and you'll quickly sense a change in your relationship. The loan workout group might more appropriately be called the *loan get-out group,* because their job is really to get their money back any way they can.

Pessimism ought to drive your relationship with your lender at this point. Assume the worst possible outcome. The bank may demand full payment of your loan within 30 days or may take immediate steps to liquidate your collateral, starting with your house. Begin to devise strategies to deal with that outcome. If it does reach this point, lenders seldom change their mind. The best you can do is to buy time.

❑ **Secret**

> For example, if you have to find another lender, you'll need interim financial statements first. They will obviously take some time to prepare. It would be reasonable, if this it the case, to counter their 30 days with a request for 90 days. The point is, give them good reasons for the extension, and convince them that their risk will be no greater as a result of the delay.

If you disagree with their approach, or if they won't agree to yours, put everything in writing. At this point, you're probably teetering on the edge of voluntary or involuntary liquidation. Call in the best advisors you can find to help you understand the options. Plenty of businesses have made it through situations like these. Determine if yours is likely to be one of them, and then devise a plan and attack it with a vengeance.

SECTION THREE

FINDING MONEY FROM INVESTORS

If you have a bright idea you want to turn into a business, or you're running a fast-track company that needs cash, money from investors may be the way to go.

Some investors are known as angels and some are known as venture—sometimes *vulture*—capitalists. Before you set out on your search for money from investors, you need to understand how to separate the good ones from the bad ones, you need to know how they're going to evaluate your proposal, and you need to know what your options are when it comes to structuring a deal.

11 HOW INVESTORS EVALUATE CAPITAL REQUESTS

While investors, both private and institutional, are less formula-based than lenders, their decision-making process uses some of the same criteria. The lender's *Five C's of Credit* might be abbreviated to the investor's *Three C's of Credibility*, although you can be sure that their evaluation of your business will be, by no means, abbreviated—quite the contrary. Character will still be the most important issue, and the focus will be on *Are You a Winner?* Conditions will deal with *Can You Pull It Off?* And Capacity will be concerned with *Will It Be Worth It?*

CHARACTER AND COMMITMENT: ARE YOU A WINNER?

People who are going to risk their hard-earned money on your company will want to know, among other things:

- Who's running the show?
- What have you done in the past?
- Were you successful?
- How successful?
- Have you run both small and large ventures and managed rapid growth?
- What experience do you have in this field?
- What do other people think of you?
- Do you surround yourself with good people who complement your talents and expertise?

152

- Do you recognize your weaknesses and your strengths?
- Are you the kind of person who will stay with it through thick and thin?

Investors will be much more thorough than lenders in their evaluation of your character and the character of your existing investors. After all, they'll be betting big bucks that you and your team can pull this off.

Background Checks

Like lenders, investors hate surprises, so be up front about absolutely everything. Their *due diligence* process, as it's called, will include interviews with dozens of people including your friends, family, former employers and employees, business associates, former and current investors, bankers, credit bureaus, competitors, industry experts, existing and potential customers, and anyone else who they think might know something about you, your investors, your business, or your industry.

Investors are great networkers—they know everyone. If a CD-ROM proposal hits investor's desks, they might very well call friends who head the CD-ROM efforts at Microsoft to check out the idea. On an entertainment industry deal, investors might even call Steven Spielberg or George Lucas. Investors' contacts with lawyers, accountants, business owners, and other investors give them access to just about anyone they want to talk to, to find out just about whatever they want to know, about you and your business.

By the same token, don't be surprised, insulted, shocked, or appalled if investors check you, your team, and your current investors for criminal records, gambling excesses, substance abuse, marital discord, radical political or religious beliefs, and other iniquities. We weren't thrilled when we discovered that one entrepreneur's partner had an FBI record and a cocaine habit, but "he was better." We were even less thrilled that he tried to hide the fact by burying the relationship in a limited partnership. It was actually the SEC who blew the whistle, but only after we'd invested a fair amount of time (fortunately no money) in their deal.

Beyond how your problems reflect on you personally, investors also must consider how those problems reflect on them, and how they might affect a future public stock offering. The SEC and stock rating agencies look for spotless backgrounds from the people involved in public offerings.

While all of the snooping around by investors might seem like an invasion of your privacy, it can also be one of the best things to happen to your business. For one thing, it's essentially free market research that should prove what you're promising. And for another thing, calls to potential customers, suppliers, investors, and bankers can do wonders for your company's credibility:

> . . . *We're calling from MegaCapital Corporation because we're considering a substantial investment in XYZ Manufacturing. What can you tell us about them . . . ?*

Your job is to steer investors in the right direction during their due diligence efforts. Investors have very short attention spans and sometimes jump to conclusions about your business or industry. Prepare a list of experts who can corroborate your pitch, and give it to your prospective investors before they ask for it. This will show that you know what you're doing, and that you know what *they're* doing. Explain any competitive sensitivities, and warn them about any skeletons in your closet or any bad blood they might encounter. Then be ready to answer the questions that will undoubtedly arise.

A word of caution, investors are easily and quickly turned off by negative feedback from the street. Be absolutely sure that you know what people are saying about you and your business before you approach investors. Furthermore, be sure that potential investors are asking the right people the right questions when they make their calls. That is, make sure they clearly understand the business you're in. Later, talk to the people you've offered as references, and find out what was discussed. If there are areas of confusion or concern, make sure you address them promptly. You can be sure investors' interest will die quickly if, after the first few calls to your customers, suppliers, and others, they don't hear what you said they would. It could be they don't know what they're talking about, it could be your references don't, and it could be you don't. In any case, it's your problem!

Credit Investigations

Since investors receive their money back only after your creditors receive theirs, you can be sure investors will conduct credit checks on you, your existing investors, and your business. If you or your existing investors have been in financial trouble, they'll think twice about writing you a six- or seven-figure check. On the other hand, there's a good chance they'll be understanding if you've merely stretched the limits of personal finance (after all, what entrepreneur hasn't). But there *is* a limit. They'll also check for any liens and encumbrances just like lenders do, so make sure there are no surprises waiting for them.

When investors evaluate where they stand in the getting-paid line, they'll be interested in any historical debts, payables, or other claims against future earnings. Investors want the bulk of their money to be put to productive use. In turnaround situations, they may be willing to have their money used to pay off debts, but they'll look for a change in management and want to see clear solutions to whatever caused the company's problems.

❏ Secret

Experienced investors can be very helpful negotiating with historical creditors since they don't want their money absorbed by past problems. What's more, they probably have experience with other workout, turnaround, and bankruptcy situations, so they'll have a better handle on what's negotiable and what isn't.

Evaluation of Existing Investors

Many a willing investor has been scorched in the pursuit of a company whose existing investors won't play ball. So potential investors are very interested in who owns what now, who's agreed to what about raising new money, and whether existing investors are willing to be diluted (have their percentage ownership reduced) as a result of the new investment.

❏ Secret

Nothing will turn off a potential investor quicker than a business owner who opens the conversation complaining about existing investors. Asking to use new investors' funds to pay off existing investors doesn't play well either. If this is such a good deal, why would your old investors want out? Resolve any differences before you approach new investors, and remember that your new investors will be your old investors in the next round of fund-raising.

Music to an Investor's Ears

From people who know you: What do you think of the team?
- The most committed I ever met; they just never give up.
- I can't think of anyone I'd trust more with my money.
- If I had the money, I'd invest in a minute.
- I've seen 'em work 48 hours straight to get the job done.
- A spotless reputation.
- Never comes unglued. They just dig in their heels and handle whatever comes along.
- An uncanny ability to attract and keep good people.
- I've never seen anyone who inspires such loyalty and devotion.
- I'd work for them in a minute.
- Not afraid to admit weaknesses.

From market experts: What do you think about the market?
- If their gizmo works, the market will be theirs.
- The rest of the industry is years behind them.
- If they were a public company, I'd buy stock right now.
- If they pull it off, they'll be filling a real void in the marketplace.
- I agree with their projections; in fact I think they're conservative.

From your customers: What do you think of the company?
- They're the answer to my prayers.
- I only wish they could ship that new product today, we need it.
- I'll buy 10 times what I order now, if they can supply them.
- The product's great. Once we show headquarters how much money these are going to save us, we'll probably replace all of our existing ones with their model.
- We've already received approval for 1,000 of them in next year's budget.
- I've been bragging to all of my industry friends about them.
- I'd like to own a piece of that company.

From existing investors: What do you think of the company? Our investment?
- I've been with them since the beginning. They've always done what they said they were going to. I believe in them.
- They're the only company I've ever invested in that regularly completes its projects on time and under budget.
- I'm happy to see your investment. I don't mind owning a smaller piece of a larger pie.
- I don't always agree with their decisions, but they always prove me wrong.
- I'm happy to wait another three to seven years for this investment to pay off.
- If I was more liquid, I'd join you and invest more.
- I'll put more money into the company if they can raise another $$$$.

CONDITIONS: CAN YOU PULL IT OFF?

The business plan you present can make or break your deal. A good one will convince investors that the market and product are real, and that you're likely to grow the way you claim you can. A poor plan will leave investors with too many unanswered questions for them to want to bother gambling on your venture. Make sure the Executive Summary is clear, concise, and inviting or they'll never even look at the rest of your masterpiece.

You need to convince investors that:

- You have a huge market.
- You have a darn good plan for reaching that market.
- You understand the market in detail (which, did we say, is huge).
- You can create, sell, and deliver a product that meets the needs of the market in a cost-effective manner.
- You understand and can effectively beat out or ward off competitors.
- You can attract, hire, and retain the kind of people you need to make your business a success.
- You can establish, maintain, and—most important of all—grow an organization.
- You have adequately estimated your income, expenses, and cash flow needs.
- They can cash out in three to seven years and will have earned between 20 and 100 percent per year.

Your emphasis must be on market not product. A product, without an adoring public that's willing to plunk down big bucks (or lots of little bucks), is merely a black hole for investor's dollars. Business graveyards are littered with great products that were developed with an "if we build it, they will come" attitude. Investors look for big hits, and the only way you'll have a big hit is if lots of customers think your product is as marvelous as you do.

An outline for a business plan, the questions each section should address, and common business plan shortcomings are provided in Chapter 21.

CAPACITY: WILL IT BE WORTH IT?

Before investors decide to invest in your business, they'll want to know that the potential returns will be commensurate with the level of risk.

Like any investment, their returns will be based on three primary
considerations:

- Can they buy at the right price?
- Can they sell at the right price?
- Will the return worth the risk?

Of course, *this* investment isn't *like any investment* in one important respect: Your investor can't simply pick up the phone and say, "Sell." In investor's terms, what you're dealing with here are issues of *exit strategy*
and *valuation*.

While some of your investors' return may come from annual profits, most of what they make will come when your company has reached
a level where it can be sold or taken public. Before going into a deal,
they'll want to know that your plans and time frames for cashing out
match their own—usually three to seven years. So include an exit strategy as part of your financial projections. It's an essential, but often
omitted, part of a pitch to investors.

How much investors will make when they cash out will depend
largely on their equity, which will be determined based on how much
your company is worth when it's sold or taken public, and how much
they own at that time. The valuation of your company at the time investors enter the deal, the extent to which any subsequent equity contributions reduced their stake, and the valuation of your company when
it's sold will determine how much they make.

DEAL PRICING

12

The price you pay for debt capital (money from a lender) is determined by an interest percentage. The price you pay for equity capital (money from investors) is determined by the percentage of your company that you give up. The value you and your investors assign to your company will determine how much ownership you'll have to relinquish.

This isn't a trivial exercise. If you say your company's *premoney valuation* is $4 million, and you're trying to raise $1 million, you'll have to give up 20 percent ownership (($4MM + $1MM) ÷ $1MM). If instead you assign a premoney value of $3 million, you'll have to give up 25 percent (($3MM + $1MM) ÷ $1MM).

Business Equity Appraisal Reports (BEAR) is a San Carlos, California company specializing in valuations and valuation software for the professional and entrepreneurial community. According to Hans Schroeder, President of BEAR, three key issues weigh heavily on the valuation of an entrepreneurial company:

- Where the business is going and how big it will be when it gets there.
- How risky this investment is, relative to other investments.
- What price has been paid for similar companies.
- How and when investors will be able to cash in their chips.

But different investors will value your business differently. An investor who's investing for strategic reasons may have lower return expectations than someone who's investing with the hopes of getting rich on your success. Time-Warner put over $100 million into an interactive cable television system back in the 1980s without much hope of ever realizing a direct financial return. But the publicity it gained from the operation, and the promises the company could make based on the technology, helped it win cable franchises that will pay for the investment many times over.

A valuation expert will work through a variety of different methods to arrive at a fair and justifiable value for your company. These methods include an *income-based valuation* that places a value on your projected performance using a discounted cash flow formula; an *asset-based valuation* where the determination of value is based on the liquidation value of assets less liabilities; and a *market multiplier-based valuation* where some multiple is assigned to your projected income, net income, or other performance measure.

MARKET MULTIPLIER

While investors will ultimately use a combination of methods to value your company, the market multiplier approach is where they'll often start. Obviously, the multiplier chosen plays a critical role in the value assigned, so they usually base their multiple on financial information from comparable public companies or from recent sales of companies in your industry. Notice, we said that your multiple will be *based* on those of others. Since, right now, you're neither a public company or ready to be sold, don't expect investors to pay public company multiples for your stock. Instead, they'll apply a valuation discount to account for the following factors:

- Unproven business plan, management team, product, marketing strategy, and so forth.
- Absence of financing alternatives.
- Lack of control by the investor.
- Lack of liquidity, meaning that investors can't cash out whenever they like.

If publicly traded companies in businesses similar to yours are valued at 10 times net pretax income, then your projected net profit (in the year that the investor wants to exit) will probably be multiplied by something between 2 and 7 instead of 10.

CAP RATE

A variation on the multiplier approach is capitalization rate valuation. The *cap rate*, as it's called, is simply the inverse of the multiplier. A

Cap Rates and Multipliers for Various Investments		
Type Investment	Cap Rate (%)	Multiplier
Government T-bills	4	25.0
High-grade corporate bonds	8	12.5
Big public stocks	10	10.0
Junk bonds	15	6.7
Small public stocks	17	5.9
Midrange closely held companies	25	4.0
Small closely held companies	30	3.3
High-tech, start-up companies	50	2.0

Investors would apply these multiples to a company's projected pretax profit for the year they expect to cash out.

Source: Business Equity Appraisor Reports (BEAR)

multiplier of 10 would equal a cap rate of 10 percent (1 ÷ 10). That number can more easily be compared with the return an investor could receive on other investments. BEAR offers the following cap rates, and their corresponding multipliers, that characterize the risk of various investment options in 1994.

The level of risk assigned to your investment will obviously reduce the multiplier assigned to your projected earnings, and thus will reduce the value assigned to your company. Therefore, it's important to document and substantiate the assumptions behind your own estimate of your company's value.

Once your investors have a good feel for what the company is going to be worth when they're ready to cash out, they can calculate how much of your equity they need to earn what *they* consider a fair return.

THE INVESTOR'S SHARE

That leads us to the most commonly used approach to deal pricing: *How Much Do They Want to Make, So How Much Do They Need to Own?*

Let's assume your investors want a rate of return equivalent to 50 percent per year compounded annually, and let's assume they won't take any money out until your company is sold. For the sake of simplicity, let's also assume that a dollar will be worth the same in four years as it is now. Let's say you want to raise $250,000 for your company, and you have a solid plan to sell out to a competitor in four years.

The first thing you need to figure out is what a reasonable value for your company will be when you sell it. That takes us back to the multiplier approach to valuation. Let's assume that companies in your industry sell for 15 times after-tax profits, and you're projecting Year 4 profits of $1 million. Because your company is an early-stage venture, we'll discount the multiple to 5 instead of 15, so your company will be valued at $5 million. Obviously, if your plan and sell-off strategy aren't so solid, the multiple and value will be lower.

Next we need to know what the $250,000 you're trying to find will be worth in four years if it's compounded annually at 50 percent. A 50 percent return in Year 1 is 150 percent of $250,000 or $375,000. If you multiply by 1.5 again for Year 2, 3, and 4, you'll find it's just over $1.25 million. If you'd like a handy rule of thumb, remember that to earn a 50 percent return in four years, your investment will need to be worth just over five times what it's worth now. Exhibit 12.1 shows the multiple that's required to produce a particular return in a given period.

Now for the punch line—the point to the whole story—what this means is that before they hand over $250,000, you're going to have to part with just over 25 percent of your company so they'll receive the $1.25 million they want when you sell it in four years for $5 million.

As Exhibit 12.2 demonstrates, if your investors have a lower expected return rate, you'll be able to keep more of your company.

Naturally you'd like to keep as much of your company as possible, but you *will* have to give up something in exchange for your investors' money. If your valuation suggests that your company will be worth $5 million, and you only offer investors 10 percent ownership for their $250,000, they simply won't give you the money because you're actually

EXHIBIT 12.1   Return on Investment Multiples

A) If your investor wants a return of:	20%	30%	40%	50%
B) And they want to cash out in year:	C) They'll need their original investment to grow by the following multiple by the end of the period			
3	1.7	2.2	2.7	3.4
4	2.1	2.9	3.8	5.1
5	2.5	3.7	5.4	7.6
6	3	4.8	7.5	11.4
7	3.6	6.3	10.5	17.1

To earn a 50% return on investment, and cash out in four years, investors' money will have to grow by 5.1 times during the period.

EXHIBIT 12.2 Equity Calculation Based on Investors' Expected Return ($000)

Return	Investment	Yr1	Yr2	Yr3	Yr4	Sale Value	Equity
20%	$250	$300	$360	$432	$518	$5,000	10.37%
30%	$250	$325	$423	$549	$714	$5,000	14.28%
40%	$250	$350	$490	$686	$960	$5,000	19.21%
50%	$250	$375	$563	$844	$1,266	$5,000	25.31%
60%	$250	$400	$640	$1,024	$1,638	$5,000	32.77%

Value of $250,000 in 4 years + company sale value of $5 million = 25.31% ownership

offering them less than a 20 percent return. If that's all the return they're going to receive, they could probably find it in a comparatively safer investment.

An important issue we didn't include in the preceding example is the extent to which subsequent rounds of equity will diminish or *dilute* early investors' ownership. If, for example, you're likely to have to give up another 20 percent ownership in the next round, initial investors will want 20 percent more, or a total of 30.4 percent (25.3% × 1.2 = 30.4) in this round. Otherwise, your first investors will only own 20.2 percent (25.3% − (20% × 25.3)) after the next financing rather than the 25.3 percent they calculated they'd require to earn a 50 percent return. If they accept the dilution of their ownership, their investment will only be worth $1,010,000 (20.2 percent of the $5 million sale price) versus $1,266,000 after four years—a difference of $256,000.

While you'll want to establish a fair value for your company in your earliest contact with a potential investor, how much equity you eventually give up will be something you negotiate as part of the deal. Just remember, if you start out unrealistically high, investors won't bother to look at your plan. In the end, the best approach is to come up with your own numbers based on the suggestions provided in this chapter, and then test your sanity and assumptions with a variety of investors and advisors.

13

STRUCTURING EQUITY

Besides offering potential investors the return they want, you'll also have to come up with a way of structuring their investment that meets your company's needs, their needs, and your own personal needs. Investment structures are as unique as the individuals and organizations investing in them, so we'll focus on the basic structures, but understand that there's lots of room for negotiation and creative arrangements. Unlike loans, investment deals rarely go the same way twice. But first a word from the lawyers.

STAYING OUT OF TROUBLE

Offering equity in your company is tricky business. If you don't play by the rules set down by federal and state securities authorities, you can find yourself in a heap of trouble. Therefore, the professionals you choose to help you in the effort must be well versed in the intricacies of the relevant laws and their practical applications.

First, you need to understand what constitutes an offering of securities. While the answer might seem obvious, it sometimes isn't. Basically, any offer of an interest in your company, in exchange for something of value from an investor (usually, but not always, cash) could be construed as a sale of securities. In some states, an interest in your company might be broadly interpreted as any potential for participation in the success of your company. Offering an ownership interest in exchange for an investor's guarantee of your debt, accepting a loan from an investor that offers future rights to ownership, and even creating certain profit-sharing or royalty arrangements could be construed as an offering of securities.

164

Advice for Avoiding Securities Law Problems

- Do not advertise, peddle, beseech, urge, implore, influence, solicit, entice, suggest, beg, promise, imply, insinuate, hint, or otherwise offer an interest in your company before you're sure that you've complied with all federal and state securities laws.

- Do not accept any money, or anything of value, from anyone in exchange for anything that could be construed as an interest in your company before you're sure that you've complied with all federal and state securities laws.

- Do not lie, fib, misrepresent, or exaggerate any facet of your business or the proposed investment. In fact, you'd be much safer to overemphasize the potential risks inherent in the deal. Sophisticated investors will understand and be able to read past the negative stuff.

- Regardless of the disclosure rules, be sure to supply investors with sufficient information for them to make an informed decision about an investment in your company.

- Be sure to document any qualifications (such as the accredited investor and sophisticated investor criteria) that are required under the securities law exemptions that you're using.

- Be sure your investors understand and comply with the resale of securities restrictions that may apply as a result of the exemptions you're using.

- Be sure to consider the potential implications of any sales that are made prior to or near the same time of any exempt offering.

- Be sure to obtain legal advice from an attorney who has experience in the kind of offering you're undertaking.

- Do not advertise, peddle, beseech, urge, implore, influence, solicit, entice, suggest, beg, promise, imply, insinuate, hint, or otherwise offer an interest in your company before you're sure that you've complied with all federal and state securities laws. *Yes, this is a repeat! Take a hint!*

Your best bet for staying out of hot water with both the securities sheriff and your investors is to move very carefully if there's even the remotest chance that what you're doing could be construed as offering an interest in your company. Even if you succeed, a wrong move now can come back to haunt you when you go to raise new money. One investor we know, in a misguided attempt to avoid a loss, sold his stock in a company in violation of securities laws. Aside from the fact that the transfer was illegal, the unfortunate purchaser holds not stock but a time bomb if the company ever wants to find new money. And the company could actually be in trouble as well because it is supposed to police the resale of securities.

Consider the advice on page 165 from Tom DeFilipps, partner with the Silicon Valley law firm of Wilson, Sonsini, Goodrich & Rosati based on their extensive experience with both private placements and public offerings.

SELLING STOCK

If you try to sell stock to the public, you'll jump through all kinds of hoops with the federal Securities and Exchange Commission (SEC) as well as affected state security authorities. You'll prepare piles of paperwork, have them endlessly reviewed by attorneys and accountants, and then the whole thing has to be approved and blessed by federal and state securities offices. If the market hasn't gone sour during the six months or so that you're putting the offer together, you'll finally find out if anyone's interested in buying your stock. By the time you reach that point, you'll probably have spent at least $500,000, and often a lot more. As a result, few small companies opt for going public as a way to raise money.

PRIVATE PLACEMENTS—EXEMPT OFFERINGS

Fortunately, if you intend to raise a relatively small amount of money, from a relatively small number of investors, you can use one of the exemptions from federal and state securities law. These exemptions allow you to do what's called a *private placement* and thereby short-circuit the complex process of going public. In any case, you'll use an *offering circular* or *private placement memorandum* to describe your deal.

A typical private placement memorandum will contain the following sections. (See box at top of page 167.)

Contrary to what you might expect, your private placement memorandum won't paint a glowing picture of your company. On the contrary, it will be filled with warnings, in bold capital letters, about the risks inherent in investing in your company. (See box on page 168.)

The Company
Risk Factors
Business and Properties
Offering Price Factors
Use of Proceeds
Capitalization
Description of Securities
Plan of Distribution
Dividends, Distributions, and Redemptions
Officers and Key Personnel of the Company
Directors of the Company
Principal Stockholders
Management Relationships, Transactions, and Remuneration
Litigation
Federal Tax Aspects
Miscellaneous Factors
Financial Statements
Management's Discussion and Analysis of Certain Relevant Factors

Chances are, when you're through reading your own private placement memorandum, even you may wonder why you have money invested in the company. On the other hand, if you do make the offer correctly, no one will ever accuse you of misrepresenting the opportunity.

Exemptions

A variety of exemptions are available with certain compliance requirements for funding limits, investor qualifications, disclosure, marketing, number of investors, and so forth.

Regulation D, Rule 504 Also known as the Small Business Exemption Rule, Reg. D, Rule 504, is intended to make it easier for qualifying small businesses to raise up to $1 million in a 12-month period

---

Sample Private Placement
Memorandum Disclaimers

... INVESTMENT IN THIS BUSINESS INVOLVES A HIGH DEGREE OF RISK, AND INVESTORS SHOULD NOT INVEST ANY FUNDS IN THIS OFFERING UNLESS THEY CAN AFFORD TO LOSE THEIR ENTIRE INVESTMENT ...

... THIS COMPANY DOES NOT HAVE THE CAPITAL THAT IT NEEDS TO ACHIEVE ITS PROJECTIONS, NOR DOES IT HAVE ANY FIRM COMMITMENTS OR ANY REASON TO BELIEVE THAT SUCH COMMITMENTS WILL BE FORTHCOMING ...

... RETURNS SUGGESTED IN THIS INVESTMENT ARE PREDICATED ON THE ABILITY TO LIQUIDATE INVESTORS' INTERESTS AT THE END OF FIVE YEARS AT A DESIGNATED LEVEL OF RETURN THAT CANNOT BE ASSURED ...

---

from an unlimited number of investors. Offerings under Rule 504 *may* be marketed by means of a general solicitation or general advertising, unlike some other types of exempt offerings.

Rule 504 does not stipulate any specific information that must be disclosed to investors, but if you want to avoid a lawsuit you'd better pay attention to the full disclosure rules that exist under the antifraud provisions of federal securities laws.

Unlike some other exceptions, investors may be allowed to resell their Rule 504 investments provided that they meet certain criteria. While the offering doesn't have to be registered with the SEC, you do have to notify the Commission within 15 days of your first sale of securities under this rule.

Regulation D, Rule 505   Rule 505 allows you to raise $5 million in a 12-month period and is sometimes referred to as the $5 million exemption rule. An unlimited number of *investors* (defined in Exhibit 13.1) and up to 35 *nonaccredited* investors may be involved.

Offerings made under this rule need to comply with certain disclosure rules, and companies should be careful to make all information that's been disclosed to accredited investors available to nonaccredited investors as well.

EXHIBIT 13.1 Definitions of Accredited Investors

An accredited investor is defined by federal securities regulations as:

- Institutional Investors (banks, brokers, dealers, insurance companies, pension funds, etc.) with total assets in excess of $5 million.
- Private business development companies.
- Tax exempt 501(c)3 organizations with total assets in excess of $5 million.
- Certain insiders such as directors, executive officers, and general partners (who do not have to meet the next two criteria below).
- Any person whose individual income exceeds $200,000 in each of the two most recent years (or joint income, with spouse, in excess of $300,000) and has a reasonable expectation for reaching the same level this year as well. Such investors must provide some evidence (as dictated by the SEC) of such status.
- Any person whose individual net worth (or joint with spouse) exceeds $1 million at the time of purchase.
- Any trust, with total assets in excess of $5 million, not formed for the specific purpose of acquiring the securities offered, whose purchase is directed by a sophisticated person.
- An entity in which all the equity owners are accredited investors.

Investors are not allowed to sell their equity for at least two years, and the offering *cannot* be made by means of general solicitation or general advertising. Like a Rule 504 filing, the offering does not have to be registered with the SEC, but you do have to notify the Commission within 15 days of your first sale of securities under this rule.

Regulation D, Rule 506 Rule 506 is similar to Rule 505 except that it allows you to raise an unlimited sum from up to 35 nonaccredited investors and an unlimited number of accredited investors with the proviso that all investors are *sophisticated*. The SEC defines a sophisticated investor as one with sufficient knowledge and experience in financial and business matters to render the investor capable of evaluating the merits and risks of the prospective investment. Companies raising money under this rule ought to prepare a questionnaire to be filled out by investors to prove that they meet the *sophisticated* criteria. The balance of the Rule 506 is similar to Rule 505.

Intrastate Offerings

Securities that are offered and/or sold only in the state where your company is both incorporated and conducting a significant portion of its business may be exempt from federal securities laws so long as the securities sold will remain in that state. Naturally, such offerings have to abide by your state's securities laws.

STATE SECURITIES LAWS

State securities laws differ from those of the SEC. Just because your offering complies with federal regulations doesn't mean it will meet your state's criteria. State securities laws are known as *Blue Sky Laws*. The Uniform Securities Act, which has been adopted by 75 percent of the states, attempts to synchronize and simplify the redundancy in the federal and state processes, but substantial differences remain.

Some state securities laws take the federal review process one step further. Federal regulators focus on making sure that all appropriate information is disclosed. They don't pass judgment on the underlying offer. On the other hand, some states, called merit states, may prohibit an offering if they do not believe that it is "fair, just, and equitable" regardless of whether or not the offer has been approved by the SEC.

❑ Secret

No matter whether you're in compliance with federal securities laws, you need to be sure that your offer or sale of securities meets the regulations of your state, and any other state where the securities will be offered. Notice we're saying *offered.* At the time of this writing, 9 states require that the private placement memorandum be registered or reviewed prior to its distribution or any *offer* of securities, 15 states require notice or registration *prior to any sale* of securities, 21 states require notice *after the sale* of securities, and 6 states don't require any filings. In addition, most states offer a variety of exemptions when selling to *institutional investors* (such as venture capital funds or banks) but each state defines that group a little differently.

Types of Investments

Convertible Senior Debt or Subordinated Debt

One approach to encouraging investors to invest is to promise them stock at a discount later, if they'll give you the money now. It's something like Wimpy, the comic strip character's, "I'll gladly pay you Tuesday for a hamburger today." The idea is that if investors will loan you money, as an inducement, you give them options or warrants for the purchase of common stock at some future date at a fixed or formula price, often at some discount over the then market value. You can structure convertible debt like any other form of debt (secured or unsecured, with high or low rates of interest and fees, deferred or currently paid interest, with a short or long term, etc.) so that investors can enjoy the best of both worlds. This is a popular mechanism with private investors.

Like lenders, investors with convertible debt are entitled to payment before stockholders in the event of liquidation, they can have steady cash flow from interest payments, and if your company is successful (or if they want to exert more control), they can convert to equity. Often convertible debt can be subordinated to conventional lenders (if the company is ever liquidated, the subordinated debt holders will be paid after other lenders), which will give your company additional borrowing capacity. As we saw earlier, lenders will usually consider subordinated debt as equity in their all important debt-to-worth calculations. The convertible debt approach is commonly used by SBICs, SSBICs and later stage investors.

Convertible Preferred Stock

Commonly used by venture capital funds, convertible preferred stock is another approach that gives investors preference over common stock holders as an inducement to invest. Such rights include the right to convert to common stock, priority in dividend payments, special voting rights, and rights to assets in the event of liquidation or business transfer. Preferred stock may or may not carry a dividend. As with convertible debt structures, the conversion feature allows investors to participate in the upside when your business is successful by allowing conversion to common stock. Convertible preferred stockholders usually receive voting rights equal to common stockholders allowing them to exert control if they need to.

Common Stock

If the company is ever liquidated, common stock owners are paid after all other creditors and investors. Therefore, sophisticated individual investors or institutional investors do not favor common stock since it offers no special rights or privileges. However, if your company is structured as a regular corporation rather than an S corporation, various classes of common stock can be created to provide certain groups of common stockholders with rights that other common stock owners may not have. S corporations may not establish different classes of stock.

14

TERMS AND CONDITIONS

The investment structure for your deal will be laid out in the closing documents. Negotiating closing documents is rarely pleasant. It's not uncommon for the whole deal to unravel at the point where pen meets paper, because this will be your first realization that you're going to be controlled. If you're like most entrepreneurs, you won't like it; unfortunately, investors tend to be control freaks as well. If you can picture two rams bashing heads on the top of a hill, you have the right image. If you find yourself in this position, let your lawyers fight it out so you won't have to worry about saying things you'll regret later. Trust us, it *will* be a memorable process.

Management rights and responsibilities, future financings, and the all-important issue of control are some of the critical issues you'll be dealing with.

MANAGEMENT

As the business owner, you want to be sure that you'll have a job at your own company in the future. You'll want to preserve your right to make you own decisions, and do things your own way. Fact is, professional investors don't want to have to run your company—there's no money in it, and it takes them away from more productive pursuits. On the other hand, your investors want to be sure they can relieve you of your duties if what you're doing isn't working the way you promised it would.

Both you and your investors will want to be sure that certain key people are compensated fairly and stay with your company (or leave if they're not performing), but you may have different criteria for performance. Take your buddy Paul who's been with you through thick and thin; he has a keen mind and a dogged work ethic, and he has been the brilliant creative member of your team. What if your investors decide you no longer need his creativity?

Other little things like salaries and bonuses and who sets them, performance measures, the opportunity for you to earn back equity through performance, causes for termination and related termination packages, and a variety of other issues may also be negotiated at this time, and are sure to create a few tense moments.

FUTURE FINANCINGS

When you're putting a deal together, you'll want to know that investors won't unreasonably delay or prevent future financings. On the other hand, your investors will want to know that their ownership interests won't be unreasonably diminished by future investors. Often they'll want a right-of-first-refusal on future financings or the right to maintain their original percentage ownership after the next round of financing. Your agreements will include appropriate clauses to address these concerns. Such issues can create havoc in a deal closing if the concepts aren't discussed early in the negotiating process. Mistakes can be very costly later when it's time to raise additional funds or share ownership with key employees, so make sure you have experienced help working out these important details.

For example, if when you go to raise more money, you learn by reading the fine print in your shareholder agreements that existing investors can keep their original percentage ownership in the event of new financings, *your* ownership will have to go down to make room for the new investors. Your investment paperwork must anticipate additional investments in future years.

CONTROLS

Unresolved issues over control will drive you crazy later. At the extreme, imagine having to negotiate with your entire board of directors every time you want to pay a bill, sign a lease, or hire a secretary.

Your closing documents will address issues like the number of board seats your investors will hold, how decisions will be made about borrowing money, selling equity, mergers or acquisitions, and reporting requirements. When it comes to control, most entrepreneurs are reluctant to become a minority stockholder. But, in fact, Venture One's research shows that by the second, and certainly by the third, round of financing, the vast majority of entrepreneurs own less than 50 percent of their company. Actually, the typical scenario at the time of an initial public offering is an 80/10/10 split among venture fund, management team, and founder.[1]

❏ **Secret**

> Equity and percentage of ownership are not what control is all about. Board seats and the terms and conditions of your deal will dictate more about who controls what than ownership percentages.

Keep in mind that conditions set in a company's first round of financing establish an important precedent for later rounds since new investors will rarely accept a deal with terms and conditions that are any less favorable than the first round. Complicated deals, with lots of ambiguous rights to future stock will only frustrate a company's negotiations with later investors. It's important, therefore, to keep the first round as simple as possible, and to establish terms and conditions that will neither discourage later rounds nor penalize early investors (that includes you, by the way).

FINDING INVESTORS

15

Your investors, their investment history, their experience in your field or with companies in your stage of growth, what role they want to play, their risk/reward appetite, how and when they want to cash out, their personalities, how you're going to work together, and whether you just plain like them will all be factors in your eventual success or failure.

CHOOSING THE RIGHT INVESTORS

When someone invests in your business, you might as well exchange rings because you're going to be together for better and especially for worse. By comparison, divorce from a private investor can make a marital breakup look like a picnic in the park. And if you do actually manage to break the relationship, you'll wear a scarlet letter for years that will send potential investors scurrying for the safety of their mutual funds. Consider the following issues when you're evaluating a potential investor.

History

Obtain a comprehensive list of the CEOs of firms in which they've invested—if they won't give you one, you've learned all you need to know. And find at least one founder whose business wasn't a shining success; after all, anyone can be easy to work with when you're making the person rich. Ask the not-so-successful CEO the following questions:

- Have the investors been of any assistance beyond their money?
- How have they reacted to setbacks and disappointments?

- If you had to do it over and had choices, would you want them as investors again?

The word on troublesome investors finds its way to the street quickly. Talk to the lawyers, financial consultants, investment bankers, accountants, and lenders for the leading growth companies about your potential investors.

Experience

Determine whether your prospective investors really understand your business or industry. You want investors who can hit the street running with you. You want investors who complement your own talents and experience. You don't want investors who need constant instructions about the most basic elements of your business; or worse yet, ones you'll have to fight every step of the way. Investors who don't understand your business will be easily spooked by unfamiliar problems. Worse yet, they may try to force you to use solutions that worked in their (unrelated) business.

You'll also want to be sure your investors have experience running or investing in businesses in your stage of growth. The disciplines required to position a start-up for significant growth are vastly different from those required by a later stage company that's positioning itself to be sold. Investors' attitudes will be biased by their experience. If they are used to running, say, an old industrial company, they will be concerned with financial consistency and steady growth in profits. The concept of plunking down big advertising bucks to buy market share for a software company will be unfamiliar and abhorrent to them.

❑ Secret

You know you're in for trouble if you ask prospective investors why they're interested in your venture and they say they want to diversify their portfolio with something a little different so they can learn about a new industry. Wrong!

Life Cycle

You need to understand where your investors are in their investment or fund life cycle. An individual or company that's already invested most of its capital will be less aggressive than one with a new source of money. Venture funds, in fact, will stop investing when they are less than fully committed so they'll have additional money for later rounds of financing for their existing portfolio companies.

You also need to consider the point where your investors are in *their* life cycle. One group of investors we've worked with entirely comprises men in their 70s. A 10-year payback strategy won't excite them much. In fact, investors in that particular group want to see deals structured with regular payments of interest or dividends, and they want to be able to cash out in two to three years.

Role

Find out whether your potential investors intend to be passive investors or active investors in your business. If they have the skills, background, and contacts your business needs, you may want them to play an active role in the business. But what if they're busy with another company that isn't performing, and you've counted on their help? Or what about the investor who's just rich and lonely, and now wants to spend all his time at your office? Or how about the investors you counted on to be passive, but who, at the sign of the first glitch, are in your face with all kinds of advice and war stories about how they used to do things back in the 1930s? Suddenly, you'll be spending all your time managing the investors, and none managing the problem or your company.

Risk Appetite

Make sure your investors understand the business risks and time frames for returns, and that you agree on them. If your business is going to take three years to turn a profit, you'd better be sure that they aren't expecting to pay off this month's Gold Card with their portion of your profits.

The best measure of investors' risk appetites is what they've been involved in before. If they've had the same nice safe job for 30 years, have 2.5 children, and until now have only invested in instruments that are backed by the full faith, credit, and printing press of the U.S. government, what do you think their reaction will be to your first business hiccup?

Exit Strategy

Make sure your investors agree with you (and each other) on an exit strategy. Especially make sure you agree on how and when they're going to take their money out. Typical exit strategies include selling the business or their equity in it, or a public offering. Another approach, seldom available from venture capital firms, but sometimes possible with private investors is a an owner buyback at some preset price or based on some formula. Be sure that their time frame for getting out matches (a) your own and (b) reality. For that matter, make sure (a) and (b) match too!

RULES OF ENGAGEMENT

Clearly delineate the rules of the game. And remember, you may be new at this, but your investors probably aren't. Who's going to run your company? How will decisions be made? How often will you meet? What information will you present at those meetings? What authority will you (and won't you) have making decisions about hiring, setting salaries, firing, borrowing money, spending money, reinvesting profits, strategic direction, and so forth? What targets are you expected to meet, and what will happen if you miss those targets? What will happen if additional capital is needed later? Are your investors willing and able to invest additional funds at the next stage of growth? How much ownership will they acquire for their investment now and at later dates if additional financing is needed? How are they going to feel if new investors dilute their ownership?

☐ **Secret**

Finally, and here's a secret you want to pay close attention to, decide whether you like your investors. That's right, if at the first meeting the chemistry is wrong and by the second or third meeting you're convinced they're jerks, don't—repeat—*don't* take their money! Arranged marriages may work in some cultures, but the entrepreneurial community isn't one of them. Even if you haven't had the money to pay bills for months, even if they're promising the equivalent of back pay and start-up expenses in exchange for reasonable equity, *don't do it.* Your business will never succeed if you're miserable because of the relationship with your investors. As numbers-oriented as a business may be, there is still a very human side to it that your heart is better at evaluating than your brain.

COMPATIBILITY

Investors will invest their money when they're comfortable with you and your team. You should feel the same way about them. You should *at least* feel, "I could work with these people," or better yet "I would enjoy and benefit from having them as partners."

You're about to embark on a long journey with your investors, and it will inevitably include some rough roads. You'll have the best chance of surviving if the partners you choose have the character, experience, and inclination to help along the way.

❑ **Secret**

If your company is good enough to attract investors, it's good enough to attract the *right* investors. Remember, money is a commodity.

16 WHY DO INVESTORS INVEST?

No two investors are alike in their interests, likes, dislikes, wants, and needs. In fact, there are some distinct differences between various types of investors. Here are some insights into the nature of private investors, other companies, institutional venture capital, SBICs, and corporate venture capital.

PRIVATE INVESTORS OR ANGELS

Finding money from angels is very different than finding money from professional venture capitalists. Angels look for a product, service, company, or entrepreneur with whom they can identify. They'll invest because your deal tickles their fancy, and because they enjoy vicarious entrepreneurship. Many are genuinely looking to "do good" by bringing their capital and experience to the aid of a fledgling business.

One private investor explains why he invests in small businesses, "I have no control over the stock market, and I don't know diddly about real estate. What I do know is how businesses operate, what they need, and what makes them successful. If, by getting involved as a minority investor and mentor I can help one in three of the businesses that I invest in become a big hit, then I stand to see a substantial return."

Private investors' analyses of a potential investment will seem to be based more on gut feel, entrepreneurial instincts, and their own business savvy than formulas and technical reports. This is not to say that they're naive or impulsive. Since most have been self-employed at some point in their life and may have run a company very much like yours, they can quickly sniff out problems in your plans. Most are genuinely street smart—which is probably how they earned enough money to be an angel in the first place.

Private investors can usually move more quickly than institutional types, sometimes (although rarely) committing to deals in a matter of hours. Angel money can be structured as friendly or patient debt (meaning debt that doesn't require regular payment of principal or interest), more formal debt, loan guarantees, pledges of collateral, royalty or profit-sharing arrangements, limited partnerships, straight equity, debt with an option for equity, convertible debt, or any number of combinations. Among professional investors, debt or subordinated debt with an option for equity is most common.

Successful Relationships with Private Investors

David Gerhardt, executive director of the Capital Network, a Texas-based computer matching service for entrepreneurs and investors, offers these tips for building successful relationships with private investors:

1. Your investors are your partners—be sure you share a common vision.

2. Hire the best advisors, ones who are experienced in the kind of deals you're trying to do.

3. Remember, you're giving investors an opportunity to make money and you should approach them on that basis.

4. Don't forget to allow room for future investment.

5. Preserve your cash at all costs.

6. Don't try to raise money when you're desperate.

7. Don't come to investors with an ironclad investment structure. Be flexible.

Structuring Private Investor Deals

To negotiate and structure deals with private investors, you need to understand what makes them tick. Why are they in the deal? Are they out to do good? Do they want to earn big returns? Are they really turned on by your industry, product, or company? Are they lonely? Are they sharks waiting for you to make a mistake so they can own your company? Are they taken by the allure of entrepreneurship? Are they truly angels, with all of the knowledge and talent you need to help make it big? Before you negotiate deals with private investors, be sure you understand their motives.

When it comes time to close a deal, make sure the structure of your deal matches your investors' needs. Don't limit yourself to the run-of-the-mill money-for-equity approach; almost anything goes. Here are a few examples of what we mean.

Pledge of a Certificate of Deposit

An investor pledged his $100,000 certificate of deposit (CD), which was only earning 5%, as collateral on a bank loan for a franchise start-up. The owner of the start-up made principal and interest payments on the loan, plus paid the investor another 1% per month on the $100,000. To mitigate the investor's risk of losing his CD in a loan default, the business owner pledged all of the company stock to the investor. That way, if the business owner defaulted, the investor could take over the business to try to recover his loss.

The investor, in effect, increased his return on the CD to 17% (the 5% he got from the bank, plus 12% per year from the business owner) in exchange for his risk. The business owner was paying a high rate on the loan (equal to the bank's rate plus 12%), but he got the money he needed to start up. Two years later, the company was established, had collateral of its own, and the lender released the CD.

Purchase on Behalf of Company/Assignment of Receipts

A small manufacturer of women's clothing could not afford to put up the $50,000 that was needed to purchase imported silk for next year's sales. The company had an excellent reputation with its buyers, and had advance orders for the finished products. A retired retailer, who was familiar with the manufacturer's reputation, purchased the goods and established a contract manufacturing relationship with the manufacturer.

When the clothing was sold, the manufacturer sent bills using a return address that belonged to the investor. As payments were received, the investor reimbursed himself the $50,000 plus 12% interest (at a time when CD's were paying 4.5%), and he also received 3% of the gross sales of $100,000 which came to $3,000 for a total of $9,000 or a return of 18%.

Letter of Credit and Goods for Funds

One angel, a wine connoisseur, provided a $75,000 standby letter of credit (L/C) to help a vineyard acquire financing to bottle the season's wine. The collateral consisted of aged wine as well as grapes still on the vine. The standby letter of credit was never drawn because the vineyard was able to repay the loan on its own from the sale of its wine.

The investor received $7,500 for the use of the L/C which was only outstanding for six months (a return of 20% less the 1% cost of the L/C). In addition, the investor received 12 cases of custom-labeled wine.

Limited Partnership

A computer game company with a strong sales record established limited partnerships to fund its games for the holiday market. Each game required a marketing budget of about $50,000. Historically, the company grossed about $200,000 on each game. Limited partners contributed $10,000 each and were repaid six months later with the proceeds of game sales. In addition, limited partners earned 5% of gross sales, which totaled $200,000 for a return of $10,000 in six months or the equivalent of 40% per year.

Senior Debt Plus Equity with Earnback

A software company needed $250,000 to launch its latest product. A group of three investors came up with the funds in the form of senior debt plus a 49% equity stake. If the company was able to pay back the debt by the end of the first year along with 15% interest (at a time when CDs were paying 6%), the investors would give back 40% of the equity. If it wasn't repaid until the end of two years, the investors would only give back 20%. And if it wasn't repaid at the end of three years, the investors would give back nothing, earn another 2% equity, and thus control the company. The investors also required a pledge of all company assets and the personal guarantee of the owner. They were willing to release their collateral, if need be, to allow the company to secure a loan that would pay them off. No provision was made for partial repayment.

INVESTMENT BY OTHER COMPANIES

When planning for the growth of your company, don't overlook the possibility of teaming up with suppliers, customers, and even competitors. Relationships with other companies may take a variety of forms:

- Joint ventures, where together you form a third entity.
- Strategic alliances, where one company contributes capital or resources to another.
- Business combinations, where you buy them, they buy you, or you merge.
- Product or division spin-offs, where one company buys part of the other, and usually retains some equity or interest in future results.
- Access to equipment, facilities, and human resources (particularly during slack time).
- Loan guarantees or other credit enhancements.
- Joint borrowing relationships where collateral-rich but cash-flow poor companies approach lenders with their collateral/cash-flow "opposites" to obtain more favorable banking terms.
- Co-op advertising, sales, distribution, customer support, equipment maintenance.
- License of intellectual property.
- Sale of limited geographic rights or foreign rights.
- Cross-manufacturing agreements.
- Cross-licensing agreements.
- Cross-distribution agreements.
- Joint marketing agreements.

Strategic alliances, particularly of high-tech companies have recently been splashed all over the headlines of newspaper business sections. But if you read carefully, you'll also see articles on recriminations, disappointments, and the dissolution of strategic alliances too. What happens is the partners often can't move past their self-interest. Good intentions based on profits, shared technology, and investment break down when it comes to execution and definable measures for success of the collaboration. The opportunity for true collaboration and mutual benefit *is* possible, but it must be based on a clear understanding of everyone's interests, expectations, and measures for success.

INSTITUTIONAL VENTURE CAPITAL

The institutional venture capital community comprises a variety of players including funds managed by venture capital partnerships, corporate venture capital, investment bankers, and the Small Business Investment Corps (SBIC). The interests and motivations of each group differ depending on their source of funding. As with private investors, it's important to understand the motivations of those you choose to pursue. This understanding will not only help you determine which funds to approach, but it will also help you tailor your business plan, valuation, and negotiating strategy.

Venture Capital Partnerships

Private partnerships represent the bulk of the venture capital community. Typically, a handful of partners manage between $100 and $200 million of invested funds, although some funds grow as large a billion dollars. The partners in these funds act as investment managers for the money they've raised from pension funds, corporations, foreign investors, insurance companies, trust funds, foundations, and wealthy individuals.

Industry Preferences   Most venture firms develop strong preferences for a certain industry, technology, location, life stage of the company in which they invest, and size of their investment. It is critical for you to find a match between your deal and the interests of the firms you pursue.

The investment interests of the venture community change with the times. In the 1980s and even the early 1990s, most venture firms would have turned their noses up at entertainment deals, but by the mid-1990s CD-ROM, multimedia entertainment, and interactive television were the talk of the industry.

Still, venture firms tend to specialize in or focus on certain types of deals such as computer hardware, software, telecommunications, biotechnology, health care, pharmaceuticals, electronics, environmental products and services, retailing, consumer products and services, media, and even environmentally and socially responsible projects. While few firms specialize in just one type of investing, specialty funds are particularly prevalent in health care, biotechnology, consumer products, and retailing.

In addition to a firm's specialties, the partners also tend to specialize in, or at least favor, certain types of deals. Before you send your business plan to a venture firm, be sure to research whether or not it is interested in deals of your type, and especially which partner(s) review deals like yours. One partner might be rich in health-care industry experience, while another might specialize in software. If the health-care specialist receives your software deal, it *might* be passed along to the right partner, but there's an equally good chance it won't. The same goes for the personal interests of the partners. If your deal has something to do with bicycles, and one of the partners happens to be a tri-athlete, it sure wouldn't hurt to make sure your plan hits that partner's desk.

We happen to think the best source for targeting venture firms, and even individual partners whose interests match your own, is another book we're writing *The Complete Guide to Venture Capital*,[1] available from John Wiley & Sons in both book and electronic form.

Life-Stage Preferences   Venture firms tend to invest in *rounds* of financing that match the company's growth needs. Sometimes early investors may commit to multiple rounds when, and if, certain benchmarks are met. Funds are generally added at the following stages of a company's life:

- Early Stage

   Seed Stage. Earliest and riskiest stage of funding. At this stage, the business may not have even been established. Funds are often needed for feasibility analysis, market testing, early product development, and business formation.

   Start-up Stage. Funds are typically needed to build an organization and continue product development.

   First Stage. Organization is in place, funds needed for manufacturing and marketing.

- Later Stage

   Second Stage. Company is fully operational, products are being shipped, but funds are needed to expand into high-growth mode. The company may or may not have made a profit at this stage.

   Third Stage. Funds are needed to support major expansion of manufacturing and marketing, or for new product development. The company is breakeven or making a profit.

- Other Stages

   Venture financing is also available for turnaround situations, management buyouts, strategic acquisitions, mezzanine funding needed prior to going public, or bridge financing for buyouts.

Vulture Capitalists   Venture capitalists are an interesting group of people. Some would describe them, and some would even describe themselves, as brilliant business people . . . and to be fair, most are. But others describe venture capitalists with words like arrogant and egotistical, or even call them predatory *vulture capitalists*. And to be fair, many are that too.

   Visitors to NEPA Venture Fund in Bethlehem, Pennsylvania, are greeted by *Vamoose*, a 2-foot high wooden sculpture of a vulture perched on a sign that says "Welcome to NEPA." According to Fred

Beste, Managing Partner of NEPA, there's a widespread impression that, by some incredible coincidence of nature, all the roughly 3,000 venture capital fund managers are arrogant, know-it-all, control-oriented jerks. Mr. Best believes the opinion is so pervasively held that several years ago he decided to use a good offense as his best defense, and made birds of prey the decorating theme in his office.

Fred says there are three reasons venture capitalists have the vulture capitalist image:

1. *In no small part, it's true.*   Venture capital is exciting, high profile, and can be very remunerative. It's also hard to get into because it's money-intensive, not people-intensive. Accordingly, many of the players are bright, high-powered Type A personalities, from top B-schools. Combine that with the fact that money, like power, tends to corrupt and lots of it tends to corrupt absolutely, and you end up with a disproportionately high industry representation of arrogant, know-it-all, control-oriented jerks. Bright jerks, in many cases; wildly successful jerks, in many cases—but jerks nonetheless. This is not to say that most fund managers are jerks, or even that most *large* fund managers are jerks. But "disproportionately high" means just what it means.

2. *Turndown rate is high.*   If a venture firm sees 1,000 investment opportunities (charitably defined) per year and invests in four or five, that means that over 99 percent of the entrepreneurs are disappointed, if not resentful. Couple this with all entrepreneurs' heartfelt conviction that their extraordinary—often industry record—projected performance is, to use their word "conservative," and VCs don't make many friends. Even though the sad truth is that the majority of the investment opportunities seen in this business feature teams that are literally kidding themselves (supreme confidence is truly the cheapest commodity in the entrepreneurial world), the end result is that venture capitalists often come off as incompetent and high-handed to the people they disappoint.

3. *Small-business press is unfavorable.*   The folks that write for entrepreneurs aren't stupid. If entrepreneurs hate venture capitalists, the press feeds the fire—with gasoline! Heartwarming stories about outside venture capital partners probably wouldn't win many kudos for *Entrepreneur* magazine, but one about VC bad guys will have readers cheering and renewing their subscriptions.

The truth is, in any industry there are great people, good people, bad people, and horrible people. Moreover, the partners who run venture firms, and who are responsible for sniffing out good deals, are typically rich in entrepreneurial experience regardless of their personality. Many got started in venture capital as a result of their own growth company's success. Obviously, each partner brings his or her own personality to the deal.

As with private investors, it's important to understand the personality of the firm and the partner who'll be handling your deal both now and after it closes. Make sure that you're dealing with someone who you trust, respect, and feel can make a contribution to your business. Find out what deals they've done in the past, and talk to the owners of both their successful and unsuccessful ventures. Research their investment history. How much equity do they take on the first round, second round, and so forth? Ask others in their investment portfolio what they would do differently if they had to do it all over again. Ask other venture firms, investors, and accounting and law professionals what they think of the firm you're considering (as with private investors, bad news travels fast). At the same time, recognize that every story has two sides. Whenever you put two strong personalities together, such as a venture capitalist and an entrepreneur, a few sparks are bound to fly. Especially when money's involved.

Corporate Venture Capital

Companies like Apple, Dow Chemical, Ford, Johnson & Johnson, Matsushita, Wal-Mart, and others have formed their own venture capital programs to systematically invest in small companies for a variety of strategic reasons. Unlike traditional venture capitalists, the companies running these funds are primarily interested in incubating promising technologies, products, or services that complement their own. As a result, their return expectations may be lower than those of traditional venture capitalists.

❏ Secret

While the large companies that run these funds obviously appreciate the role that entrepreneurship plays in innovation, they remain large companies with all of the cultural baggage that most entrepreneurs disdain. It's important therefore, to make sure that you clearly understand the motivation for their investments, their expectations, how you'll be measured, the extent of your autonomy, and how and when they plan to exit the investment. As with any investor, be sure you can deal with the personalities of both the investing organization and the contact person.

On the plus side, corporate venture capitalists not only represent deep pockets, but also can provide access to other valuable corporate resources.

Investment Banking Firms

Investment banking firms are broker/dealer firms, blessed by the SEC, that make their money helping companies go public. To enter on the ground floor of opportunities, some firms have established their own venture capital pools to help incubate companies they can later take public. The goals and interests of their funds management differ little from those of traditional venture capital firms.

Small Business Investment Corps

The Small Business Investment Corps (SBIC) leverages private money with federal dollars to establish venture funds. SBICs and Special Small Business Investment Corps (SSBICs, which fund socially or economically disadvantages persons), are privately owned and operated; but they're licensed, regulated, and in part, funded by the Small Business Administration. As of October 1993, the SBA reported that 177 licensed SBICs were managing approximately $2.6 billion in investment funds, and 103 SSBICs managed another $503 million. Nearly 40 percent of the SBICs are operated or controlled by commercial banks (representing 64% of the investment dollars). On average, bank-run funds manage investment pools of less than $10 million each, smaller than traditional venture capital funds.

The official goal of the SBIC/SSBIC program is to stimulate the flow of equity capital and long-term loan funds for small business growth and development. They provide both long-term (5–20 years) debt and equity investments. In 1993, SBICs funded almost 2,000 mostly equity investments averaging $405,000 each for a total of $806.3 million. SBICs generally invest only in later stage companies (management buyouts, strategic acquisitions, mezzanine funding needed prior to going public, or bridge financing for buyouts). They look for a 20 to 30 percent return on their investment, slightly lower than the expectation of traditional venture capitalists.

Names of local SBICs are available from your local SBA office or by calling the SBA's Associate Administrator for Investment at 202-205-6510.

THE INVESTMENT PACKAGE

Once you've decided on the type of investor you think you should pursue, its time to put together a formal business plan that will help you in the door.

Venture proposals take the form of a business plan which, like a loan proposal, may be your only chance to convince someone of the value of your concept. It should be thorough, concise, and presented with the readers' interests in mind—namely, how *they* will make money by investing in your deal. According to one venture capitalist, "Most proposals fail to convince me that the owner has a clear idea about why this venture is going to be a big hit. All too often, they focus on the neat technology or gadget that they've invented rather than on how they're going to bring it to market and manage its growth so we can make money."

At the simplest level, your business plan needs to communicate enough about you, your venture, and the investment opportunity to make investors want to meet you to learn more. If it leaves too many unanswered questions, it won't adequately convince anyone of anything except that you don't know how to write a business plan. If it's too long and boring, you won't hold the attention of your reader. As in the Goldilocks story, it has to be *just right*.

GENERAL COMMENTS ABOUT BUSINESS PLANS

The format for a business plan will differ depending on the nature of the business and the purpose for the plan. For that reason, canned business plan formats rarely work; they have an uncanny knack for giving readers the distinct impression that they're looking at an amateur effort. The fact is, and this should be no secret, the thought process involved in creating the plan is as important as the plan itself. Shortcuts don't help.

Neatness counts! Don't even think about submitting a handwritten or, for that matter, typewritten business plan. In this day and technological age, there's simply no excuse for typos, white-out, or misspellings (we always have to have the computer's spelling checker check *that* one). If you can't manage to make your business plan look professional—the plan that's supposed to help you raise thousands or millions of dollars—how are you possibly going to manage a successful business?

Note: Have investors sign a confidentiality agreement, but go easy on this, especially with institutional investors.

❑ Secret

> Don't insist that investors sign a nondisclosure agreement before you'll send them the plan. Especially don't tell people you won't talk about your concept until they sign—there's no quicker way to turn off an investor. Aside from the implied mistrust, if your hot-shot idea is so easy to copy that just telling someone about it will compromise your chances, they won't be interested in it as venture deal. If they're professionals, their confidentiality is implied, so have them either mail the agreement back when they receive the plan, or pick it up if and when you meet with them.

EXECUTIVE SUMMARY

This is the first and most important part of your business plan. If it's good, investors might even read or at least, peruse the rest of the plan. If it isn't good—if it doesn't hold their attention, tell them what they want to know, intrigue them, and give them reason to think that investing in this deal could make them lots of money—the rest of the plan won't be read. You can't imagine how many poorly prepared business plans for dumb ideas an investor has to wade through to find one that looks like it might have a chance of making some money. If yours looks like another hare-brained idea for a better mousetrap written by a techno-nerd with no concept for market or marketing, you can safely assume it will be sent back with a polite form letter saying, "Thanks, but no thanks."

Tips for Structuring Your Business Plan

- Start with an attractive cover. Maybe put the most impressive thing about the venture right up front—
  52% Return Expected on Negotiated Sale to IBM in Four Years
- Include your name, address, and phone number on the cover page.
- Assign a number to each copy of the plan that you distribute, and record recipient's name and telephone number.
- Include a table of contents and tabs for major sections.
- Early in the plan (perhaps on the cover or in the table of contents), include a statement that goes something like this: *The contents of the plan are confidential and proprietary. Readers are not permitted to copy or distribute the plan, in whole or part, without the express consent of the Company.*
- Make your plan easy to read and easy on the eye by choosing an easy-to-read font and font size.
- Use bold type to emphasize key points or, better yet, use about a third of each page width for bold margin notes that summarize key points.
- Use charts and other visual aids to summarize data (but make the background data available too).
- Be sure to include a last-revised-date on the plan.
- Number the pages.
- Put it in a three-ring binder or some other binding that will make it easy for readers to make copies if they want to show it to associates.
- Include any appropriate disclosures and disclaimers needed to comply with securities law.
- Be sure to document your sources of information. Sentences that start with "Experts agree . . ." are always suspect.
- Name drop—if impressive people or companies use, endorse, or have anything to do with your product or company, be sure to mention them—but assume they'll be contacted for verification/opinions.
- Include testimonials, relevant articles, or anything else that supports your contention that you have terrific prospects for success.
- Include photos or samples of your product if feasible.
- Include a list of customers, suppliers, investors, industry experts, and other references.

The executive summary should be no more than two to four pages long. It should briefly summarize the history of your company, describe your product or service, the proprietary or intellectual property components, the size and nature of the market, the percentage of the market you expect to capture, how you expect to capture it, key customers or alliances, your unique competitive advantages, your management team, your historical and anticipated financial performance, your financing need, an approximate valuation for your firm, the proposed exit strategy, and the returns that investors can expect. Since each of those topics will be covered in greater depth in the body of the plan, write the executive summary *after* you've written the rest of the plan.

To emphasize, investors have incredibly short attention spans. If you're lucky enough to have them to pick up your plan at all, you've got to get their adrenaline pumping quickly or you're going to lose them.

COMPANY DESCRIPTION

In this, the first full section of the plan, describe your company—where it's been and where it's going. If the company's been around a while, include a chronology of events or achievements that led you to where you are today. *Do not* leave out any information about past problems that may surface in the investors' due diligence process.

This section should include answers to the following questions:

- Where and when was the company was started?
- What is its present legal form (S corporation, proprietorship, partnership, C corporation, etc.)?
- How has your company evolved to this point?
- What changes are anticipated postfinancing?

MARKETING SECTION

This section must include information about your products and services, about the industry in which you operate, about the size of the market and your segment of it, about your competition and the advantages you have over them, and about how you're going to price, promote, and distribute your products. If product development is a significant part of your venture, include the details in a separate section.

All too often, entrepreneurs devote entirely too much attention to the product portion of this section, and not enough to the market and competition sections. Success will require a lot more than a cool product.

Don't be product driven. We repeat, *Do Not Be Product Driven!* A market-driven approach is much more attractive to investors, because it's much more likely to be successful.

❑　Secret

Products won't make money for your company. *Customers* who buy your products will make money for your company, for you, and for your investors. It's not an exaggeration to say that a well-defined market need with a fuzzy product concept is far more likely to be funded than a well-defined product with a fuzzy market concept.

Here's what your marketing section should include:

- Products and/or Services.
- Industry overview.
- Market size.
- Customers.
- Competitors.
- Product and/or service positioning (relative to competitors).
- Pricing.
- Advertising and promotion.
- Distribution.
- Service and warranty policies (if applicable).
- Product development plans (if appropriate).
- Key marketing risks, potential problems, and solutions.

Here are the questions the section should answer:

- What are the company's major and minor products and services (now and in the future)?
- What are the proprietary aspects to those products and services (e.g., patents, trade secrets, copyrights, other exclusivity, etc.)?
- What's the compelling need for your product or service?
- Who are the existing or potential customers?
- How will you identify and reach them?
- Why will they buy from you?
- How big is the market for your product (document your estimates)?

- What market segment will you serve, and how big is that segment (document your estimates)?
- How much of your target market segment can you capture? How quickly?
- How are you going to do it?
- What makes you so sure that you'll be able to capture market share?
- Have you conducted any market tests? What were the results?

Investors are bored to death with back-of-an-envelope market strategies that go something like this: "The market for our whiz-bang bicycle accessory (which we've described in exquisite detail) includes a gajullion Chinese. Since they all ride bicycles, we've projected that even a 1 percent market share will yield a bazillion customers, so we're obviously gonna be rich. And that's just the Chinese market, worldwide sales prospects are truly phenomenal!" Yeah, right . . . next plan.

Other investor pet peeves include:

- Failure to acknowledge, name, and understand primary and secondary competitors.
- Use of national statistics to document a local or regional business.
- Broad, unsubstantiated assumptions.
- Overly aggressive assumptions about market share that will be captured.
- Lack of knowledge on how your market segments (if you think it doesn't, you don't know near enough about your market).
- Failure to document how you're going to find, reach, and convert customers.
- Failure to understand the risks inherent in your marketing plan.

Fact of the matter is, this section is *the* pivotal section of your plan because all of your financial assumptions will hinge on the success or failure of your marketing. If you can't convince investors that you clearly understand your market and your marketing strategy, your projections (and for that matter your company) will be meaningless.

OPERATIONS SECTION

This section will include information about your company's management (including brief biographies for key people), organizational structure, staffing, ownership, advisors, location, facilities, and product manufacturing or service delivery.

Here's what your operations section should include:

- Management.
- Staffing and availability of labor.
- Compensation strategy and plans.
- Organization chart.
- Breakdown of ownership.
- Key advisors.
- Board of directors.
- Location and facilities.
- Relevant licensing and insurance issues.
- Key suppliers and vendors.
- Production and/or service delivery plan.
- Key operations risk and potential problems.

Here are the questions the operations section should answer:

- Who are the present owners and investors? How much did each contribute for what ownership? What's the structure of their ownership? Are there any impediments to raising additional equity?
- Who are the other key players in the company (now and in the future)? What qualifications and experience do they bring to the table?
- Who in the firm will manage the finances? What is that person's qualifications?
- What's your present and future staffing plan?
- How will you retain good people?
- Are there any management or employment contracts or special relationships?
- Who are your formal and even informal advisors? Why were they chosen?
- What's the structure of the board of directors? Who's included?
- Where is the company located? What are the facilities like?
- Are there any required license, regulatory, or insurance issues?
- Who are your key vendors? Are there any special relationships?
- How will you produce your products and deliver your services?

Investor pet peeves in this section include:

- Failure to demonstrate that you and other key people have the background and experience necessary to run the proposed company.
- Failure to consider growth issues (when an investor asks, "What are you going to do when you're getting ten thousand phone calls a week?" you'd better not answer, "That would be a nice problem to have." Instead you need to have a real plan for handling growth.
- Failure to think through labor and staffing issues, particularly when the type people you need are in short supply.
- Unusual insider deals with employees, family, or investors.
- Failure to employ appropriate advisors for your size company.
- Failure to understand key risks inherent in the operating plan.

FINANCIAL SECTION

This section, and the attached financial statements, should document, justify, and convince investors of your present and future financing needs. Key historical and projected financial information should be summarized with tables, graphs and other visual aids. The section should conclude with details about the proposed deal, future financing needs, and their potential effect on early investors, and an exit strategy showing the potential return on investors' money.

Here's what your financial section should include:

- Summary/Analysis of historical and projected performance.
- Projected income statement (3–5 years, quarterly for the first two years).
- Projected balance sheet (3–5 years, annual).
- Cash flow projections (3–5 years, quarterly for the first two years).
- Break-even and sensitivity analysis.
- Assumptions (for all projections).
- Ratio analyses as appropriate.
- Schedule of financing needs (3–5 years).
- Use of funds.
- Valuation.
- Proposed investment structure.
- Discussion of future financing needs and options.
- Investor exit strategy.

Here are the questions the financial section should answer:

- How has your company performed in the past?
- How do you expect to perform in the future? Why?
- How will the company finance its growth?
- What if everything doesn't go as planned?
- What value have you assigned to the company and why?
- What's the deal that you're offering investors?
- How will future financings affect early investors?
- How and when will investors cash out?
- What evidence do you have to support your assumptions about the exit strategy?

Investor pet peeves in this section include:

- Insufficiently documented assumptions about the company's growth.
- Failure to include the effects of seasonality and business cycles in your projections.
- Unrealistically quick ramp-up of sales (so-called hockey stick growth curves).
- Underestimating your cash flow needs.
- Spreadsheet-itis, a chronic condition that results from letting your computer spit out reams of useless, unsubstantiated numbers that you begin to believe.
- Income and expenses that grow by some formula that has no basis in reality.
- Projections that include dates and events already in the past, particularly if you're off your target.

❑ **Secret**

Use a Month 1, Month 2, Month 3 . . . convention rather than running this risk.

- Large income or expense categories that are lumped together without backup information about the components.

- Mistakes in spreadsheets.
- Canned business plans and spreadsheet templates that have not been customized for your business.
- Failure to anticipate future financing needs.
- Unrealistic company valuation.
- Failure to document how investors will make money in the deal.
- Failure to recognize investors' expected returns.

Every column, every row, and every entry on your spreadsheet needs to be thoroughly thought out and justified. After all, this isn't just an exercise for the benefit of investors. If you underestimate your financing needs, there's a good chance that you'll have to give up the controlling interest in your company to solve the problem.

ATTACHMENTS AND SUPPORTING MATERIALS

Include copies of any and all materials that might support your proposal. Here are some items you might include:

- Résumés (all owners, key employees, and advisors).
- References.
- Timetables and implementation schedules.
- Sample marketing materials.
- Price lists.
- Product samples, renderings, and photos.
- Competitor information including samples and ads.
- Testimonials.
- Customer list (existing/potential).
- Industry data and research.
- Relevant articles.

Once your plan is done, have a few trusted advisors and friends read it as a dry run. What questions do they have once they're finished? Remedy any problems or deficiencies before you send it out to prospective investors. The rewrite process will be frustratingly ongoing, so develop an efficient process for sending updates to plan recipients once it's been distributed. Particularly in fast-growing ventures, a month-old plan can be stale, misleading, or even wrong.

18 | THE DECISION— BEHIND CLOSED DOORS

So what happens to your business plan once it reaches the desk of a potential investor? Someone (usually) opens it and logs it in along with the many others they received that day. The first cut comes when someone determines your plan involves the type and stage of business that they like. Next, that same someone decides who in the office should read it. Based on our advice, you've already addressed it to the partner who's likely to be interested, so your plan should scoot straight to that person's desk. And, yes, packaging matters. A good-looking plan won't necessarily be funded if the contents are weak, but a scraggly looking one, regardless of contents might not even have a chance.

FIRST GLANCE

Now for the hard part—getting investors to just read your plan! They probably have at least several, probably many, and possibly a whole stack of boring, self-important, pie-in-the sky works of fantasy sitting on their desk. So assuming that your business plan is the best that it can possibly be, and that your executive summary is a tasteful work of art, what's the best thing you can do to be on the top of the stack?

THE ONCE OVER

Investors who decide to read your plan will start by skimming the executive summary. If they have a glimmer of interest, they'll also skim the management profiles to decide if the people you've surrounded yourself with appear to have the right skills and background. Next, they'll flip to the "good parts" to see if the plan has the financial depth to really provide the level of return you offered in the summary. If your valuation is even remotely reasonable, they'll flip to your financial projections. If they're still interested at that point (and nothing else has interrupted them), they'll skim (and maybe even *read*) the rest of the plan.

❑ **Secret**

The best way to ensure your plan is read is to have it referred in by someone who is known to and respected by the investor. The letterhead of your referral on the cover of your plan will do more good than just about anything else you could do at this stage. Investors don't like to waste time any more than anyone else, so when someone they trust suggests they should look at your plan, they'll spend time on it rather than take a chance on an unknown.

If your plan doesn't make it past these initial checkpoints, they'll probably put it down and move on to another. If you're lucky, they'll send it back in a week or two with a delicately worded decline. If they were interested but your plan failed only one or two of their criteria, it will probably sit somewhere on a desk until they have time to consider a few real dogs. After reading a few works of sheer fiction, they may decide yours wasn't that bad after all. Or it may just sit in the "maybe" pile until someone calls to see where things stand.

LET'S GET TOGETHER

Assuming your package passes the sniff test, whoever reviews your plan will probably talk it over with a few other people including partners, other investment firms, and maybe a few industry people. If they're still excited about it in a few days or weeks, they'll call or send you a letter to indicate that they're interested and want to meet. The date for the meeting will be much too far in the future to suit your taste and bank balance, but don't give the appearance of being desperate by pushing too hard. *Everything* will take longer than you want. And, by the way, it ain't over 'til it's over. No matter how excited and encouraging investors seem along the way, don't spend the money 'til you have it.

Now, this first meeting is very—repeat—*very* important! It's your first and maybe your last chance to prove you have the character, commitment, and capability to pull it off. You have to go in ready to dazzle them, so even if you're up to your butt in alligators, and even if you're worn out from talking to other potential investors, you can't afford to be down. Find a way to reacquire your sincere, confident enthusiasm, and approach this new investor meeting as though it was your first.

You'll probably meet with one or more of the firm's partners/associates—and possibly one or more consultants whom they'll invite without asking you. They may or may not have thoroughly reviewed your plan (assume they haven't), and expect that they'll have a number of key issues on their mind. If you can, find out ahead of time through one of the underlings how long you'll have to make your pitch, prepare thoroughly, and then be flexible.

❑ Secret

Investors are notorious for short attention spans (they've heard it all a million times before) so plan to make your presentation *very* short (10–15 minutes) and to the point. Then be flexible enough to follow their lead, but don't let the session wander out of control by letting them distract you from your key points. By all means, answer their questions and address their concerns, but don't forget you're the boss of the company you're trying to have them fund. They're also using this meeting as an opportunity to judge how you handle yourself.

DON'T BE A STRANGER

Assuming that the meeting goes well, don't expect to hear from them right away; they'll think about it for a few days or even weeks. During this time, it doesn't hurt to call and touch base once a week, but don't be a pest.

If they're interested, they'll ask for an extensive list of references. Be sure investors have been alerted for any sensitivities, skeletons in your closet, or other potential surprises that could short-circuit their interest in your deal.

The whole process is probably moving much too slowly to suit you because you need the money now; but, as with lenders, desperation doesn't play well in investor circles. It's OK to let them know that there are good reasons to move quickly, but don't let them think that you have a financial crisis because of poor planning.

I'LL SHOW YOU MINE IF . . .

During the investor's formal due diligence process, which can take weeks or months, you'll likely be barraged with questions and requests for additional information. If not, drop the investor a note periodically with relevant information about your company or the industry that will help keep your deal in the limelight.

Sometime during the due diligence process, you'll also be talking about valuation and other key issues in the deal. Be open and honest about your needs and wants, but you must understand the investor's perspective as well.

DOING IT

The rest of the process is a matter of dotting the *i*'s and crossing the *t*'s, which is by no means as simple as it sounds. Remember, throughout the process your primary responsibility is to run your company, and the deal isn't done until it's done! The help of informed advisors who have closed similar deals in the past is an essential part of this process, so be sure you have the right people on your team. Nothing is more frustrating and potentially disastrous to negotiations than the use of naive accountants, lawyers, or other advisors.

The investment community is very small and tight. If you're talking to other firms, your investors will know it. If your deal has been declined, potential investors will call those who declined you to find out why. This is not to say that you should only talk to one firm, but understand that investors talk to each other. And realize, as in borrowing money, that you'll rarely be successful at changing the mind of an investor who has decided to pass on your deal. By the time you put together a new business plan that addresses the investor's original concerns, your deal will be considered stale. Trying to spruce it up or cast the deal in a different light is rarely successful.

THE MORNING AFTER

Once the deal is done, it's vital to your mutual success that you maintain a good relationship with your investors—you want to be sure they respect you in the morning, to coin a phrase. Make sure you've accurately represented all of the facts while you were selling your deal, because if you didn't, it won't be pretty when they discover you've snowed them.

Do's and Don'ts for Finding Money from Investors

Do:
- Start looking before you need the money.
- Search for "most likely" investors.
- Develop a strong business plan.
- Write a spectacular executive summary.
- Consider your investor's needs and wants.
- Remember investors have short attention spans.
- Make sure your projections are realistic, not wishful.
- Include high and low scenarios in your numbers.
- Document your assumptions.
- Explain your use of their funds.
- Be open, honest, and forthright.
- Focus on who's going to buy your product.
- Offer a reasonable valuation.
- Establish the credibility of your team.
- Thoroughly check out potential investors.
- Involve professionals with experience.

Don't:
- Misrepresent anything or hide problems.
- Expect investor's money to pay off past problems.
- Accept funding from people you don't trust or like.
- Spend their money before you get it.
- Underestimate your financial needs.
- Count on money to solve your problems.
- Be greedy with equity.
- Allow yourself to be taken by "miracle workers."
- Let desperation make your decisions.
- Give up.

From here on out, you'll want to keep your investors (by now you ought to consider them to be your partners) informed about all that's going on—the good *and* the bad.

WHAT IF THEY SAY "NO"

Investors *will* decline your deal. Accept that as a fact of entrepreneurial life. You may have to approach as many as a hundred investors before you finally snag one. Raising money from investors is hard work! Even if you're the kind of person who loves the thrill of the chase, rejection is bound to wear on you. After all, they're not just rejecting your investment proposal, they're rejecting you, and all that you believe in. The nerve!

Fact is, you should be working on a number of investors from the very beginning. You can't afford to put all your eggs in one basket. When you're declined, you need to take a deep breath, dust off your ego, and go on to the next investor with all the enthusiasm and determination you can muster.

If you were "referred in" by someone the investors know and trust, they'll look a little harder before they decide to pass on your deal. They'll call the referral source if they have any questions or need more information. More likely, your referral source will follow up with them first. Either way, even if the deal is declined, investors will offer a lot more honest feedback to someone they know than they would to you. This feedback is priceless. It will clue you in to how you need to tighten up your plan and may also offer the names of some other potential investors.

As you might suspect by now, the money-raising process can easily become a full time job. Unfortunately, most entrepreneurs already have one—starting or running their company. Since doing *that* job well is also crucial to the money-raising process, you'll find that qualified advisors can be a big help in contacting new investors, following up with old ones, fielding questions, and negotiating the deal.

HOW MUCH MONEY DO YOU NEED?

Now that you know where to find money and how to obtain it, let's figure out how much you *really* need. Your dreams will quickly turn to nightmares if you underestimate your need for cash.

You don't need a degree in accounting to read this section or, for that matter, to run a business. If each time you come across pages of numbers, you're suddenly overtaken by an urge to do something else (similar, perhaps, to the feeling you have when it's time to pay your taxes) take heart, you're not alone.

What successful business owners do know is how to read past the accounting-ese to determine the health and financial needs of their company. What they know is that the financial statements they look at bear little resemblance to the company they run day to day. Financial statements are about esoteric accounting concepts like assets, liabilities, revenues, expenses, and profits that have little to do with running your company day to day. What really matters is cash flow.

❏ **Secret**

And this is perhaps the most important secret in this book: You can't eat profits.

19

CASH IS KING

Consider, if you will, fictitious Surgical Products Company, a highly profitable manufacturer of postoperative medical supplies for home use. During start-up, they hired people, purchased manufacturing equipment and raw materials, ran the machinery to produce their introductory products, and then paid a sales team to sell them. Their salespeople, it turned out, were very successful at generating orders at prices that offered a good profit.

They sold $2,000 in Month 1, $5,000 in Month 2, $10,000 in Month 3, and sales continue to grow by $5,000 a month. Their cost of production is only 45 percent of sales, which leaves a healthy gross profit margin of 55 percent—more than enough to cover operating expenses and still produce a profit.

Sounds great, right? Well, maybe not. Some time this month, they'll collect part of the money customers owe them from last month. The balance of their receivables will be collected in 60 or 90 days. Meanwhile, they're working overtime to fill this month's orders. They're paying for the extra supplies they ordered last month in anticipation of continued growth, plus they're ordering more supplies for next month's sales, hiring more people, expanding their facility, and so forth. With any luck, the sales trend will continue and they'll do it all over again, but bigger next month, the month after, and so on. And so on, that is, as long as their cash flow holds up.

As it turns out Surgical Products Company, in spite of the success, is actually in real danger of going, make that *growing*, broke!

Exhibit 19.1 shows that even with 30-day terms from their suppliers, this successful manufacturer is $24,000 in the red by the end of Month 6. And, by the way, those numbers don't include any other operating expenses—little things like rent, telephone, office supplies, and payroll,

EXHIBIT 19.1 Growing Broke Surgical Products Company

Assume:
Cost of Goods Sold = 45%.
Accounts Receivabe are collected 20% in 30 days, 40% in 60 days, and 40% in 90 days.
Accounts Payable are paid in 30 days.
Two months inventory should be on hand at all times.

		Month -2	Month -1	Month 1	Month 2	Month 3	Month 4	Month 5	Month 6
Sales $ (,000 omitted)		$0	$0	$2	$5	$10	$15	$25	$30
					This shows the delay between sales and the collection of cash from those sales.				
Cash in from Sales									
Sales Collected in 30 Days	20%				$0	$1	$2	$3	$5
Sales Collected in 60 Days	40%				$0	$1	$2	$4	$6
Sales Collected in 90 Days	40%				$0	$0	$1	$2	$4
Total Cash Collected From Sales		$0	$0	$0	$0	$2	$5	$9	$15
Inventory Needs	Inventory is ordered two months before anticipated sales.								
Cost of Goods This Month	45%			$1	$2	$5	$7	$11	$14
Plus: Desired Ending Inventory	2 months	$0	$3	$7	$11	$18	$25	$29	$34
Equals: Total Inventory Needed			$3	$8	$14	$23	$32	$41	$47
					The prior month's ending inventory becomes next month's beginning inventory.				
Less: Beginning Inventory		$0	$0	$3	$7	$11	$18	$25	$29
Equals: Purchases This Month			$3	$5	$7	$11	$14	$16	$18
	Materials are paid for one month after purchase.								
Cash Out for Inventory		$0	$0	$3	$5	$7	$11	$14	$16
Net Cash before Operating Expenses		$0	$0	($3)	($4)	($5)	($6)	($5)	($1)
Beginning Cash		$0	$0	$0	($3)	($7)	($12)	($19)	($23)
Ending Cash Balance		$0	$0	($3)	($7)	($12)	($19)	($23)	($24)

By the end of the Month 6 the company is $24,000 in the red even before any operating expenses.

not to mention groceries for the owner. The fact is, they can forget those extra people and expansion plans . . . they don't even have the cash flow to support what they're doing now.

So what's cash flow, and where do you find it? On one level, cash flow is a very simple concept. Your business has to generate more cash than it uses if you're going to survive. It almost sounds too obvious; that's what profitability is all about, right? But what a lot of people don't understand is that you can't spend profits unless they're cash profits. Paper profits aren't worth the paper they're printed on when it comes to survival and growth.

Let's look first at some common misunderstandings about what your financial statements do and don't tell you, and what cash flow is and isn't. Again, don't worry, this isn't going to be an accounting course. We're just going to take a look at the essentials, so you'll know how to figure how much money you need to find.

CASH FLOW ISN'T PROFIT—AND VICE VERSA

Exhibit 19.2 shows a simplified accrual-based Income Statement Summary for Surgical Products Company after its first four years in business.

The Income Statement tells us that Surgical Products Company is a growing and profitable company. Unfortunately, it doesn't tell us anything about its cash flow and therefore the company's true financial health. Accrual-based accounting, commonly used by businesses, records income when sales are made (regardless of when cash is received) and records expenses when they're incurred (regardless of when cash is paid).

For example, assume you sold $100,000 worth of goods in December, collected $45,000, and billed your customers for the balance. Under an accrual accounting system, you'd count the entire $100,000 in December and book it as last year's income. Under a cash accounting system, you'd count the $45,000 as last year's income, and book the remaining $55,000 when you collect it this year. The same would be true for your expenses. Thus, an accrual accounting system reflects what the business earned in December, but it doesn't tell us anything about cash flow. Exhibit 19.2 and the following explanation show why.

Revenue

The company didn't actually collect $1,440,000 in cash from sales in Year 4 because some customers didn't pay at the time of sale. In fact, the company has $221,000 in Accounts Receivable, but you don't know *that* unless you look at their Balance Sheet Summary (Exhibit 19.3). Those receivables are the equivalent of almost two months' sales that haven't produced any cold hard cash. They'll collect *that* cash when, and if, their customers pay. The point is, a portion of the company's cash is sitting in their customer's checking accounts. So don't confuse total income with total cash coming in.

Actually, to further confuse the issue, the company had some cash come in during Year 4 that didn't show up as sales or income. That cash was collected from customers who owed them money at the end of the prior year, yet another reason the Income Statement Summary doesn't tell the whole story.

Cost of Goods Sold

Cost of Goods Sold (or COGS) is the cost of materials and supplies that go into producing the company's products. But the company didn't

EXHIBIT 19.2 Surgical Products Company Income Statement Summary

($,000 omitted)	Year 1	Year 2	Year 3	Year 4
Total Income				
Product 1	$0	$301	$679	$715
Product 2	$404	$490	$497	$523
Product 3	$0	$190	$192	$202
Total Income	$404	$981	$1,368	$1,440

> They didn't collect cash from all their customers. In fact, the company still needed to collect $221 at the end of the year which will show up as Accounts Receivable on the Balance Sheet.

	Year 1	Year 2	Year 3	Year 4
Cost of Goods Sold				
Product 1	$0	$181	$408	$422
Product 2	$182	$216	$219	$235
Product 3	$0	$95	$96	$99
Total Cost of Goods Sold	$182	$491	$722	$756

> They didn't pay for all their purchases. They still owe $108 at the end of the year which will show up as Account Payable on the Balance Sheet.

	Year 1	Year 2	Year 3	Year 4
Gross Profit	$222	$490	$646	$684
Gross Profit Margin%	55.00%	49.93%	47.21%	47.49%
Operating Expenses				
Sales Salaries/Benefits	$65	$125	$165	$183
Administrative Salaries/Benefits	$55	$110	$136	$151
Occupancy	$13	$18	$19	$21
Marketing	$40	$55	$75	$83
Insurance	$30	$50	$59	$66
Equipment Leases	$25	$45	$84	$0
Professional Fees	$2	$4	$5	$6
Depreciation	$0	$0	$0	$60
Other Operating Expenses	$14	$18	$24	$27
Total Operating Expenses	$244	$425	$567	$597
Operating Expense %	60.40%	43.32%	41.47%	41.46%

> Depreciation is not a cash expense. Actually the company paid $180 in cash for this equipment, but that will show up on the Balance Sheet.

	Year 1	Year 2	Year 3	Year 4
Interest on Debt	$0	$0	$0	$18
Net Income before Taxes	($22)	$65	$79	$69
Net Income %	-5.40%	6.61%	5.74%	4.78%
Taxes	$0	$13	$24	$21
After-Tax Income	($22)	$52	$55	$48

actually spend $756,000 in cash for supplies in Year 4. What really happened was they received materials and supplies along with a bill, which they'll probably pay in 30 days. At the end of Year 4, in fact, the company still owed $108,000 to vendors (or the equivalent of almost two months' purchases). Of course, like Accounts Receivable, you wouldn't know *that* unless you look at their Balance Sheet, in this case under Accounts Payable.

On the other hand, in January of Year 4, cash went out for bills that were still outstanding at the end of the prior year, but that won't show up on the Year 4 Income Statement because the expense was already accounted for in Year 3.

Also, due to a variety of accounting conventions, that $756,000 in Costs of Goods Sold only represents an approximation of the real cost of materials that were used to produce the company's products in this accounting period. After all, if the company purchased surgical steel in bulk at the end of last year because prices were scheduled to increase this year, no one really knows which hunk of metal was used in a particular product. Is it a piece that they bought at last year's price, or is it a piece that they've purchased since? Accounting rules establish a methodology for assigning a cost to raw materials, but when those costs show up on an income statement, they tell the owner very little about how much cash went out for raw materials in the accounting period the statement covers.

Operating Expenses

While this example assumes that operating expenses were paid as incurred, some of these expenses often slip into the "pay later" category and therefore don't represent an immediate cash drain. For that matter, the company probably paid a few of the "pay later" bills from Year 3 in Year 4.

Depreciation

When a company buys equipment, it's not allowed to deduct the total cost for that equipment immediately. Instead, it is supposed to estimate the useful life of the equipment, divide the purchase price by the expected life, and deduct only that portion each year. That may make some sense from an accounting point of view, but not from a cash flow perspective. The company put out, let's say, $180,000 in cash to buy equipment in Year 4; but its Income Statement only shows an expense of

$60,000 since the useful life of the equipment is estimated to be three years.

To add insult to injury, Uncle Sam will want to collect taxes on the paper profits, which are based on a deduction of only $60,000 for depreciation, even though the company paid out $180,000 for equipment.

Interest Expense

The company paid $18,000 in interest in Year 4. That shows up as an expense on the Income Statement. But most loans include payments of principal *and* interest, which don't show up on the Income Statement. Payment of the principal portion of the loan shows up on the company's Balance Sheet as a reduction to the loan balance.

So how much cash *did* the company produce in Year 4? How did it pay for the equipment purchase? It certainly didn't come out of cash profits. Well, to answer that, we'll have to look at the company's Balance Sheet. Never fear, we promised not to make this an accounting course. We simply need to figure out how this company is going to pay its bills.

CASH FLOW ISN'T NET WORTH

Unfortunately, balance sheets are even less useful than income statements when it comes to tracking cash. True, there's an entry on the balance sheet called "cash," which contributes to another entry called "Net Worth," but they don't tell us about cash flow.

A company's balance sheet is simply a snapshot, at a point in time, of what it owns (those are assets), what it owes (those are liabilities), and what's left (that's company equity comprising money that's been invested and money that the company has collected over time through profits).

A balance sheet is similar to an X ray. If you take an X ray of your arm today and break it tomorrow today's film, by itself, is worthless. However, when compared with a new X ray, it does offer a clue to how things have changed. Take a look at the Balance Sheet Summary in Exhibit 19.3 that compares the first four years for Surgical Products Company.

All we know about cash from looking at the Balance Sheet in Year 4 is that the company had $51,000 in cash on the last day of the year. Who cares? That was then, this is now.

If we work at it, using the Balance sheet and the Income Statement, we could piece together how much cash this company generated in Year

EXHIBIT 19.3   Surgical Products Company Balance Sheet Summary

($,000 omitted)	Year 1	Year 2	Year 3	Year 4
Assets				
Current Assets				
Cash	$5	$7	$9	$51
Accounts Receivable	$31	$89	$137	$221
Inventory	$11	$35	$71	$85
Total Current Assets	$47	$131	$217	$357

> Increases in Assets reduce cash. For example more customers owe us $ at the end of this year than they did at the end of last year.

	Year 1	Year 2	Year 3	Year 4
Equipment	$0	$0	$0	$180
Less Accumulated Depreciation	$0	$0	$0	($60)
Net Equipment	$0	$0	$0	$120

> The purchase of $180 in equipment required cash.

	Year 1	Year 2	Year 3	Year 4
Total Assets	$47	$131	$217	$477
Liabilities				
Current Liabilities				
Accounts Payable	$17	$49	$80	$108
Line of Credit	$0	$0	$0	$50
Total Current Liabilities	$17	$49	$80	$158

> Increases in Liabilities increase cash. For example, we borrowed money during the year which supplied cash.

	Year 1	Year 2	Year 3	Year 4
Long-Term Debt	$0	$0	$0	$135
Total Liabilities	$17	$49	$80	$293
Net Worth				
Common Stock	$52	$52	$52	$52
Retained Earnings	($22)	$30	$85	$132
Total Net Worth	$30	$82	$137	$184
Total Liabilities and Net Worth	$47	$131	$217	$477

4. When assets such as accounts receivable and inventory go up from one year to the next they actually drain cash. If receivables go down from one year to the next, it means you collected cash. For example, if you had receivables of $200,000 at the end of last year (which you collected this year), and receivables of $150,000 at the end of this year (which you'll collect next year), you have $50,000 more cash now than you did at the end of last year.

On the other side of the equation, an increase in liabilities (as strange as it may seem) supplies cash. If the balance on your line of credit . . . a liability . . . is higher this year than it was last, you have more borrowed cash to spend. If accounts payable . . . another liability . . . are higher at the end of the year this year, it means you're using more trade credit now, and hence have more cash.

CASH FLOW ISN'T WORKING CAPITAL

Working Capital represents the difference between those things a business expects to convert to cash in the near term and those things they expect to require cash in the same period. Conveniently, these items are grouped together on the Balance Sheet as Current Assets (e.g., Cash, Accounts Receivable, and Inventory) and Current Liabilities (e.g., Short Term Loans and Accounts Payable). Current Assets minus Current Liabilities equals Working Capital.

As we see on the Balance Sheet Summary for Surgical Products Company (Exhibit 19.3) Working Capital grew from $137,000 in Year 3 ($217,000 in Current Assets minus $80,000 in Current Liabilities) to $199,000 in Year 4 ($357,000 in Current Assets minus $158,000 in Current Liabilities). While Working Capital grew from Year 3 to Year 4, it doesn't represent cash. In fact, most of the growth in Working Capital was the result of an increase in Accounts Receivable which will take some time to collect.

Working Capital is actually a leading indicator of future cash. The $199,000 in Working Capital at the end of Year 4, while it isn't cash, does predict that more things are going to supply cash in the near term than those that will require it. Of course, that assumes the receivables are good ones, and that the company's inventory can and will be converted into salable items. Remember, a company with a Current Ratio of 2:1 is considered healthy. But, aside from the Cash portion of Current Assets, you can't spend Working Capital.

CASH FLOW IS CASH!

We've seen that cash flow can't be found on an Income Statement, it can't be found on a Balance Sheet, and it isn't the same thing as Working Capital. So what *is* it, and if it's so dang important why isn't there some financial statement that makes it easier to understand? Well, it turns out there is. Enter the Uniform Commercial Analysis (UCA) Cash Flow Report. The UCA Cash Flow Report, shown in Exhibit 19.4,

EXHIBIT 19.4 Surgical Products Company Uniform Commercial Analysis (UCA) Cash Flow Summary

	Year 2	Year 3	Year 4
($,000 omitted)			
Net Sales	$981	$1,368	$1,440
Change in A/R	($58)	($48)	($84)
Cash from Sales	$923	$1,320	$1,356

This year's Sales, plus the collection of last year's A/R, less new A/R from this year's sales = Cash from Sales

	Year 2	Year 3	Year 4
Cost of Goods	($491)	($722)	($756)
Change in Inv	($24)	($36)	($14)
Change in A/P	$33	$31	$28
Cash Production Costs	($483)	($727)	($742)

This year's Cost of Goods Sold, plus last year's inventory and payables, less new inventory and payables = Cash Production Costs

	Year 2	Year 3	Year 4
Selling, General and Admin Expenses	($425)	($567)	($537)
Cash Operating Costs	($425)	($567)	($537)
Income Tax Expense	($13)	($24)	($21)
Taxes Paid	($13)	($24)	($21)
Cash after Operations	**$2**	**$2**	**$55**

Cash produced from Sales, less cash used for inventory and payables, less cash operating costs, less taxes paid = Cash produced by operations.

	Year 2	Year 3	Year 4
Interest	$0	$0	($18)
Cash Financing Costs	$0	$0	($18)
Cash after Financing Costs	**$2**	**$2**	**$37**
Capital Expenditures	$0	$0	($180)
Financing Surplus/Deficit	**$2**	**$2**	**($143)**
Change in Short-Term Debt	$0	$0	$50
Change in Long-Term Debt	$0	$0	$135
Total External Financing	**$0**	**$0**	**$185**

Cash from operations, less cash paid for financing and equipment, plus cash from the increase in debt = net CASH generated by the company.

	Year 2	Year 3	Year 4
Financing Surplus+Ext Financing	**$2**	**$2**	**$42**
Change in Cash	**$2**	**$2**	**$42**

incorporates elements of both an Income Statement and Balance Sheet, but the bottom line (literally) is cash.

Finally, we're talking cash. As you can see, a cash flow statement is much more useful than an income statement or balance sheet because it not only deals in terms of cash, but it also highlights where the cash is coming from. Businesses that aren't generating cash from their own efforts (the "Cash after Operations" line) can't survive very long unless they have an unlimited supply of lenders and investors to solve their cash flow problems.

Surgical Products Company generated $55,000 in Cash from Operations (which you may have noticed, isn't far off their Income Statement profit of $48,000, but that's only coincidental). Then they paid $18,000 in interest on their loans, they purchased $180,000 in equipment, and borrowed $185,000 from lenders (a $135,000 equipment loan and a $50,000 line of credit). As a result of all that, their checking account went up by $42,000 in cash—money they can actually spend.

20 DEVELOPING CASH FLOW PROJECTIONS

Because cash flow is so vital to your business success, lenders and investors will insist on seeing a cash flow projection for two to three years into the future. They'll also want to see projected income statements and balance sheets for the same period. If lenders and investors don't believe your projections, they won't lend to, or invest in, your company.

But you're not just preparing projections for their benefit. If you underestimate your cash needs, you could find yourself in a position where you can't pay your bills and you can't borrow any more money (which leads to insolvency). If investors are involved in your company and you need more cash than you originally estimated, you might have to give up a controlling interest to induce them into coughing up more cash (which leads to ulcers).

Here, then, are the steps you need to follow to prepare cash flow projections for your new wholesale coffee and tea business called *Coffee & Tea Emporium* (see Exhibit 20.1 for the finished product).

PROJECT MONTHLY SALES

Start your projection with a forecast of the number of units you'll sell each month. Companies with multiple products should make a projection for each product. Be sure to account for a realistic phase-in of sales, particularly if you're a new business or developing a new product. Also be sure to reflect any seasonal fluctuations.

Next, project your sales by multiplying the number of units by your projected price. It's best to have a separate field or table for prices so that you can easily play with different pricing scenarios. Remember, the goal here is to predict, as accurately as possible, how cash is going to

EXHIBIT 20.1   Coffee & Tea Emporium ... *Wholesalers of Exotic Coffee and Tea* ... Cash Flow Projection

($,000 omitted)

	Month -2	Month -1	Month 1	Month 2	Month 3	Month 4	Month 5	Month 6	Month 7	Month 8	Month 9	Month 10	Month 11	Month 12	Total Yr1
Sales (# Cases):															
Coffee	0	0	50	75	100	125	150	300	450	550	650	700	700	700	4550
Tea	0	0	38	56	75	94	113	225	338	413	488	525	525	525	3413
Sales $ (,000)															
Coffee ($110/Case)	$0.0	$0.0	$5.5	$8.3	$11.0	$13.8	$16.5	$33.0	$49.5	$60.5	$71.5	$77.0	$77.0	$77.0	$500.5
Tea ($80/Case)	$0.0	$0.0	$3.0	$4.5	$6.0	$7.5	$9.0	$18.0	$27.0	$33.0	$39.0	$42.0	$42.0	$42.0	$273.0
Total Income	$0.0	$0.0	$8.5	$12.8	$17.0	$21.3	$25.5	$51.0	$76.5	$93.5	$110.5	$119.0	$119.0	$119.0	$773.5
Cash In From Sales															
Sales Collected in 30 Days (50%)				$4.3	$6.4	$8.5	$10.6	$12.8	$25.5	$38.3	$46.8	$55.3	$59.5	$59.5	$327.3
Sales Collected in 60 Days (40%)					$3.4	$5.1	$6.8	$8.5	$10.2	$20.4	$30.6	$37.4	$44.2	$47.6	$214.2
Sales Collected in 90 Days (10%)						$0.9	$1.3	$1.7	$2.1	$2.6	$5.1	$7.7	$9.4	$11.1	$41.7
Total Cash Collected From Sales	$0.0	$0.0	$0.0	$4.3	$9.8	$14.5	$18.7	$23.0	$37.8	$61.2	$82.5	$100.3	$113.1	$118.2	$583.1

This reflects the delay between sales and the collection of cash from those sales.

	Month -2	Month -1	Month 1	Month 2	Month 3	Month 4	Month 5	Month 6	Month 7	Month 8	Month 9	Month 10	Month 11	Month 12	Total Yr1
Inventory Needs															
Cost of Goods This Month (51%)			$4.3	$6.5	$8.7	$10.8	$13.0	$26.0	$39.0	$47.7	$56.4	$60.7	$60.7	$60.7	$394.5
Plus: Desired Ending Inventory (2 months)		$10.8	$15.2	$19.5	$23.8	$26.0	$39.0	$65.0	$86.7	$104.0	$117.0	$121.4	$121.4	$121.4	
Equals: Total Inventory Needed		$10.8	$19.5	$26.0	$32.5	$49.9	$78.0	$112.7	$143.1	$164.7	$177.7	$182.1	$182.1		
Less: Beginning Inventory		$0.0	$10.8	$15.2	$19.5	$23.8	$26.0	$39.0	$65.0	$86.7	$104.0	$117.0	$121.4	$121.4	
Equals: Purchases This Month		$10.8	$8.7	$10.8	$13.0	$26.0	$39.0	$47.7	$56.4	$60.7	$60.7	$60.7	$60.7		
Cash Needed for Inventory	$0.0	$0.0	$10.8	$8.7	$10.8	$13.0	$26.0	$39.0	$47.7	$56.4	$60.7	$60.7	$60.7	$60.7	

This section reflects the effect of having to order inventory in advance of sales.
The prior month's ending inventory becomes the next month's beginning inventory.
This section reflects the one month delay in paying bills.

	Month -2	Month -1	Month 1	Month 2	Month 3	Month 4	Month 5	Month 6	Month 7	Month 8	Month 9	Month 10	Month 11	Month 12	Total Yr1
Cash Needed for Operating Expenses															
Payroll			$2.0	$4.0	$6.0	$6.0	$6.0	$6.0	$8.0	$8.0	$8.0	$8.0	$8.0	$8.0	$80.0
Benefits			$0.6	$1.2	$1.8	$1.8	$1.8	$1.8	$2.4	$2.4	$2.4	$2.4	$2.4	$2.4	$24.0
Office Expense			$2.0	$2.0	$2.0	$3.0	$3.0	$3.0	$4.0	$4.0	$4.0	$4.0	$4.0	$4.0	$36.0
Professional Fees			$2.0						$2.0						$4.0
Marketing		$10.0			$3.0	$3.0	$3.0	$3.0	$3.0	$3.0	$3.0	$3.0	$3.0	$3.0	$42.0
Insurance		$5.0													$5.0
Other Expenses		$3.0	$4.0	$5.0	$5.0	$6.0	$6.0	$7.0	$7.0	$8.0	$8.0	$9.0	$9.0		$78.0
Total Operating Expenses	$20.0	$17.6	$16.2	$16.2	$19.8	$19.8	$19.8	$24.8	$23.4	$23.4	$27.4	$25.4	$26.4	$26.4	$269.0

Project expenses in the month they're likely to be paid and be sure to include a start-up period.

	Month -2	Month -1	Month 1	Month 2	Month 3	Month 4	Month 5	Month 6	Month 7	Month 8	Month 9	Month 10	Month 11	Month 12	Total Yr1
Other Cash Out															
Line of Credit Interest			$0.0	$0.0	$0.2	$0.3	$0.6	$0.9	$1.2	$1.3	$1.4	$1.4	$1.2		$8.5
Dividends															
Equipment Purchases	$35.0														
Total Other Uses of Cash	$35.0	$0.0	$0.0	$0.0	$0.0	$0.0	$0.2	$0.3	$0.6	$0.9	$1.2	$1.3	$1.4	$1.2	$8.5

This is calculated as 10% of the outstanding line of credit balance.

EXHIBIT 20.1 (Continued)

	Month -2	Month -1	Month 1	Month 2	Month 3	Month 4	Month 5	Month 6	Month 7	Month 8	Month 9	Month 10	Month 11	Month 12
Total Sources of Cash														
Cash Collected from Sales	$0.0	$0.0	$0.0	$4.3	$9.8	$14.5	$18.7	$23.0	$37.8	$61.2	$82.5	$100.3	$113.1	$118.2
Total Uses of Cash														
Cash Needed for Inventory	$0.0	$0.0	$10.8	$8.7	$10.8	$13.0	$26.0	$39.0	$47.7	$56.4	$60.7	$60.7	$60.7	$60.7
Cash Needed for Operating Expenses	$20.0	$17.6	$16.2	$16.2	$19.8	$19.8	$19.8	$24.8	$23.4	$23.4	$27.4	$25.4	$26.4	$26.4
Other Uses of Cash	$35.0	$0.0	$0.0	$0.0	$0.0	$0.2	$0.3	$0.6	$0.9	$1.2	$1.3	$1.4	$1.4	$1.2
Total Uses	$55.0	$17.6	$27.0	$24.9	$30.6	$33.0	$46.1	$64.4	$72.0	$80.9	$89.4	$87.5	$88.5	$88.3
Net Cash from Business Activities	($55.0)	($17.6)	($27.0)	($20.6)	($20.9)	($18.5)	($27.4)	($41.4)	($34.2)	($19.7)	($7.0)	$12.8	$24.5	$29.9
Less: Beginning Cash Balance	$0.0	$45.0	$27.4	$50.4	$29.7	$28.9	$30.4	$32.9	$31.5	$27.3	$27.6	$30.6	$43.4	$37.9
Equals: Cash Before Financing	($55.0)	$27.4	$0.4	$29.7	$8.9	$10.4	$2.9	($8.5)	($2.7)	$7.6	$20.6	$43.4	$67.9	$67.8
Financing Activities														
Line of Credit	$0.0	$0.0	$0.0	$0.0	$20.0	$20.0	$30.0	$40.0	$30.0	$20.0	$10.0	$0.0	($30.0)	($50.0)
Owner Contribution	$100.0	$0.0	$0.0										$0.0	$0.0
Investor Contributions	$0.0	$0.0	$50.0										$0.0	$0.0
Total Financing	$100.0	$0.0	$50.0	$0.0	$20.0	$20.0	$30.0	$40.0	$30.0	$20.0	$10.0	$0.0	($30.0)	($50.0)
Line of Credit Balance	$0.0	$0.0	$0.0	$0.0	$40.0	$70.0	$110.0	$140.0	$160.0	$170.0	$170.0	$140.0	$90.0	
Ending Cash Balance	$45.0	$27.4	$50.4	$29.7	$28.9	$30.4	$32.9	$31.5	$27.3	$27.6	$30.6	$43.4	$37.9	$17.8

Beginning Cash this month equals Ending Cash from last month.

The company's cash account is low, so you project borrowing on your line of credit to keep your cash balance around $30.

When your cash balance is high, you begin to pay off the line of credit.

By the end of Year 1, you have invested $100, outsiders have invested $50, and you owe $90 on a line of credit which reached a high of $170 in Month 9.

come and go. You won't do yourself or anyone else any favors by being aggressive about your rate of growth.

PROJECT YOUR CASH RECEIPTS

If, by some miracle, you can collect from all of your customers at the time of purchase (cash, check, or credit cards), your cash income will match your sales. But if, like most businesses, you bill for all or part of your sales, then you won't collect the cash until your customers decide to pay you. In your projections, be pessimistic about how quickly you'll be paid.

Exhibit 20.2 (top) shows how your cash receipts will look if you assume you'll collect 50 percent of your accounts receivable in 30 days, 40 percent in 60 days, and 10 percent in 90 days. Notice that in spite of $8,500 in sales in Month 1, your forecast shows that you'll collect no cash. Instead, you'll collect $4,300 in 30 days (50% of $8,500), $3,400 in 60 days (40% of $8,500) and $900 in 90 days (10% of $8,500, rounded).

DETERMINE INVENTORY AND COST OF GOODS SOLD

If you're a manufacturer, distributor, wholesaler, retailer, or other company that requires inventory, you next have to project how much inventory you want on hand in each period based on expected sales. Since you don't ever want to run out of inventory, you'll want to maintain some margin over what you think you'll actually need. So, let's say you've decided that at the end of each month you want to have enough inventory on hand to cover the next two months' sales.

Exhibit 20.2 (bottom) shows how you'd calculate your inventory and purchasing needs if the product costs 51 percent of its selling price to produce or purchase. For example, in the month before start-up (Month − 1), the company has to order $10,800 in inventory to cover the first two months' sales. This is because you expect to sell $8,500 in Month 1 and $12,800 in Month 2. Since it costs you 51 percent of the selling price to purchase the coffee and tea, that's $4,300 in Month 1 (51% of $8,500, rounded) and $6,500 in Month 2 (51% of $12,800, rounded), or $10,800 in total.

The amount of inventory the company needs for the next two months ($10,800) plus the amount you'll need for this month's sales (in this case, none because the business hasn't started yet) equals the total inventory needed. If you had any inventory left at the end of last month

EXHIBIT 20.2 Coffee & Tea Emporium Projected Cash Collected from Sales (Top) and Cash Needed for Inventory (Bottom).

($,000 omitted)

Sales $	$/Case	Month 1	Month 2	Month 3	Month 4
Coffee	$110	$5.5	$8.3	$11.0	$13.8
Tea	$80	$3.0	$4.5	$6.0	$7.5
Total Income		**$8.5**	**$12.8**	**$17.0**	**$21.3**
Cash In from Sales					
Sales Collected in 30 Days	50%	$0.0	$4.3	$6.4	$8.5
Sales Collected in 60 Days	40%	$0.0	$0.0	$3.4	$5.1
Sales Collected in 90 Days	10%	$0.0	$0.0	$0.0	$0.9
Total Cash Collected From Sales		**$0.0**	**$4.3**	**$9.8**	**$14.5**

This month's sales won't be collected this month.

Instead, you'll bill your customers and collect 50% in 30 days, 40% in 60 days, and the remaining 10% in 90 days.

Inventory Needs

	Month -1	Month 1	Month 2	
Cost of Goods This Month (COGS) 51%	$0.0	$4.3	$6.5	= 51% of this month's sales.
Plus: Desired Ending Inventory (2 months)	$10.8	$15.2	$19.5	= next two months' COGS since we want two month's inventory on hand at the end of each
Equals: Total Inventory Needed	$10.8	$19.5	$26.0	= inventory for this months' sales plus the next two months needs.
Less: Beginning Inventory	$0.0	$10.8	$15.2	= last months' ending inventory is this month's beginning inventory.
Equals: Purchases This Month	$10.8	$8.7	$10.8	= what you need to buy this month.
Cash Needed for Inventory		**$0.0**	**$10.8**	**$8.7** = bills you'll pay in 30 days.

(which you didn't because this is your first inventory purchase), you'd subtract that from the total needed to arrive at the amount you'll have to purchase. In this case, again because this is your first inventory purchase and you had no sales, you'll have to purchase $10,800.

DETERMINE HOW MUCH CASH YOU NEED FOR INVENTORY

What your inventory actually costs you in cash will depend on how quickly you pay your bills. Assuming you pay your bills in 30 days, the $10,800 in inventory purchased the month prior to start-up will be paid in Month 1 as Exhibit 20.3 shows.

PROJECT YOUR MONTHLY OPERATING EXPENSES

Now you need to project all of your regular monthly operating expenses. Naturally, you'll want to reflect when the cash will actually go out for those expenses. For example, if the premium for next year's insurance is due this year, it should be included in this year's cash flow. Likewise, if you pay rent, health insurance, or payroll taxes on a quarterly basis, the expenses should be shown in the month they'll actually be paid.

On the first run of your cash flow, you'll want to itemize as many expenses as possible, but later you might want to collapse some items into broader categories. (Lenders and investors often want all the details, in addition to the summary information, so keep them on a separate spreadsheet.) For example, you might develop an advertising budget that includes each ad as a separate item, because some require payment well in advance of when the ad will run. Then, when you finalize the numbers, you can summarize them under one line called Advertising or Marketing. Don't include noncash items such as Depreciation.

Exhibit 20.1 shows the full cash flow pro forma for Coffee & Tea Emporium and demonstrates how your projection of operating expenses might look in finished form. Note that a number of items such as rent deposits, office supplies, and initial marketing expenses are shown in the month prior to opening. Other periodic expenses, such as professional fees, are shown in the month they're likely to be paid.

SUBTRACT ANY OTHER USES OF CASH

Subtract all nonoperating expenses such as principal payments on loans, equipment purchases, and dividends paid. Exhibit 20.1 shows the purchase of a $35,000 piece of equipment the month prior to start-up, and interest payments on a line of credit you project you'll need to solve your cash flow problems. If your company is making payments on a term loan or paying dividends, they'll show up in this section as well.

CALCULATE TOTAL CASH SOURCES, USES, AND NET CASH

Total Sources of Cash includes Cash Collected from Sales, and Total Uses of Cash includes Cash Needed for Inventory, Cash Needed for Operating Expenses, and Other Uses of Cash. Total Sources less Total Uses will equal Net Cash from Business Activities. Now add your Beginning Cash Balance (which is really last month's Ending Cash Balance), and you'll have Cash before Financing.

Exhibit 20.1 shows Total Sources of Cash in Month 1 of $0 and Total Uses of Cash of $27,000. The company's Beginning Cash Balance for Month 1 is $27,400, so their Cash before Financing that month is forecast to be $400.

SOLVE FOR THE FINANCING NEEDED

If your projected cash account is in the red, or close to it, you have a few choices. You can: (1) kick in more of your own money; (2) you can find a lender, investor, or both to plug up the hole; or (3) you can change your plan. In the case of Coffee & Tea Emporium, Exhibit 20.1 shows you've found an investor to kick in $50,000 so you wound up Month 1 with an Ending Cash Balance of $50,400. This is your Beginning Cash Balance for Month 2.

Now, if you can't raise the money you've projected you'll need, and you opt for changing your plan, understand that *isn't* the same thing as just changing your spreadsheet. The good thing about computer spreadsheets is that they make it easy to change scenarios. The bad thing about computer spreadsheets is that they make it *too* easy to change scenarios. If your first cash flow projection shows that you need more money than you can possibly find, it's altogether too easy to just tweak a few assumptions, poke a few buttons on your keyboard and, miracle of miracles, it all *seems* to work.

When we say change your plan, we mean you need to change how your business is going to operate. We can't emphasize this point enough. *Do not* back into your sales or expense assumptions by starting with how much money you think you can raise. Likewise, if once you've started raising money, you learn you can't find nearly as much as you project you'll need, don't simply change your projections to make it *look* like it will work. *It won't!*

One of our clients put together a well-researched plan that showed the need for $300,000 in start-up capital for a software business. The plan included a budget of $150,000 for product advertising which he believed would be necessary to bring the new software to market. After shopping for investors for months, he finally found someone who agreed to put $125,000 in the company and to personally loan him $25,000 to cover mounting personal bills.

The investor argued that the ad budget was much too high because his manufacturing business only spent about $6,000 a year. In desperation, and against our advice, the entrepreneur revised his spreadsheets to "prove" that the company could make it on the reduced amount. He

EXHIBIT 20.3 Coffee & Tea Emporium Breakeven Sensitivity Analysis

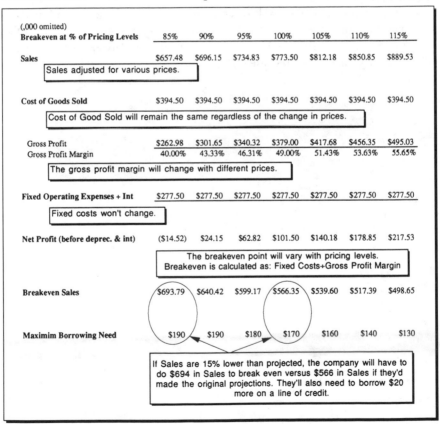

(,000 omitted) Breakeven at % of Pricing Levels	85%	90%	95%	100%	105%	110%	115%
Sales	$657.48	$696.15	$734.83	$773.50	$812.18	$850.85	$889.53
Sales adjusted for various prices.							
Cost of Goods Sold	$394.50	$394.50	$394.50	$394.50	$394.50	$394.50	$394.50
Cost of Good Sold will remain the same regardless of the change in prices.							
Gross Profit	$262.98	$301.65	$340.32	$379.00	$417.68	$456.35	$495.03
Gross Profit Margin	40.00%	43.33%	46.31%	49.00%	51.43%	53.63%	55.65%
The gross profit margin will change with different prices.							
Fixed Operating Expenses + Int	$277.50	$277.50	$277.50	$277.50	$277.50	$277.50	$277.50
Fixed costs won't change.							
Net Profit (before deprec. & int)	($14.52)	$24.15	$62.82	$101.50	$140.18	$178.85	$217.53
The breakeven point will vary with pricing levels. Breakeven is calculated as: Fixed Costs+Gross Profit Margin							
Breakeven Sales	$693.79	$640.42	$599.17	$566.35	$539.60	$517.39	$498.65
Maximim Borrowing Need	$190	$190	$180	$170	$160	$140	$130

If Sales are 15% lower than projected, the company will have to do $694 in Sales to break even versus $566 in Sales if they'd made the original projections. They'll also need to borrow $20 more on a line of credit.

then sold 45 percent of his company to the investor and went to work finishing the software. A year later, the software was done, but there was no money left for advertising. As he'd originally projected, the company needed about $150,000 for marketing. Without the funds for even a reasonable market test, the company was unable to find additional money and eventually went down the tubes.

CONDUCT A SENSITIVITY ANALYSIS

Once you've done your cash flow projections, you should test some "what if" scenarios. What if sales are off by 5, 10, or 15 percent (too high or too low)? What if your prices were higher or lower by 5, 10, or 15 percent? What if you collect your receivables slower than you expected? What if you pay your bills slower than projected? At what point do you break even or have just enough sales to cover your expenses (in dollars and in units)?

Lenders and investors will be comforted by a high case and low case scenario. Summarize your "what if's" in an easy-to-read chart or table. As an example, Exhibit 20.3 (p. 225) is a combined breakeven and sensitivity analysis at various sales levels.

FINDING HIDDEN CASH TREASURES | 21

Before you finalize how much money you'll need to borrow or find from investors, let's look at some often overlooked sources of cash flow that come with few or no strings attached. They don't require personal guarantees, fancy business plans, or your firstborn as collateral, but they may require a bit of creativity. Some will seem obvious, and some you may even be using already; but we'd feel remiss if we'd didn't mention these practically free ways to find money.

Aside from borrowing money or finding investors, you can increase cash flow by increasing income, reducing expenses, speeding the flow of cash coming in, and slowing the flow of cash going out.

INCREASE YOUR REVENUE

Assuming you're already working as hard as you can at peddling your wares, the quickest way to increase revenue is to raise your prices.

❑ **Secret**

Even though you may lose customers at the higher prices, you'll probably still make more money.

For example, if you sell 500 items for $100 with a Cost of Goods Sold of $75, your revenue will be $50,000 with a gross profit of $12,500 (that's $25 per unit, or 25% gross profit margin). Now let's say you raise your price by 5 percent to $105 per unit, but in so doing you sell 10 percent fewer units. Your sales will be 450 units (500 less 10%), your revenue

EXHIBIT 21.1   How Much Business Can I Afford to Lose If I Raise My Prices?

% Increase	New Price/Unit	Cost/ Unit	Gross Profit Unit $	Gross Profit Unit %	Sales in Units	Total Revenue	Gross Profit	% Change
None	$100	$75	$25	25.0%	500	$50,000	$12,500	0.00%
5%	$105	$75	$30	28.6%	396	$41,666	$12,500	20.60%
10%	$110	$75	$35	31.8%	324	$35,714	$12,500	35.10%
15%	$115	$75	$40	34.8%	271	$31,250	$12,500	45.70%

> If you raise prices by 5%, you can sell 396 units and make the same gross profit that you would have selling 500 units at the old price.

will be $47,250 (450 units at $105 each), and your Cost of Goods Sold is still $75/unit. So your new gross profit is $30 per unit ($105 − $75), and your gross profit margin is 28.6 percent ($30 ÷ $105). So now your gross profit is actually $13,500 . . . $1000 more than it was originally, in spite of the lost business. In fact, as Exhibit 21.1 demonstrates, if you raise your price by 5 percent, you can sell about 20 percent fewer units and still make the same gross profit.

❑ Secret

Don't lower your prices figuring you'll make it up on volume. It's a *very* dangerous strategy, Exhibit 21.2 shows that if you *reduce* your price by just 5%, just to keep the same gross profit of $12,500, you'll have to sell 157 more units.

EXHIBIT 21.2   How Much Business Do You Have to Produce to Make Up for a Price Cut?

% Decrease	New Price/Unit	Cost/ Unit	Gross Profit Unit $	Gross Profit Unit %	Sales in Units	Total Revenue	Gross Profit	% Change
0%	$100	$75	$25	25.0%	500	$50,000	$12,500	0%
5%	$95	$75	$20	21.1%	657	$62,500	$12,500	31.60%
10%	$90	$75	$15	16.7%	925	$83,333	$12,500	85.20%
15%	$85	$75	$10	11.8%	1470	$125,000	$12,500	194.10%

> If you lower prices by 5%, you'll have to sell 657 units to make the same gross profit that you made selling 500 units at the old price.

Wow, that's a lot of tamales! So if you have a nice little 15 percent off sale to increase traffic, you'll have to sell almost *three times more* units just to stay even, to say nothing of increasing revenue (which is what we're trying to do here, after all). Not only will you be out of business if you don't meet the new volumes, but you'll be exhausted and out of business! Think twice, no think *three times*, before you lower prices. Just because the people next door do it, doesn't mean you should too.

Aside from raising prices, you may want to think about some other ways to increase income. Here's some ideas to help you start:

- Provide sales-based incentives.
- Establish sales goals.
- Establish referral relationships with related businesses and/or customers.
- Offer incentives for repeat businesses.
- Consider government contracts.
- Offer paid consulting services.
- Consider representing related product lines.
- Fill production slack time with jobs that can utilize similar equipment.
- Market your product more effectively or differently.
- Charge premium prices for specialty or rush jobs.
- Reduce customer returns by improving quality control practices.
- Get free advertising by sending newsworthy stories to the local press.
- Offer charitable donations that will provide your company with visibility.
- Add new products or services.
- Educate your customers about the other products and services you offer.

DECREASE YOUR EXPENSES

Once you've done everything you can to boost your top line (revenue), you'll want to look for ways to reduce expenses. The tactics you'll use will vary with the severity of your cash flow problem, but in general you'll want to focus your attention on your company's largest expenses first.

❏ **Secret**

Blanket cost-cutting measures, such as chopping every item by 10 percent, rarely work. Your focus should be on those items that will reduce the ratio of expenses to sales. For example, cutting your advertising budget will reduce your expenses, but it's likely to reduce sales too. So while you've lowered expenses, you may have lost a lot more in sales, and the ratio of expenses to sales will be worse. Here are some true cost-cutting ideas:

- Develop and use an effective financial reporting system.
- Test your expense ratios against others in your industry.
- Develop and use budgets.
- Make managers/employees part of the budgeting process.
- Establish budget-based incentives.
- Immediately follow up on expenses that are over budget.
- Offer employee incentives for cost-saving ideas.
- Make all employees part of the financial management process.
- Have a contingency plan if revenue isn't as planned.
- Take immediate action if a financial downturn is imminent.
- Consider a zero-based budgeting process.
- Understand your fully-allocated product costs.
- Evaluate each product and service on a breakeven basis.
- Monitor costs closely on large jobs.
- Avoid fixed price contracts.
- Measure your advertising and promotional effectiveness.
- Have suppliers co-op advertising and promotion.
- Train your people in good buying strategies.
- Cross-check invoices with shipments received.
- Require approval for large purchases.
- Fully evaluate the cost/benefit of equipment purchases.
- Require that large budget items be periodically bid.
- Evaluate your insurance programs for options such as higher deductibles, higher co-pay, or self insurance.
- Establish a preventive maintenance program for buildings and equipment.

- Develop production standards (how long it should take to produce a product).
- Provide adequate training to improve employee effectiveness.
- Measure employee effectiveness.
- Consider the use of contractors versus employees or vice versa.
- Consider a shortened or extended work week or shifts.
- Consider flextime or work-at-home programs.
- Closely manage employee overtime.
- Pay salespeople on collections not sales.
- Reflect customer discounts in sales commissions.
- Continually evaluate employee benefits.
- Be suspicious of employee theft and pilferage.
- Require all employees to take vacations at least once a year (since this is the easiest way to spot theft).
- Be suspicious of telephone fraud.
- Consider a profit-sharing program (preferably one that's tied to cash flow).
- Look for tax credits for handicapped or low-income workers.
- Offer equity or royalty-based payments for vendors, consultants, employees.

SPEED UP CASH COMING IN

Next in your search for cash, look at how well you're managing cash and soon-to-be-cash assets such as accounts receivable.

In the case of accounts receivable, the sooner you have your customer's money, the sooner you can use it. If you're selling to people who aren't paying you quickly enough, or heaven forbid, not paying you at all, you might as well start a bank because, in effect, you're financing *their* cash flow problems.

Don't let someone else's cash crunch become your own. If, instead of paying you in 30 days as your policy dictates, your customers pay you on average every 60 days, you may find it impossible to stay afloat. Here's an example that demonstrates the point. Assume you have annual credit sales of $1,000,000. If customers pay you in:

60 days your average A/R balance will be
$$(\$1{,}000{,}000 \div (365 \div 60)) = \$164{,}473$$
30 days your average A/R balance will be
$$(\$1{,}000{,}000 \div (365 \div 30)) = \underline{\$\ 82{,}169}$$
Your loss in cash flow will be: $\$\ 82{,}304$

So if you tolerate a slip in your receivables from 30 to 60 days, you'll have $80,000 less when it comes time to pay your own bills.

Here are some other suggestions for managing cash and accounts receivable:

- Keep tight controls over cash.
- Track daily, weekly, monthly cash flow.
- Invoice immediately on completion of jobs.
- Check work flow for bottlenecks in billing, mailing invoices, and making deposits.
- Compare your payment policies to those of your competitors.
- Require cash on delivery for questionable accounts.
- Evaluate customer creditworthiness before extending credit.
- Require and check credit references rather than relying on outside reports.
- Establish and enforce credit limits.
- Inform new customers of credit policies.
- Require personal guarantees, stock pledges, or collateral on questionable accounts.
- Periodically check on customer credit standings.
- Produce and use regular Accounts Receivable Agings.
- Establish and enforce late payment penalties.
- Don't allow late-pay customers to take early-payment discounts.
- Immediately follow up on slow-pay accounts.
- Stop selling to customers who owe you money.
- Remember the squeaky wheel gets greased—hound your bad debts.
- Consider legal action or collection agency services for bad debt.
- Accelerate deposits.
- Invest excess cash in higher yielding accounts.
- Offer incentives for your customers to pay early.
- Require customer deposits to cover your up-front costs.

- Collect progress payments on large jobs.
- Consider using bank cash management services (sweep accounts, lockbox, cash concentration services, balance reporting).

SLOW DOWN CASH GOING OUT

Inventory and payables represent significant uses of cash. Inadequate controls in these areas can cost your company a bundle in precious cash flow.

Focusing on inventory first, the following example demonstrates the effect of a build-up from thirty days to sixty days inventory-on-hand. Assume annual inventory purchases of $500,000. Assuming you keep:

30 days-on-hand inventory level ($500,000/(365/30)) = $41,084
60 days-on-hand inventory level ($500,000/(365/60)) = $82,192

Your loss in cash flow will be: $41,108

So if you let your inventory grow from 30 to 60 days-on-hand, you'll have $41,000 less when your bills come due at the end of the month. Certainly, you don't want to run the risk of not having enough inventory, but if you can reduce the level you carry through better tracking and inventory controls, you can put cash back in your pocket.

Here are a few inventory management suggestions that may help your cash flow:

- Have customers supply raw materials.
- Monitor inventory defects that inflate inventory costs.
- Monitor inventory levels by item.
- Investigate just-in-time inventory options.
- Investigate supplier floor-plan financing or consignment alternatives.

Properly managed accounts payable, on the other hand, can free up cash.

Trade credit is the unsecured financing that your suppliers provide to you in the form of extended payment terms. Because vendors have a primary interest in obtaining your business, they're more lenient than other money sources. They'll extend you credit when no one else will, they won't require collateral, and they won't want to see your business plan or tax returns. During periods of growth and during tough times, good relationships with trade creditors can make or break your business. Because suppliers have a vested interest in your survival, they'll often work out special payment terms if you can show them it's in their interest to do so.

Here's how trade credit works: To encourage your purchase, suppliers will ship you goods or provide services and then wait 15, 30, 45, 60, or even 90 days to be paid. In other words, they give you an interest-free loan for the amount of your purchase until the due date. Suppliers in certain industries will even offer payment terms that match your sales cycle, particularly in seasonal businesses where inventory must be purchased well in advance of the sales season.

If you don't think trade credit is a real source of money, consider this scenario: You're a start-up company. All of your sales are made on credit. You collect 50 percent of your accounts receivable in 30 days, 40 percent in 60 days, and the balance in 90 days. At the end of each month you want enough inventory on hand to cover the next two months of sales. Exhibit 21.3 shows what would happen if you paid your vendors in 30 days or 60 days or, heaven forbid, if they required cash on delivery.

With 30-day payment terms, your cash account will be down $14,900 after you've collected your account receivables and paid your vendors (and that doesn't even count the rest of your operating expenses like salaries, office expense, and advertising). On one hand, if instead of 30-day terms, your vendors gave you 60-day payment terms, you'd only be down $1,900 at the end of Month 4. On the other hand, if they made you pay cash on delivery of goods, you'd be down a whopping $40,900 at the end of Month 4.

Without trade credit, you can't continue to grow unless you find some investor with deep pockets to solve your ongoing cash flow problem. And, if your suppliers ever put you on COD terms, you might as well hang it up. On the other hand, if you can convince suppliers to agree to more flexible terms, you can save yourself a great deal of *It's-Friday-afternoon-and-the-payroll's-due-but-we-ain't-got-the-money* anguish.

Some creative ideas you might try as bargaining chips to negotiate longer payment terms and some other ideas for improving cash flow through payables management include:

- Agree to buy exclusively from one vendor for some period of time.
- Agree to pay a higher price for longer payment terms.
- Create a long-term interest-bearing note for your balance due while you pay for new goods on standard terms.
- Offer your personal guarantee or other collateral.
- Barter inventory for good or services.
- Offer to take new inventory on consignment and pay as a percentage of the selling price, when sold.

EXHIBIT 21.3 Effect on Cash Flow of Paying Bills in 30 days, 60 days, or C.O.D.

Cash Flow based on 30-Day Payables

		Month -2	Month -1	Month 1	Month 2	Month 3	Month 4	Month 5	Month 6
Total Income		$0.0	$0.0	$8.5	$12.8	$17.0	$21.3	$25.5	$51.0
Cash In From Sales									
Sales Collected in 30 Days	50%	$0.0	$0.0	$0.0	$4.3	$6.4	$8.5	$10.7	$12.8
Sales Collected in 60 Days	40%	$0.0	$0.0	$0.0	$0.0	$3.4	$5.1	$6.8	$8.5
Sales Collected in 90 Days	10%	$0.0	$0.0	$0.0	$0.0	$0.0	$0.9	$1.3	$1.7
Total Cash Collected From Sales		$0.0	$0.0	$0.0	$4.3	$9.8	$14.5	$18.7	$23.0
Inventory Needs									
Cost of Goods This Month	51%	$0.0	$0.0	$4.3	$6.5	$8.7	$10.9	$13.0	$26.0
Plus: Desired Ending Inventory	2 months	$0.0	$10.9	$15.2	$19.5	$23.9	$39.0	$65.0	$86.7
Equals: Total Inventory Needed		$0.0	$10.9	$19.5	$26.1	$32.5	$49.9	$78.0	$112.7
Less: Beginning Inventory		$0.0	$0.0	$10.9	$15.2	$19.5	$23.9	$39.0	$65.0
Equals: Purchases This Month		$0.0	$10.9	$8.7	$10.9	$13.0	$26.0	$39.0	$47.7
Cash Out for Inventory		$0.0	$0.0	$10.9	$8.7	$10.9	$13.0	$26.0	$39.0
Net Cash		$0.0	$0.0	($10.9)	($4.4)	($1.1)	$1.5	($7.3)	($16.0)
Cumulative Cash		$0.0	$0.0	($10.9)	($15.3)	($16.3)	($14.9)	($22.2)	($38.2)

> With 30-day payment terms, the company's cash flow after inventory purchases is ($14,900) at the end of the Month 4.

Cash Flow based on 60-Day Payables

	Month -2	Month -1	Month 1	Month 2	Month 3	Month 4	Month 5	Month 6
Cash Out for Inventory	$0.0	$0.0	$0.0	$10.9	$8.7	$10.9	$13.0	$26.0
Net Cash	$0.0	$0.0	$0.0	($6.6)	$1.1	$3.6	$5.7	($3.0)
Cumulative Cash	$0.0	$0.0	$0.0	($6.6)	($5.5)	($1.9)	$3.8	$0.8

> With 60-day payment terms, the company's cash flow after inventory purchases is ($1,900) at the end of the Month 4.

Cash Flow based on C. O. D. Payment Terms

	Month -2	Month -1	Month 1	Month 2	Month 3	Month 4	Month 5	Month 6
Cash Out for Inventory	$0.0	$10.9	$8.7	$10.9	$13.0	$26.0	$39.0	$47.7
Net Cash	$0.0	($10.9)	($8.7)	($6.6)	($3.2)	($11.5)	($20.3)	($24.7)
Cumulative Cash	$0.0	($10.9)	($19.5)	($26.1)	($29.4)	($40.9)	($61.2)	($85.9)

> With C. O. D. payment terms, the company's cash flow after inventory purchases is ($40,900) at the end of Month 4.

- Take advantage of trade discounts whenever possible.
- Learn suppliers' invoice cycles and don't buy the day before billing.
- Open a checking account in Alaska, and use it for your payables. Float helps.

You don't want to alienate your suppliers by stringing them along unnecessarily, but on the other hand why look a gift-horse in the mouth.

One company's aged account receivable is another company's improved cash flow. The best strategy is to find that optimal point where you're paying as slowly as possible, but not so slowly that you appear to be a bad credit risk.

Incidentally, it's best to establish a payment policy and stick with it as best you can. Just like you, your suppliers watch their customer's accounts for changes in payment patterns as a sign of possible financial trouble.

Also remember that the door swings both ways. If you happen to be flush with cash at a time when your supplier is cash-tight, you'll improve your relationship if you speed up your payments a bit to help the vendor out. Besides, taking trade discounts and paying quicker can represent big savings for you.

❑ **Secret**

If your supplier offers a 2 percent discount on invoices paid within 10 days versus their standard 30-day no interest terms, and you can borrow at anything less than 37.2 percent (and *that* shouldn't be too hard these days), you'll actually make money even if you have to borrow the needed funds to take advantage of the discount. Exhibit 21.4 demonstrates the point.

STRATEGIC SOURCES OF CASH

Finally, in your quest for the ever-elusive cash, you might want to consider a wholesale change in your company's mode of operation. Here are some ideas to start your creative juices going in this direction.

- Diversify, find other sources of revenue.
- Focus product emphasis on cash cows.
- If cash flow is very seasonal, find other products to even it out.
- Offer new products to the same customers.
- Offer the same products to new customers.
- Offer new products to new customers.
- Consider spinning off products or services.
- Consider buying complementary businesses.
- Consider selling limited marketing or distribution rights.
- Consider franchising.

EXHIBIT 21.4   Is It Worth Taking a Trade Discount?

Assume Your Supplier's Terms Are:
2% discount if paid in 10 days, otherwise 100% due in 30 days

To determine if it's worth borrowing money to take the trade discount, you first have to figure out what the trade discount is worth on an annual basis. Here's the formula:

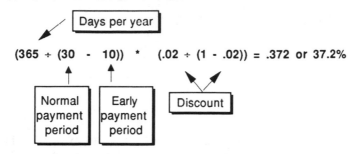

$$(365 \div (30 - 10)) * (.02 \div (1 - .02)) = .372 \text{ or } 37.2\%$$

Days per year

Normal payment period

Early payment period

Discount

In other words, if you can borrow at less than 2% for 20 days (or an annual rate 37.2% per year), you'll save money.

- Consider selling locations.
- Consider slowing your pace of growth.
- Become a specialist in something (and charge accordingly).
- Don't try to be all things to all people.
- Find a market niche and concentrate your efforts.
- Be on the lookout for the next business trend.
- Plan at least five years into the future.
- Develop strategic alliances with larger companies, customers, distributors, and even competitors.
- Develop joint marketing relationships with others.
- Involve your employees in suggesting and implementing cash management strategies.

AFTERWORD

Finding money to start a new business or to help an existing business grow *is* possible. The process can seem overwhelming, but it doesn't have to be if you understand lenders and investors—how they operate and how to approach them. Once you're successful finding money, you'll have created flexibility for your business that can go a long way toward resolving problems before they become costly or unmanageable. Better yet, you'll have made it possible to take advantage of opportunities that might otherwise have been out of reach.

As Arthur Clarke put it, "The future ain't what it used to be." To effectively manage the financing of your business in an environment of change, you need to constantly plan, research, act, and adjust.

PLAN

When Alice asked the Cheshire Cat which road she should take at a crossroads in Wonderland, he asked her where she was going. She said she didn't really know, and the Cat replied that it didn't really matter, then, which road she took. Your company is the same; if you don't know where you're going you can't pick the right road to success. Planning for your business needs to be an ongoing, top-priority process.

RESEARCH

Keep track of significant occurrences in your industry, and keep track of your performance compared with others in your industry. At the same time, a budget based on the income and expense pro formas you prepared as part of the financing process will show how you are doing compared with what you thought you could do. New financing techniques and sources are always being developed, especially for new and growing companies, so stay current. Use your local libraries and librarians; they're the most underutilized resource you have available to your business. And don't forget on-line information services accessed through your computer. Keyword retrieval of industry news can help you keep ahead. Research what's going on constantly, especially by reading everything you can put your hands on.

ACT

When it comes to finding money, start on your next round early. It always takes longer than you think it will, and you want to avoid giving the impression that chronic cash shortages and "emergency" visits to the bank are standard operating procedure. It's not an exaggeration to say that you should *always* be looking for the next round of financing. You have to *do* something. Take action.

ADJUST

Your ongoing planning, your research, and your actions should keep your company nimble and on its toes. Run your business on the premise that five years from now you'll be doing something entirely different. You may be selling to different markets, you may be creating different products, you may even be running a different company. As the world changes, as your customers' needs and wants change, you'll have to adjust to changing reality. Our hero is an entrepreneur who brags that he's working on his second million. "Gave up on the first," he admits. That's exactly the undefeatable spirit it takes to adjust and, ultimately, to succeed.

> *One can never consent to creep*
> *when one feels the impulse to soar*
>
> Helen Keller

NOTES

PREFACE

1. *The State of Small Business: A Report of the President,* transmitted to Congress 1993, GPO ISSN 0735-1437, Table A-5, p. 156.

CHAPTER THREE

1. *Loan Profiles Fiscal Year 1992,* SBA Office of Financial Assistance, Washington DC, 1993.
2. *The States and Small Business,* SBA Office of Advocacy, Government Printing Office, ISBN 0-16-041654-X.
3. *Ibid.*
4. *Barter Basics,* Barter Advantage, New York, 1990.

CHAPTER FOUR

1. *Annual Statement Studies,* Robert Morris Associates, Philadelphia, 1994.

CHAPTER FIVE

1. *The Gambler,* words and music by Don Schlitz, © 1976.

CHAPTER FOURTEEN

1. *Venture One 1993 Entrepreneurial Investment Report,* Venture One, San Francisco, CA, 1993.

CHAPTER SIXTEEN

1. Kate Lister and Tom Harnish, *Compendium of Venture Capital,* New York: John Wiley & Sons, Fall 1995 release.

APPENDIX

American Credit Indemnity
100 East Pratt Street
5th Floor
Baltimore MD 21202
800-879-1224, 410-554-0770
Leading provider of credit
insurance.

Baker Hill Financial
655 West Carmel Drive
Suite 100
Carmel IN 46032
800-821-4455, 317-571-2000
Software for financial analysis
(STAN). Used by the nation's largest
banks.

Bank of Commerce
1060 Eighth Avenue
Suite 201
San Diego CA 92101
619-232-2266
The largest bank SBA lender in the
western United States.

Business Equity Appraisal Reports
865 Laurel Street
San Carlos CA 94070
800-548-3288, 415-592-6041

Provider of exceptional valuation
software and valuation studies for
entrepreneurs and advisors.

Center for Venture Research
University of New Hampshire
Whittemore School of Business and
Economics
Durham NH 03824-3556
603-862-3369
Leading researcher on
entrepreneurship and private
investment capital.

CFI ProServices, Inc.
400 SW Sixth Street
Suite 200
Portland OR 97204
800-274-7280, 503-274-7280
Provider of software for bank legal
forms (Laser Pro® Closing Program
used by many of the nation's largest
banks).

CoreStates Bank
Centre Square—West Tower
1500 Market Street—39th Floor
Philadelphia PA 19102
215-973-3100

One of the largest small business lenders in the eastern United States.

Coopers & Lybrand
2400 Eleven Penn Center
Philadelphia PA 19103-2962
215-963-8263
Accounting services and consulting for entrepreneurial companies.

Export-Import Bank of the United States
811 Vermont Avenue NW
Washington DC 20571
202-565-3946
International financing and insurance programs.

The Fair Isaac Company, Inc.
120 North Redwood Drive
San Rafael CA 94903-1996
415-472-2211
Industry leader in credit scoring for consumer and commercial loans.

First Interstate Bank of California
1055 Wilshire Boulevard
Mail Sort B10-10
Los Angeles CA 90017
213-580-6374
Commercial bank serving the entrepreneurial community.

GE Capital Administrative Office
260 Long Ridge Road
Stamford CT 06927
203-357-4000
Largest leasing company in the world.

Heller, Ehrman, White & McAuliffe
525 University Avenue
Suite 1100
Palo Alto CA 94301-1900
415-324-7000

Leading West Coast technology law firm with an extensive corporate, intellectual property, litigation, and tax practice.

Inc.
38 Commercial Wharf
Boston MA 02110
617-248-8000
Leading business magazine focusing on the entrepreneurial community.

NEPA Venture Fund
Ben Franklin Technology Center
125 Goodman Drive
Bethlehem PA 18015
610-865-6550
Venture fund specializing in early stage ventures.

Riviera Finance
225 Avenue I
Suite 201
Redondo Beach CA 90277
310-792-2010
Accounts receivable factoring for the entrepreneurial community.

Robert Morris Associates
1650 Market Street—Suite 2300
One Liberty Place
Philadelphia PA 19103-7398
215-851-0585
Nonprofit association serving the banking community. Publisher of *Annual Statement Studies* and other excellent resources for understanding how bankers evaluate borrowers.

Sontag & Associates
966 Old Eagle School Road
Wayne PA 19087
610-964-1866

Regional accounting firm specializing in services for small and medium-size businesses.

The Capital Network
8920 Business Park Drive
Austin TX 78759-7405
512-794-9398
A nonprofit computerized matching network for entrepreneurs and private investors.

The Edwards Research Group
PO Box 95101
Newton MA 02195
800-963-1993, 617-244-8414
Research on the factoring industry. Publisher of the annual *Directory of American Factors*.

Union Bank
530 B Street
Suite 520
San Diego CA 92101
619-230-4175

Commercial bank serving the small-business community. SBA lender including 504 program.

Venture One
345 Spear Street
East Tower, Suite 520
San Francisco CA 94105-1657
415-357-2100
Preeminent research firm specializing in tracking the business progress and financing plans of privately held, venture-backed companies.

Wilson Sonsini Goodrich & Rosati
650 Page Mill Rd
Palo Alto CA 94304-1050
415-493-9300
A leading Silicon Valley law firm with extensive experience in private placements and public offerings.

INDEX